Robust Python
Write Clean and Maintainable Code

Patrick Viafore

Beijing • Boston • Farnham • Sebastopol • Tokyo

Robust Python

by Patrick Viafore

Published by O'Reilly Media, Inc., 1005 Gravenstein Highway North, Sebastopol, CA 95472.

O'Reilly books may be purchased for educational, business, or sales promotional use. Online editions are also available for most titles (*http://oreilly.com*). For more information, contact our corporate/institutional sales department: 800-998-9938 or *corporate@oreilly.com*.

Acquisitions Editor: Amanda Quinn

Development Editor: Sarah Grey

Production Editor: Kristen Brown

Copyeditor: Justin Billing

Proofreader: Shannon Turlington

Indexer: Ellen Troutman-Zaig

Interior Designer: David Futato

Cover Designer: Karen Montgomery

Illustrator: Kate Dullea

July 2021:   First Edition

Revision History for the First Edition

2021-07-12:   First Release
2022-12-16:   Second Release

See *http://oreilly.com/catalog/errata.csp?isbn=9781098100667* for release details.

978-1-098-10066-7

[LSI]

Table of Contents

Part II. Defining Your Own Types

Part III.   Extensible Python

Part IV.   Building a Safety Net

Preface

Noted software engineer and entrepreneur Marc Andreesen famously declared that "software is eating the world" (*https://oreil.ly/tYaNz*). This was back in 2011, and has only become more true over time. Software systems continue to grow in complexity and can be found in all facets of modern life. Standing in the middle of this ravenous beast is the Python language. Programmers often cite Python as a favorite language (*https://oreil.ly/RUNNh*), and it can be found everywhere: from web applications, to machine learning, to developer tools, and more.

Not all that glitters is gold, though. As our software systems become more complex, it becomes harder to understand how our mental models map onto the real world. If left unchecked, software systems bloat and become brittle, earning the frightening moniker "legacy code." These codebases often come with warnings such as, "Do not touch these files; we don't know why, but it breaks when you do," and, "Oh, only So-and-So knows that code, and they left for a high-paying Silicon Valley job two years ago." Software development is a young field, but these sort of statements should be terrifying to developers and businesspeople alike.

The truth is, to write systems that last, you need to be deliberate in the choices you make. As stated by Titus Winters, Tom Manshreck, and Hyrum Wright, "Software engineering is programming integrated over time."[1] Your code might last a long time —I've stepped into projects whose code was written while I was in elementary school. How long will your code last? Will it last longer than your tenure at your current job (or when you finish maintaining that project)? How do you want your code to be received in a few years when someone is building core components from it? Do you want your successors to thank you for your foresight, or curse your name for the complexities you bore into this world?

---

1 Titus Winters, Tom Manshreck, and Hyrum Wright. *Software Engineering at Google: Lessons Learned from Programming over Time.* Sebastopol, CA: O'Reilly Media, Inc., 2020.

Python is a wonderful language, but it occasionally makes building for the future tricky. Some proponents of other programming languages have decried Python as "not production-grade" or "useful for prototyping only," but the truth is that many developers only scratch the surface, rather than learning all the tools and tricks for writing robust Python. Throughout this book, you'll learn how to do better. You'll journey through numerous ways to make Python clean and maintainable. Your future maintainers will enjoy working with your code, as it was designed up front to make things easy. So go, read this book, look toward the future, and build awesome software that will last.

Who Should Read This Book

This book is for any Python developer who is looking to grow the code they work on in a sustainable and maintainable fashion. This is not intended to be your first Python text; I expect that you have written Python before. You should be comfortable with Python control flow, and have worked with classes before. If you are looking for a more introductory text, I suggest reading *Learning Python* (*https://oreil.ly/iIl2K*) by Mark Lutz (O'Reilly) first.

While I will be covering many advanced Python topics, the goal of this book is not to be a how-to for using all of Python's features. Instead, the features are a backdrop for a larger conversation about robustness and how your choices impact maintainability. At times I will discuss strategies that you should rarely use, if at all. That is because I want to illustrate first principles of robustness; the journey of understanding why and how we make decisions in code is more important than knowing what tools to use in an optimal scenario. In practice, the optimal scenario is a rare occurence. Use the principles in this book to draw your own conclusions from your codebase.

This book is not a reference book. You might call it a discussion book. Each chapter should be a starting point for developers in your organization to discuss, together, how best to apply these principles. Start a book club, discussion group, or lunch and learn to foster communication. I have proposed discussion topics in each chapter to get the converstation started. When you come across these topics, I encourage you to stop and reflect on your current codebase. Talk among your peers and use these topics as a springboard for discussing the state of your code, processes, and workflows. If you are interested in a reference book about the Python language, I heartily recommend *Fluent Python* (*https://oreil.ly/PVbON*) by Luciano Ramalho (O'Reilly; a second edition is forthcoming in late 2021).

A system can be robust in many different ways. It can be security hardened, scalable, fault-tolerant, or less likely to introduce new errors. Each one of these facets of robustness warrants a full book; this book is focused on preventing the developers who inherit your code from creating new faults in your system. I will show you how to communicate to future developers, how to make their lives easier through architectural patterns, and how to catch errors in your codebase before they make it into production. This book zeroes in on the robustness of your Python codebase, not the robustness of your system as a whole.

I will be covering a wealth of information, from many different areas of software, including software engineering, computer science, testing, functional programming, and object-oriented programming (OOP). I do not expect you to have a background in these fields. There are sections where I explain things at a beginner level; this is often to deconstruct how we think about core fundamentals of the language. This is, for the most part, an intermediate-level text.

Ideal readers include:

- Developers currently working in a large codebase, looking to find better ways to communicate with their colleagues
- Primary codebase maintainers, looking for ways to help lessen the burden of future maintainers
- Self-taught developers who can write Python really well but need to better understand why we do the things we do
- Software engineering graduates who need a reminder of practical advice for development
- Senior developers looking for a way to tie their design rationale to first principles of robustness

This book focuses on writing software over time. If a lot of your code is a prototype, throwaway, or disposable in any other fashion, the advice in this book will end up creating more work than is necessary for your project. Likewise if your project is small—say, under one hundred lines of Python. Making code maintainable does add complexity; there's no doubt about that. However, I'll guide you through minimizing that complexity. If your code lives longer than a few weeks or grows to a considerable size, you need to consider the sustainability of your codebase.

About This Book

This book covers a wide swath of knowledge, across many chapters. It is broken up into four parts:

Part I, "Annotating Your Code with Types"
We'll start with types in Python. Types are fundamental to the language, but are not often examined in great detail. The types you choose matter, as they convey a very specific intent. We'll examine type annotations and what specific annotations communicate to the developer. We'll also go over typecheckers and how those help catch bugs early.

Part II, "Defining Your Own Types"

> After covering how to think about Python's types, we'll focus on how to create your own types. We'll walk through enumerations, data classes, and classes in depth. We'll explore how making certain design choices in designing a type can increase or decrease the robustness of your code.

Part III, "Extensible Python"

> After learning how to better express your intentions, we'll focus on how to enable developers to change your code effortlessly, building with confidence on your strong foundation. We'll cover extensibility, dependencies, and architectural patterns that allow you to modify your system with minimal impact.

Part IV, "Building a Safety Net"

> Lastly, we'll explore how to build a safety net, so that you can gently catch your future collaborators when they do fall. Their confidence will increase, knowing that they have a strong, robust system that they can fearlessly adapt to their use case. Finally, we'll cover a variety of static analysis and testing tools that will help you catch rogue behavior.

Each chapter is mostly self-contained, with references to other chapters where applicable. You can read this book from cover to cover, or bounce around to chapters that suit your fancy. Chapters grouped in each part will be related to one another, but there will be fewer relations between book parts.

All code examples were run using Python 3.9.0, and I'll try to call out when you need a specific Python version or later to run examples (such as Python 3.7 for the use of data classes).

Throughout this book, I will be doing most of my work on the command line. I ran all of these commands from an Ubuntu operating system, but most tools should work just as well on Mac or Windows systems. In some cases, I will show how certain tools interact with integrated development environments (IDEs), such as Visual Studio Code (VS Code). Most IDEs use the command-line options underneath the hood; most of what you learn on the command line will translate directly to IDE options.

This book will be presenting many different techniques that can improve the robustness of your code. However, there are no silver bullets in software development. Trade-offs are the heart of solid engineering, and there is no exception in the methods that I present. I will be transparent about benefits and drawbacks as I discuss these topics. You will know more about your systems than I will, and you are best suited to choose which tool is appropriate for which job. All I am doing is stocking your toolbox.

Conventions Used in This Book

The following typographical conventions are used in this book:

Italic
> Indicates new terms, URLs, email addresses, filenames, and file extensions.

`Constant width`
> Used for program listings, as well as within paragraphs to refer to program elements such as variable or function names, databases, data types, environment variables, statements, and keywords.

`Constant width bold`
> Shows commands or other text that should be typed literally by the user.

`Constant width italic`
> Shows text that should be replaced with user-supplied values or by values determined by context.

This element signifies a tip or suggestion.

This element signifies a general note.

This element indicates a warning or caution.

Using Code Examples

Supplemental material (code examples, exercises, etc.) is available for download at *https://github.com/pviafore/RobustPython*.

If you have a technical question or a problem using the code examples, please send email to *bookquestions@oreilly.com*.

This book is here to help you get your job done. In general, if example code is offered with this book, you may use it in your programs and documentation. You do not need to contact us for permission unless you're reproducing a significant portion of the code. For example, writing a program that uses several chunks of code from this book does not require permission. Selling or distributing examples from O'Reilly books does require permission. Answering a question by citing this book and quoting example code does not require permission. Incorporating a significant amount of example code from this book into your product's documentation does require permission.

We appreciate, but generally do not require, attribution. An attribution usually includes the title, author, publisher, and ISBN. For example: "*Robust Python* by Patrick Viafore (O'Reilly). Copyright 2021 Kudzera, LLC, 978-1-098-10066-7."

If you feel your use of code examples falls outside fair use or the permission given above, feel free to contact us at *permissions@oreilly.com*.

O'Reilly Online Learning

 For more than 40 years, *O'Reilly Media* has provided technology and business training, knowledge, and insight to help companies succeed.

Our unique network of experts and innovators share their knowledge and expertise through books, articles, and our online learning platform. O'Reilly's online learning platform gives you on-demand access to live training courses, in-depth learning paths, interactive coding environments, and a vast collection of text and video from O'Reilly and over two hundred other publishers. For more information, visit *http:// oreilly.com*.

How to Contact Us

Please address comments and questions concerning this book to the publisher:

O'Reilly Media, Inc.
1005 Gravenstein Highway North
Sebastopol, CA 95472
800-998-9938 (in the United States or Canada)
707-829-0515 (international or local)
707-829-0104 (fax)

We have a web page for this book, where we list errata, examples, and any additional information. You can access this page at *https://oreil.ly/robust-python*.

Email *bookquestions@oreilly.com* to comment or ask technical questions about this book.

For news and information about our books and courses, visit *http://oreilly.com*.

Find us on Facebook: *http://facebook.com/oreilly*

Follow us on Twitter: *http://twitter.com/oreillymedia*

Watch us on YouTube: *http://youtube.com/oreillymedia*

Acknowledgments

I would like to acknowledge my incredible wife, Kendall. She is my support and sounding board, and I appreciate everything she did to make sure that I had the time and space to write this book.

No book is written in isolation, and this book is no exception. I stand on the shoulders of giants in the software industry, and I appreciate all who came before me.

I also would like to thank everyone who was involved in reviewing this book to make sure that my messaging was consistent and that my examples were clear. Thank you to Bruce G., David K., David P., and Don P. for providing early feedback and helping me decide on a direction for this book. Thank you to my tech reviewers Charles Givre, Drew Winstel, Jennifer Wilcox, Jordan Goldmeier, Nathan Stocks, and Jess Males for their invaluable feedback, especially where things really only made sense in my head but not on paper. Lastly, thank you to anyone who read the early release draft and was kind enough to email me their thoughts, especially Daniel C. and Francesco.

I'd like to thank everyone who helped transform my final draft into something production-worthy. Thank you to Justin Billing for diving deep as a copyeditor and helping refine the presentation of my ideas. Thank you to Shannon Turlington for proofreading; the book is much more polished because of you. A big thank you goes to Ellen Troutman-Zaig, who produced a fantastic index that I was blown away by.

Lastly, I could not do this without the fabulous team at O'Reilly. Thank you to Amanda Quinn for helping me through the proposal process and helping me develop focus for the book. Thank you to Kristen Brown for making the production stage incredibly easy for me. Thank you to Kate Dullea, who converted my MS Paint-quality sketches into clean, crisp illustrations. Also, I would like to give a tremendous thank you to my developmental editor, Sarah Grey. I looked forward to our weekly meetings, and she was fantastic in helping me craft a book for a broad audience, while still letting me dive deep into technical details.

## CHAPTER 1

Introduction to Robust Python

This book is all about making your Python more manageable. As your codebase grows, you need a specific toolbox of tips, tricks, and strategies to build maintainable code. This book will guide you toward fewer bugs and happier developers. You'll be taking a hard look at how you write code, and you'll learn the implications of your decisions. When discussing how code is written, I am reminded of these wise words from C.A.R. Hoare:

> There are two ways of constructing a software design: One way is to make it so simple that there are obviously no deficiencies, and the other way is to make it so complicated that there are no obvious deficiencies. The first method is far more difficult.[1]

This book is about developing systems the first way. It will be more difficult, yes, but have no fear. I will be your guide on your journey to leveling up your Python game such that, as C.A.R. Hoare says above, *there are obviously no deficiencies* in your code. Ultimately, this is a book all about writing *robust* Python.

In this chapter we're going to cover what *robustness* means and why you should care about it. We'll go through how your communication method implies certain benefits and drawbacks, and how best to represent your intentions. "The Zen of Python" (*https://oreil.ly/SHq8i*) states that, when developing code, "There should be one -- and preferably only one -- obvious way to do it." You'll learn how to evaluate whether your code is written in an obvious way, and what you can do to fix it. First, we need to address the basics. What is *robustness* in the first place?

---

1 Charles Antony Richard Hoare. "The Emperor's Old Clothes." *Commun. ACM* 24, 2 (Feb. 1981), 75–83. *https://doi.org/10.1145/358549.358561*.

Robustness

Every book needs at least one dictionary definition, so I'll get this out of the way nice and early. Merriam-Webster offers many definitions for *robustness* (*https://oreil.ly/ 2skKO*):

1. having or exhibiting strength or vigorous health
2. having or showing vigor, strength, or firmness
3. strongly formed or constructed
4. capable of performing without failure under a wide range of conditions

These are fantastic descriptions of what to aim for. We want a *healthy* system, one that meets expectations for years. We want our software to *exhibit strength*; it should be obvious that this code will stand the test of time. We want a *strongly constructed* system, one that is built upon solid foundations. Crucially, we want a system that is *capable of performing without failure*; the system should not become vulnerable as changes are introduced.

It is common to think of a software like a skyscraper, some grand structure that stands as a bulwark against all change and a paragon of immortality. The truth is, unfortunately, messier. Software systems constantly evolve. Bugs are fixed, user interfaces get tweaked, and features are added, removed, and then re-added. Frameworks shift, components go out of date, and security bugs arise. Software changes. Developing software is more akin to handling sprawl in city planning than it is constructing a static building. With ever changing codebases, how can you make your code robust? How can you build a strong foundation that is resilient to bugs?

The truth is, you have to accept change. Your code will be split apart, stitched together, and reworked. New use cases will alter huge swaths of code—and that's OK. Embrace it. Understand that it's not enough that your code can easily be changed; it might be best for it to be deleted and rewritten as it goes out of date. That doesn't diminish its value; it will still have a long life in the spotlight. Your job is to make it easy to rewrite parts of the system. Once you start to accept the ephemeral nature of your code, you start to realize that it's not enough to write bug-free code for the present; you need to enable the codebase's future owners to be able to change your code with confidence. That is what this book is about.

You are going to learn to build strong systems. This strength doesn't come from rigidity, as exhibited by a bar of iron. It instead comes from flexibility. Your code needs to be strong like a tall willow tree, swaying in the wind, flexing but not breaking. Your software will need to handle situations you would never dream of. Your codebase needs to be able to adapt to new circumstances, because it won't always be you maintaining it. Those future maintainers need to know they are working in a healthy codebase. Your codebase needs to communicate its strength. You must write Python code in a way that reduces failure, even as future maintainers tear it apart and reconstruct it.

Writing robust code means deliberately thinking about the future. You want future maintainers to look at your code and understand your intentions easily, not curse your name during late-night debugging sessions. You must convey your thoughts, reasoning, and cautions. Future developers will need to bend your code into new shapes—and will want to do so without worrying that each change may cause it to collapse like a teetering house of cards.

Put simply, you don't want your systems to fail, especially when the unexpected happens. Testing and quality assurance are huge parts of this, but neither of those bake quality completely in. They are more suited to illuminating gaps in expectations and offering a safety net. Instead, you must make your software stand the test of time. In order to do that, you must write *clean and maintainable* code.

Clean code expresses its intent clearly and concisely, in that order. When you look at a line of code and say to yourself, "ah, that makes complete sense," that's an indicator of clean code. The more you have to step through a debugger, the more you have to look at a lot of other code to figure out what's happening, the more you have to stop and stare at the code, the less clean it is. Clean code does not favor clever tricks if it makes the code unreadable to other developers. Just like C.A.R. Hoare said earlier, you do not want to make your code so obtuse that it will be difficult to understand upon visual inspection.

The Importance of Clean Code

Having clean code is paramount to having robust code; consider it table stakes for any meaningful project. There are often specific practices tied to writing clean code, including:

- Organizing your code in an appropriately granular fashion
- Providing good documentation
- Naming your variables/functions/types well
- Keeping functions short and simple

While the motifs of clean code weave throughout this book, I will not be dedicating substantial time to these specific practices. There are other books that capture clean code practices much better. I recommend *Clean Code* by Robert C. Martin (Prentice Hall), *The Pragmatic Programmer* by Andy Hunt and Dave Thomas (Addison-Wesley), and *Code Complete* by Steve McConnell (Microsoft Press). All three of these books greatly improved my skills as a developer and are great resources for anyone looking to grow.

While you should absolutely strive to write code cleanly, you must be prepared to work in codebases that aren't a shining example of cleanliness. Software development is a messy endeavor, and there will be times where the purity of clean code will be sacrificed for various reasons, both business and technical. Use the advice given in this book to help drive toward cleaner code through discussions about maintainability.

Maintainable code is code that…well, can be easily maintained. Maintenance begins immediately after the first commit and continues until not a single developer is looking at the project anymore. Developers will be fixing bugs, adding features, reading code, extracting code for use in other libraries, and more. Maintainable code makes these tasks frictionless. Software lives for years, if not decades. Focus on your maintainability *today*.

You don't want to be the reason systems fail, whether you are actively working on them or not. You need to be proactive in making your system stand the test of time. You need a testing strategy to be your safety net, but you also need to be able to avoid falling in the first place. So with all that in mind, I offer my definition of robustness in terms of your codebase:

> A robust codebase is resilient and error-free in spite of constant change.

Why Does Robustness Matter?

A lot of energy goes into making software do what it's supposed to, but it's not easy to know when you're done. Development milestones are not easily predicted. Human factors such as UX, accessibility, and documentation only increase the complexity. Now add in testing to ensure that you've covered a slice of known and unknown behaviors, and you are looking at lengthy development cycles.

The purpose of software is to provide value. It is in every stakeholder's interests to deliver that full value as early as possible. Given the uncertainty around some development schedules, there is often extra pressure to meet expectations. We've all been on the wrong end of an unrealistic schedule or deadline. Unfortunately, many of the tools to make software incredibly robust only add onto our development cycle in the short term.

It's true that there is an inherent tension between immediate delivery of value and making code robust. If your software is "good enough," why add even more complexity? To answer that, consider how often that piece of software will be iterated upon. Delivering software value is typically not a static exercise; it's rare that a system provides value and is never modified again. Software is ever-evolving by its very nature. The codebase needs to be prepared to deliver value frequently and for long periods of time. This is where robust software engineering practices come into play. If you can't painlessly deliver features quickly and without compromising quality, you need to re-evaluate techniques to make your code more maintainable.

If you deliver your system late, or broken, you incur real-time costs. Think through your codebase. Ask yourself what happens if your code breaks a year from now because someone wasn't able to understand your code. How much value do you lose? Your value might be measured in money, time, or even lives. Ask yourself what happens if the value isn't delivered on time? What are the repercussions? If the answers to these questions are scary, good news, the work you're doing is valuable. But it also underscores why it's so important to eliminate future errors.

Multiple developers work on the same codebase simlutaneously. Many software projects will outlast most of those developers. You need to find a way to communicate to the present and future developers, without having the benefit of being there in person to explain. Future developers will be building off of *your* decisions. Every false trail, every rabbit hole, and every yak-shaving[2] adventure will slow them down, which impedes value. You need empathy for those who come after you. You need to step into their shoes. This book is your gateway to thinking about your collaborators and maintainers. You need to think about sustainable engineering practices. You need to write code that lasts. The first step to making code that lasts is being able to communicate through your code. You need to make sure future developers understand your intent.

What's Your Intent?

Why should you strive to write clean and maintainable code? Why should you care so much about robustness? The heart of these answers lies in communication. You're not delivering static systems. The code will continue to change. You also have to consider that maintainers change over time. Your goal, when writing code, is to deliver value. It's also to write your code in such a way that other developers can deliver value just as quickly. In order to do that, you need to be able to communicate reasoning and intent without ever meeting your future maintainers.

Let's take a look at a code block found in a hypothetical legacy system. I want you to estimate how long it takes for you to understand what this code is doing. It's OK if you're not familiar with all the concepts here, or if you feel like this code is convoluted (it intentionally is!).

---

2 Yak-shaving describes a situation where you frequently have to solve unrelated problems before you can even begin to tackle the original problem. You can learn about the origins of the term at *https://oreil.ly/4iZm7*.

```
# Take a meal recipe and change the number of servings
# by adjusting each ingredient
# A recipe's first element is the number of servings, and the remainder
# of elements is (name, amount, unit), such as ("flour", 1.5, "cup")
def adjust_recipe(recipe, servings):
    new_recipe = [servings]
    old_servings = recipe[0]
    factor = servings / old_servings
    recipe.pop(0)
    while recipe:
        ingredient, amount, unit = recipe.pop(0)
        # please only use numbers that will be easily measurable
        new_recipe.append((ingredient, amount * factor, unit))
    return new_recipe
```

This function takes a recipe and adjusts every ingredient to handle a new number of servings. However, this code prompts many questions.

- What is the pop for?
- What does recipe[0] signify? Why is that the old servings?
- Why do I need a comment for numbers that will be easily measurable?

This is a bit of questionable Python, for sure. I won't blame you if you feel the need to rewrite it. It looks much nicer written like this:

```
def adjust_recipe(recipe, servings):
    old_servings = recipe.pop(0)
    factor = servings / old_servings
    new_recipe = {ingredient: (amount*factor, unit)
                    for ingredient, amount, unit in recipe}
    new_recipe["servings"] = servings
    return new_recipe
```

Those who favor clean code probably prefer the second version (I certainly do). No raw loops. Variables do not mutate. I'm returning a dictionary instead of a list of tuples. All these changes can be seen as positive, depending on the circumstances. But I may have just introduced three subtle bugs.

- In the original code snippet, I was clearing out the original recipe. Now I am not. Even if it's just one area of calling code that is relying on this behavior, I broke that calling code's assumptions.
- By returning a dictionary, I have removed the ability to have duplicate ingredients in a list. This might have an effect on recipes that have multiple parts (such as a main dish and a sauce) that both use the same ingredient.
- If any of the ingredients are named "servings" I've just introduced a collision with naming.

Whether these are bugs or not depends on two interrelated things: the original author's intent and calling code. The author intended to solve a problem, but I am unsure of why they wrote the code the way they did. Why are they popping elements? Why is "servings" a tuple inside the list? Why is a list used? Presumably, the original author knew why, and communicated it locally to their peers. Their peers wrote calling code based on those assumptions, but as time wore on, that intent became lost. Without communication to the future, I am left with two options of maintaining this code:

- Look at all calling code and confirm that this behavior is not relied upon before implementing. Good luck if this is a public API for a library with external callers. I would spend a lot of time doing this, which would frustrate me.
- Make the change and wait to see what the fallout is (customer complaints, broken tests, etc.). If I'm lucky, nothing bad will happen. If I'm not, I would spend a lot of time fixing use cases, which would frustrate me.

Neither option feels productive in a maintenance setting (especially if I have to modify this code). I don't want to waste time; I want to deal with my current task quickly and move on to the next one. It gets worse if I consider how to call this code. Think about how you interact with previously unseen code. You might see other examples of calling code, copy them to fit your use case, and never realize that you needed to pass a specific string called "servings" as the first element of your list.

These are the sorts of decisions that will make you scratch your head. We've all seen them in larger codebases. They aren't written maliciously, but organically over time with the best intentions. Functions start simple, but as use cases grow and multiple developers contribute, that code tends to morph and obscure original intent. This is a sure sign that maintainability is suffering. You need to express intent in your code up front.

So what if the original author made use of better naming patterns and better type usage? What would that code look like?

```python
def adjust_recipe(recipe, servings):
    """
    Take a meal recipe and change the number of servings
    :param recipe: a `Recipe` indicating what needs to be adusted
    :param servings: the number of servings
    :return Recipe: a recipe with serving size and ingredients adjusted
                    for the new servings
    """
    # create a copy of the ingredients
    new_ingredients = list(recipe.get_ingredients())
    recipe.clear_ingredients()

    for ingredient in new_ingredients:
```

```
        ingredient.adjust_proportion(Fraction(servings, recipe.servings))
    return Recipe(servings, new_ingredients)
```

This looks much better, is better documented, and expresses original intent clearly. The original developer encoded their ideas directly into the code. From this snippet, you know the following is true:

- I am using a `Recipe` class. This allows me to abstract away certain operations. Presumably, inside the class itself there is an invariant that allows for duplicate ingredients. (I'll talk more about classes and invariants in Chapter 10.) This provides a common vocabulary that makes the function's behavior more explicit.

- Servings are now an explicit part of a `Recipe` class, rather than needing to be the first element of the list, which was handled as a special case. This greatly simplifies calling code, and prevents inadvertent collisions.

- It is very apparent that I want to clear out ingredients on the old recipe. No ambiguous reason for why I needed to do a `.pop(0)`.

- Ingredients are a separate class, and handle fractions (*https://oreil.ly/YxUHK*) rather than an explicit `float`. It's clearer for all involved that I am dealing with fractional units, and can easily do things such as `limit_denominator()`, which can be called when people want to restrict measuring units (instead of relying on a comment).

I've replaced variables with types, such as a recipe type and an ingredient type. I've also defined operations (`clear_ingredients`, `adjust_proportion`) to communicate my intent. By making these changes, I've made the code's behavior crystal clear to future readers. They no longer have to come talk to me to understand the code. Instead, they comprehend what I'm doing without ever talking to me. This is *asynchronous communication* at its finest.

Asynchronous Communication

It's weird writing about asynchronous communication in a Python book without mentioning `async` and `await`. But I'm afraid I have to discuss asynchronous communication in a much more complex place: *the real world*.

Asynchronous communication means that producing information and consuming that information are independent of each other. There is a time gap between the production and consumption. It might be a few hours, as is the case of collaborators in different time zones. Or it might be years, as future maintainers try to do a deep dive into the inner workings of code. You can't predict when somebody will need to understand your logic. You might not even be working on that codebase (or for that company) by the time they consume the information you produced.

Contrast that with *synchronous communication.* Synchronous communication is the exchange of ideas live (in real time). This form of direct communication is one of the best ways to express your thoughts but unfortunately, it doesn't scale, and you won't always be around to answer questions.

In order to evaluate how appropriate each method of communication is when trying to understand intentions, let's look at two axes: proximity and cost.

Proximity is how close in time the communicators need to be in order for that communication to be fruitful. Some methods of communication excel with real-time transfer of information. Other methods of communication excel at communicating years later.

Cost is the measure of effort to communicate. You must weigh the time and money expended to communicate with the value provided. Your future consumers then have to weigh the cost of consuming the information with the value they are trying to deliver. Writing code and not providing any other communication channels is your baseline; you have to do this to produce value. To evaluate additional communication channels' cost, here is what I factor in:

Discoverability
　　How easy was it to find this information outside of a normal workflow? How ephemeral is the knowledge? Is it easy to search for information?

Maintenance cost
　　How accurate is the information? How often does it need to be updated? What goes wrong if this information is out of date?

Production cost
　　How much time and money went into producing the communication?

In Figure 1-1, I plot some common communication methods' cost and proximity required, based on my own experience.

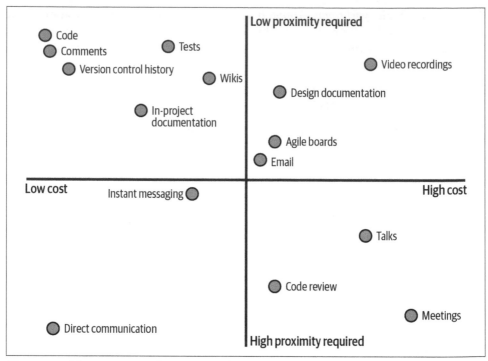

Figure 1-1. Plotting cost and proximity of communcation methods

There are four quadrants that make up the cost/proximity graph.

Low cost, high proximity required
> These are cheap to produce and consume, but are not scalable across time. Direct communication and instant messaging are great examples of these methods. Treat these as snapshots of information in time; they are only valuable when the user is actively listening. Don't rely on these methods to communicate to the future.

High cost, high proximity required
> These are costly events, and often only happen once (such as meetings or conferences). These events should deliver a lot of value at the time of communication, because they do not provide much value to the future. How many times have you been to a meeting that felt like a waste of time? You're feeling the direct loss of value. Talks require a multiplicative cost for each attendee (time spent, hosting space, logistics, etc.). Code reviews are rarely looked at once they are done.

High cost, low proximity required
> These are costly, but that cost can be paid back over time in value delivered, due to the low proximity needed. Emails and agile boards contain a wealth of information, but are not discoverable by others. These are great for bigger concepts

that don't need frequent updates. It becomes a nightmare to try and sift through all the noise just to find the nugget of information you are looking for. Video recordings and design documentation are great for understanding snapshots in time, but are costly to keep updated. Don't rely on these communication methods to understand day-to-day decisions.

Low cost, low proximity required

These are cheap to create, and are easily consumable. Code comments, version control history, and project READMEs all fall into this category, since they are adjacent to the source code we write. Users can view this communication years after it was produced. Anything that a developer encounters during their day-to-day workflow is inherently discoverable. These communication methods are a natural fit for the first place someone will look after the source code. However, your code is one of your best documentation tools, as it is the living record and single source of truth for your system.

Discussion Topic

This plot in Figure 1-1 was created based on generalized use cases. Think about the communication paths you and your organization use. Where would you plot them on the graph? How easy is it to consume accurate information? How costly is it to produce information? Your answers to these questions may result in a slightly different graph, but the single source of truth will be in the executable software you deliver.

Low cost, low proximity communication methods are the best tools for communicating to the future. You should strive to minimize the cost of production and of consumption of communication. You have to write software to deliver value anyway, so the lowest cost option is making your code your primary communication tool. Your codebase becomes the best possible option for expressing your decisions, opinions, and workarounds clearly.

However, for this assertion to hold true, the code has to be cheap to consume as well. Your intent has to come across clearly in your code. Your goal is to minimize the time needed for a reader of your code to understand it. Ideally, a reader does not need to read your implementation, but just your function signature. Through the use of good types, comments and variable names, it should be crystal clear what your code does.

Self-Documenting Code

The wrong response to Figure 1-1 is "Self-documenting code is all I need!" Code should absolutely self-document *what* is being done, but can't cover every use case of communication. For example, version control will give you a history of changes. Design documents discuss sweeping ideals that are not local to any one code file. Meetings (when done right) can be an important event for synchronizing plan execution. Talks are great for sharing ideas with a large audience all at once. While this book focuses on what you can do in your code, don't throw away any other valuable means of communication.

Examples of Intent in Python

Now that I've talked through what intent is and how it matters, let's look at examples through a Python lens. How can you make sure that you are correctly expressing your intentions? I will take a look at two different examples of how a decision affects intentions: collections and iteration.

Collections

When you pick a collection, you are communicating specific information. You must pick the right collection for the task at hand. Otherwise, maintainers will infer the wrong intention from your code.

Consider this code that takes a list of cookbooks and provides a mapping between authors and the number of books written:

```python
def create_author_count_mapping(cookbooks: list[Cookbook]):
    counter = {}
    for cookbook in cookbooks:
        if cookbook.author not in counter:
            counter[cookbook.author] = 0
        counter[cookbook.author] += 1
    return counter
```

What does my use of collections tell you? Why am I not passing a dictionary or a set? Why am I not returning a list? Based on my current usage of collections, here's what you can assume:

- I pass in a list of cookbooks. There may be duplicate cookbooks in this list (I might be counting a shelf of cookbooks in a store with multiple copies).

- I am returning a dictionary. Users can look up a specific author, or iterate over the entire dictionary. I do not have to worry about duplicate authors in the returned collection.

What if I wanted to communicate that no duplicates should be passed into this function? A list communicates the wrong intention. Instead, I should have chosen a set to communicate that this code absolutely will not handle duplicates.

Choosing a collection tells readers about your specific intentions. Here's a list of common collection types, and the intention they convey:

List

This is a collection to be iterated over. It is *mutable*: able to be changed at any time. Very rarely do you expect to be retrieving specific elements from the middle of the list (using a static list index). There may be duplicate elements. The cookbooks on a shelf might be stored in a list.

String

An immutable collection of characters. The name of a cookbook would be a string.

Generator

A collection to be iterated over, and never indexed into. Each element access is performed lazily, so it may take time and/or resources through each loop iteration. They are great for computationally expensive or infinite collections. An online database of recipes might be returned as a generator; you don't want to fetch all the recipes in the world when the user is only going to look at the first 10 results of a search.

Tuple

An immutable collection. You do not expect it to change, so it is more likely to extract specific elements from the middle of the tuple (either through indices or unpacking). It is very rarely iterated over. The information about a specific cookbook might be represented as a tuple, such as (`cookbook_name, author, page count`).

Set

An iterable collection that contains no duplicates. You cannot rely on ordering of elements. The ingredients in a cookbook might be stored as a set.

Dictionary

A mapping from keys to values. Keys are unique across the dictionary. Dictionaries are typically iterated over, or indexed into using dynamic keys. A cookbook's index is a great example of a key to value mapping (from topic to page number.)

Do not use the wrong collection for your purposes. Too many times have I come across a list that should not have had duplicates or a dictionary that wasn't actually being used to map keys to values. Every time there is a disconnect between what you intend and what is in code, you create a maintenance burden. Maintainers must pause, work out what you really meant, and then work around their faulty assumptions (and your faulty assumptions, too).

Dynamic Versus Static Indexing

Depending on the collection type you are using, you may or may not want to use a *static index*. A static index is what you get when you use a constant literal to index into the collection, such as my_list[4] or my_dict["Python"]. In general, lists and dictionaries will not often need a use case for this. You have no guarantee that the collection has the element you are looking for at that index, due to their dynamic nature. If you are looking for specific fields in these types of collections, this is a good sign that you need a user-defined type (explored in Chapters 8, 9 and 10). It is safe to statically index into a tuple, since they are fixed size. Sets and generators are never indexed into.

Exceptions to this rule include:

- Getting the first or last element of a sequence (my_list[0] or my_list[-1])
- Using a dictionary as an intermediate data type such as when reading JSON or YAML
- Operations on a sequence dealing specifically with fixed chunks (e.g., always splitting after the third element or checking for a specific character in a fixed-format string)
- Performance reasons for a specific collection type

In contrast, *dynamic indexing* occurs whenever you index into a collection with a variable that is not known until runtime. This is the most appropriate choice for lists and dictionaries. You'll see this when iterating over collections or searching for a specific element with an index() function.

These are basic collections, but there are more ways to express intent. Here are some special collection types that are even more expressive in communicating to the future:

frozenset
    A set that is immutable.

OrderedDict
    A dictionary that preserves order of elements based on insertion time. As of CPython 3.6 and Python 3.7, built-in dictionaries will also preserve order of elements based on insertion of time.

```
defaultdict
```
A dictionary that provides a default value if the key is missing. For example, I could rewrite my earlier example as follows:

```
from collections import defaultdict
def create_author_count_mapping(cookbooks: list[Cookbook]):
    counter = defaultdict(lambda: 0)
    for cookbook in cookbooks:
        counter[cookbook.author] += 1
    return counter
```

This introduces a new behavior for end users—if they query the dictionary for a value that doesn't exist, they will receive a 0. This might be beneficial in some use cases, but if it's not, you can just return `dict(counter)` instead.

```
Counter
```
A special type of dictionary used for counting how many times an element appears. This greatly simplifies our above code to the following:

```
from collections import Counter
def create_author_count_mapping(cookbooks: list[Cookbook]):
    return Counter(book.author for book in cookbooks)
```

Take a minute to reflect on that last example. Notice how using a `Counter` gives us much more concise code without sacrificing readability. If your readers are familiar with `Counter`, the meaning of this function (and how the implementation works) is immediately apparent. This is a great example of communicating intent to the future through better selection of collection types. I'll explore collections further in Chapter 5.

There are plenty of additional types to explore, including `array`, `bytes`, and `range`. Whenever you come across a new collection type, built-in or otherwise, ask yourself how it differs from other collections and what it conveys to future readers.

Iteration

Iteration is another example where the abstraction you choose dictates the intent you convey.

How many times have you seen code like this?

```
text = "This is some generic text"
index = 0
while index < len(text):
    print(text[index])
    index += 1
```

This simple code prints each character on a separate line. This is perfectly fine for a first pass at Python for this problem, but the solution quickly evolves into the more

Pythonic (code written in an idiomatic style that aims to emphasize simplicity and is recognizable to most Python developers):

```
for character in text:
    print(character)
```

Take a moment and reflect on why this option is preferable. The for loop is a more appropriate choice; it communicates intentions more clearly. Just like collection types, the looping construct you select explicitly communicates different concepts. Here's a list of some common looping constructs and what they convey:

for *loops*

for loops are used for iterating over each element in a collection or range and performing an action/side effect.

```
for cookbook in cookbooks:
    print(cookbook)
```

while *loops*

while loops are used for iterating as long as a certain condition is true.

```
while is_cookbook_open(cookbook):
    narrate(cookbook)
```

Comprehensions

Comprehensions are used for transforming one collection into another (normally, this does not have side effects, especially if the comprehension is lazy).

```
authors = [cookbook.author for cookbook in cookbooks]
```

Recursion

Recursion is used when the substructure of a collection is identical to the structure of a collection (for example, each child of a tree is also a tree).

```
def list_ingredients(item):
    if isinstance(item, PreparedIngredient):
        list_ingredients(item)
    else:
        print(ingredient)
```

You want each line of your codebase to deliver value. Furthermore, you want each line to clearly communicate what that value is to future developers. This drives a need to minimize any amount of boilerplate, scaffolding, and superfluous code. In the example above, I am iterating over each element and performing a side effect (printing an element), which makes the for loop an ideal looping construct. I am not wasting code. In contrast, the while loop requires us to explicitly track looping until a certain condition occurs. In other words, I need to track a specific condition and mutate a variable every iteration. This distracts from the value the loop provides, and provides unwanted cognitive burden.

Law of Least Surprise

Distractions from intent are bad, but there's a class of communication that is even worse: when code actively surprises your future collaborators. You want to adhere to the *Law of Least Surprise*; when someone reads through the codebase, they should almost never be surprised at behavior or implementation (and when they are surprised, there should be a great comment near the code to explain why it is that way). This is why communicating intent is paramount. Clear, clean code lowers the likelihood of miscommunication.

 The *Law Of Least Surprise*, also known as the *Law of Least Astonishment*, states that a program should always respond to the user in the way that astonishes them the least.[3] Surprising behavior leads to confusion. Confusion leads to misplaced assumptions. Misplaced assumptions lead to bugs. And that is how you get unreliable software.

Bear in mind, you can write completely correct code and still surprise someone in the future. There was one nasty bug I was chasing early in my career that crashed due to corrupted memory. Putting the code under a debugger or putting in too many print statements affected timing such that the bug would not manifest (a true "heisenbug").[4] There were literally thousands of lines of code that related to this bug.

So I had to do a manual bisect, splitting the code in half, see which half actually had the crash by removing the other half, and then do it all over again in that code half. After two weeks of tearing my hair out, I finally decided to inspect an innocuous sounding function called getEvent. It turns out that this function was actually *setting* an event with invalid data. Needless to say, I was very surprised. The function was completely correct in what it was doing, but because I missed the intent of the code, I overlooked the bug for at least three days. Surprising your collaborators will cost their time.

A lot of this surprise ends up coming from complexity. There are two types of complexity: *necessary complexity* and *accidental complexity*. Necessary complexity is the complexity inherent in your domain. Deep learning models are necessarily complex; they are not something you browse through the inner workings of and understand in a few minutes. Optimizing object–relational mapping (ORM) is necessarily complex; there is a large variety of possible user inputs have to be accounted for. You won't be able to remove necessary complexity, so your best bet would be to try and contain it,

---

3 Geoffrey James. *The Tao of Programming*. *https://oreil.ly/NcKNK*.

4 A bug that displays different behavior when being observed. *SIGSOFT '83: Proceedings of the ACM SIGSOFT/ SIGPLAN software engineering symposium on High-level debugging*.

lest it sprawls across your codebase and ends up becoming accidental complexity instead.

In contrast, accidental complexity is complexity that produces superfluous, wasteful, or confusing statements in code. It's what happens when a system evolves over time and developers are jamming features in without reevaluating old code to determine whether their original assertions hold true. I once worked on a project where adding a single command-line option (and associated means of programmatically setting it) touched no fewer than 10 files. Why would adding one simple value ever need to require changes all over the codebase?

You know you have accidental complexity if you've ever experienced the following:

- Things that sound simple (adding users, changing a UI control, etc.) are non-trivial to implement.
- Difficulty onboarding new developers into understanding your codebase. New developers on a project are your best indicators of how maintainable your code is right now—no need to wait years.
- Estimates for adding functionality are always high, yet you slip the schedule nonetheless.

Remove accidental complexity and isolate your necessary complexity wherever possible. Those will be the stumbling blocks for your future collaborators. These sources of complexity compound miscommunication, as they obscure and diffuse intent throughout the codebase.

Discussion Topic

What accidental complexities do you have in your codebase? How challenging would it be to understand simple concepts if you were dropped into the codebase with no communication to other developers? What can you do to simplify complexities identified in this exercise (especially if they are in often-changing code)?

Throughout the rest of the book, I will look at different techniques for communicating intent in Python.

Closing Thoughts

Robust code matters. Clean code matters. Your code needs to be maintainable for the entire lifetime of the codebase, and in order to ensure that outcome, you need to put active foresight into what you are communicating and how. You need to clearly embody your knowledge as close to the code as possible. It will feel like a burden to continuously look forward, but with practice it becomes natural, and you start reaping the benefits as you work in your own codebase.

Every time you map a real-world concept to code, you are creating an abstraction, whether it is through the use of a collection or your decision to keep functions separate. Every abstraction is a choice, and every choice communicates something, whether intentional or not. I encourage you to think about each line of code you are writing and ask yourself, "What will a future developer learn from this?" You owe it to future maintainers to enable them to deliver value at the same speed that you can today. Otherwise, your codebase will get bloated, schedules will slip, and complexity will grow. It is your job as a developer to mitigate that risk.

Look for potential hotspots, such as incorrect abstractions (such as collections or iteration) or accidental complexity. These are prime areas where communication can break down over time. If these types of hotspots are in areas that change often, they are a priority to address now.

In the next chapter, you're going to take what you learned from this chapter and apply it to a fundamental Python concept: types. The types you choose express your intent to future developers, and picking the correct types will lead to better maintainability.

## PART I

Annotating Your Code with Types

Welcome to Part I, where I will focus on *types* in Python. Types model the behavior of your program. Beginner programmers understand that there are different types in Python, such as `float` or `str`. But what is a type? How does mastering types make your codebase stronger? Types are a fundamental underpinning of any programming language, but, unfortunately, most introductory texts gloss over just how types benefit your codebase (or if misused, those same types increase complexity).

Tell me if you've seen this before:

```
>>>type(3.14)
<class 'float'>

>>>type("This is another boring example")
<class 'str'>

>>> type(["Even", "more", "boring", "examples"])
<class 'list'>
```

This could be pulled from almost any beginner's guide to Python. You will learn about the `int`, `str`, `float`, and `bool` data types, and all sorts of other things the language offers. Then, boom, you move on, because let's face it, this Python is not flashy. You want to dive into the cool stuff, like functions and loops and dictionaries, and I don't blame you. But it's a shame that many tutorials never revisit types and give them their proper due. As users dig deeper, they may discover type annotations (which I cover in the next chapter) or start writing classes, but often miss out on the fundamental discussion about when to use types appropriately.

That's where I'll start.

## CHAPTER 2

Introduction to Python Types

To write maintainable Python, you must be aware of the nature of types and be deliberate about using them. I'll start by talking about what a type actually is and why that matters. I'll then move on to how the Python language's decisions about its type system affects the robustness of your codebase.

What's in a Type?

I want you to pause and answer a question: without mentioning numbers, strings, text, or Booleans, how would you explain what a type is?

It's not a simple answer for everyone. It's even harder to explain what the benefits are, especially in a language like Python where you do not have to explicitly declare types of variables.

I consider a type to have a very simple definition: a communication method. Types convey information. They provide a representation that users and computers can reason about. I break the representation down into two different facets:

Mechanical representation
    Types communicate behaviors and constraints to the Python language itself.

Semantic representation
    Types communicate behaviors and constraints to other developers.

Let's go learn a little more about each representation.

Mechanical Representation

At its core, computers are all about binary code. Your processor doesn't speak Python; all it sees is the presence or absence of electrical current on circuits going through it. Same goes for what's in your computer memory.

Suppose your memory looked like the following:

```
0011001010001001000101001001000100100010000010101
0010101010101000000111111110010010100111110100100
0100100010010100101011101111011010101010101010101

010100000100000101010100

10100100100100010101000101001001010101001001001001
0001111010101101011010010101110000000000000000000111
```

Looks like a bunch of gibberish. Let's zoom in on the middle part there:

```
01010000 01000001 01010100
```

There is no way to tell exactly what this number means by itself. Depending on computer architecture it is plausible that this could represent the number 5259604 or 5521744. It could also be the string "PAT." Without any sort of context, you can't know for certain. This is why Python needs types. Type information gives Python what it needs to know to make sense of all the ones and zeroes. Let's see it in action:

```python
from ctypes import string_at
from sys import getsizeof
from binascii import hexlify

a = 0b01010000_01000001_01010100
print(a)
>>> 5259604

# prints out the memory of the variable
print(hexlify(string_at(id(a), getsizeof(a))))
>>> b'0100000000000000607c05499555000001000000000000054415000'

text = "PAT"
print(hexlify(string_at(id(text), getsizeof(text))))
>>>b'0100000000000000a00f0649955500000300000000000000375c9f1f02'
   b'acdbe4e5379218b77f00000000000000000000050415400'
```

 I am running CPython 3.9.0 on a little-endian machine, so if you see different results, don't worry, there are subtle things that can change your answers. (This code is not guaranteed to run on other Python implementations such as Jython or PyPy.)

These hex strings display the contents of the memory containing a Python object. You'll find pointers to the next and previous object in a linked list (for garbage collection purposes), a reference count, a type, and the actual data itself. You can see the bytes at the end of each returned value to see the number or string (look for the bytes 0x544150 or 0x504154). The important part of this is that there is a type encoded into that memory. When Python looks at a variable, it knows exactly what type everything is at runtime (just as when you use the type() function.)

It's easy to think that this is the only reason for types—the computer needs to know how to interpret various blobs of memory. It is important to be aware of how Python uses types, as it has some implications for writing robust code, but even more important is the second representation: semantic representation.

Semantic Representation

While the first definition of types is great for lower-level programming, it's the second definition that applies to every developer. Types, in addition to having a mechanical representation, also manifest a semantic representation. A semantic representation is a communication tool; the types you choose communicate information across time and space to a future developer.

Types tell a user what behaviors they can expect when interacting with that entity. In this context, "behaviors" are the operations that you associate with that type (plus any preconditions or postconditions). They are the boundaries, constraints, and freedoms that a user interacts with whenever they use that type. Types used correctly have low barriers to understanding; they become natural to use. Conversely, types used poorly are a hindrance.

Consider the lowly int. Take a minute to think about what behaviors an integer has in Python. Here's a quick (noncomprehensive) list I came up with:

- Constructible from integers, floats, or strings
- Mathematical operations such as addition, subtraction, division, multiplication, exponentiation, and negation
- Relational comparison such as <, >, ==, and !=
- Bitwise operations (manipulating individual bits of a number) such as &, |, ^, ~, and shifting
- Convertible to a string using str or repr functions
- Able to be rounded through ceil, floor, and round methods (even though they return the integer itself, these are supported methods)

An int has many behaviors. You can view the full list if you if you type help(int) into your interactive Python console.

Now consider a `datetime`:

```
>>>import datetime
>>>datetime.datetime.now()
datetime.datetime(2020, 9, 8, 22, 19, 28, 838667)
```

A `datetime` is not that different from an `int`. Typically, it's represented as a number of seconds or milliseconds from some epoch of time (such as January 1, 1970). But think about the behaviors a `datetime` has (I've italicized the differences in behavior from an integer):

- Constructible from a *string, or a set of integers representing day/month/year/etc.*
- Mathematical operations such as addition of *time deltas* and subtraction of *both time deltas and other `datetime` objects*
- Relational comparison
- *No bitwise operations available*
- Convertible to a string using `str` or `repr` functions
- *Is not* able to be rounded through `ceil`, `floor`, or `round` methods

A `datetime` supports addition, but not of other datetimes. We only add time deltas (such as adding a day or adding a week). Multiplying and dividing really don't make sense for a `datetime`. Similarly, rounding dates is not a supported operation in the standard library. However, `datetimes` do offer comparison and string formatting operations with similar semantics to an integer. So even though `datetime` is at heart an integer, it contains a constrained subset of operations.

 Semantics refers to the meaning of an operation. While `str(int)` and `str(datetime.datetime.now())` will return differently formatted strings, the meaning is the same: I am creating a string from a value.

Datetimes also support their own behaviors, to further distinguish them from integers. These include:

- Changing values based on time zones
- Being able to control the format of strings
- Finding what weekday it is

Again, if you'd like a full list of behaviors, type `import datetime; help(datetime.datetime)` into your REPL.

A `datetime` is more specific than an `int`. It conveys a more specific use case than just a plain old number. When you choose to use a more specific type, you are telling future contributors that there are operations that are possible and constraints to be aware of that aren't present in the less specific type.

Let's dive into how this ties into robust code. Say you inherit a codebase that handles the opening and closing of a completely automated kitchen. You need to add in functionality to be able to change closing time (say, for extending a kitchen's hours on holidays).

```python
def close_kitchen_if_past_cutoff_time(point_in_time):
    if point_in_time >= closing_time():
        close_kitchen()
        log_time_closed(point_in_time)
```

You know you need to be operating on `point_in_time`, but how do you get started? What type are you even dealing with? Is it a `str`, `int`, `datetime`, or some custom class? What operations are you allowed to perform on `point_in_time`? You didn't write this code, and you have no history with it. The same problems exist if you want to call the code as well. You have no idea what is legal to pass into this function.

If you make an incorrect assumption one way or the other, and that code makes it to production, you will have made the code less robust. Maybe that code doesn't lie on a codepath that is executed often. Maybe some other bug is hiding this code from being run. Maybe there aren't a whole lot of tests around this piece of code, and it becomes a runtime error later on. No matter what, there is a bug lurking in the code, and you've decreased maintainability.

Responsible developers do their best not to have bugs hit production. They will search for tests, documentation (with a grain of salt, of course—documentation can go out of date quickly), or calling code. They will look at `closing_time()` and `log_time_closed()` to see what types they expect or provide, and plan accordingly. This is a correct path in this case, but I still consider it a suboptimal path. While an error won't reach production, they are still expending time in looking through the code, which prevents value from being delivered as quickly. With such a small example, you would be forgiven for thinking that this isn't that big a problem if it happens once. But beware of death by a thousand cuts: any one slice isn't too detrimental on its own, but thousands piled up and strewn across a codebase will leave you limping along, trying to deliver code.

The root cause is that the semantic representation was not clear for the parameter. As you write code, do what you can to express your intent through types. You can do it as a comment where needed, but I recommend using type annotations (supported in Python 3.5+) to explain parts of your code.

```
def close_kitchen_if_past_cutoff_time(point_in_time: datetime.datetime):
    if point_in_time >= closing_time():
        close_kitchen()
        log_time_closed(point_in_time)
```

All I need to do is put in a : <type> after my parameters. Most code examples in this book will utilize type annotations to make it clear what type the code expects.

Now, as developers come across this code, they will know what's expected of point_in_time. They don't have to look through other methods, tests, or documentation to know how to manipulate the variable. They have a crystal clear clue on what to do, and they can get right to work performing the modifications they need to do. You are conveying semantic representation to future developers, without ever directly talking to them.

Furthermore, as developers use a type more and more, they become familiar with it. They won't need to look up documentation or help() to use that type when they come across it. You begin to create a vocabulary of well-known types across your codebase. This lessens the burden of maintenance. When a developer is modifying existing code, they want to focus on the changes they need to make without getting bogged down.

Semantic representation of a type is extremely important, and the rest of Part I will be dedicated to covering how you can use types to your advantage. Before I move on, though, I need to walk through some fundamental structural elements of Python as a language, and how they impact codebase robustness.

Discussion Topic

Think about types used in your codebase. Pick a few and ask yourself what their semantic representations are. Enumerate their constraints, use cases, and behaviors. Could you be using these types in more places? Are there places where you are misusing types?

Typing Systems

As discussed earlier in the chapter, a type system aims to give a user some way to model the behaviors and constraints in the language. Programming languages set expectations about how their specific type systems work, both during code construction and runtime.

Strong Versus Weak

Typing systems are classified on a spectrum from weak to strong. Languages toward the stronger side of the spectrum tend to restrict the use of operations to the types that support them. In other words, if you break the semantic representation of the type, you are told (sometimes quite loudly) through a compiler error or a runtime error. Languages such as Haskell, TypeScript, and Rust are all considered strongly typed. Proponents advocate strongly typed languages because errors are more apparent when building or running code.

In contrast, languages toward the weaker side of the spectrum will not restrict the use of operations to the types that support them. Types are often coerced into a different type to make sense of an operation. Languages such as JavaScript, Perl, and older versions of C are weakly typed. Proponents advocate the speed with which developers can quickly iterate on code without fighting language along the way.

Python falls toward the stronger side of the spectrum. There are very few implicit conversions that happen between types. It is noticeable when you perform illegal operations:

```
>>>[] + {}
TypeError: can only concatenate list (not "dict") to list

>>> {} + []
TypeError: unsupported operand type(s) for +: 'dict' and list
```

Contrast that with a weakly typed language, such as JavaScript:

```
>>> [] + {}
"[object Object]"

>>> {} + []
0
```

In terms of robustness, a strongly typed language such as Python certainly helps us out. While errors still will show up at runtime instead of at development time, they still will show up in an obvious `TypeError` exception. This reduces the time taken to debug issues significantly, again allowing you to deliver incremental value more quickly.

Are Weakly Typed Languages Inherently Not Robust?

Codebases in weakly typed languages can absolutely be robust; by no means am I dumping on those languages. Consider the sheer amount of production-grade JavaScript that the world runs on. However, a weakly typed language requires extra care to be robust. It's easy to mistake the type of a variable and make incorrect assumptions. Developers come to rely very heavily on linters, tests, and other tools to improve maintainability.

Dynamic Versus Static

There is another typing spectrum I need to discuss: static versus dynamic typing. This is fundamentally a difference in handling mechanical representation of types.

Languages that offer static typing embed their typing information in variables during build time. Developers may explicitly add type information to variables, or some tool such as a compiler infers types for the developer. Variables do not change their type at runtime (hence, "static"). Proponents of static typing tout the ability to write safe code out of the gate and to benefit from a strong safety net.

Dynamic typing, on the other hand, embeds type information with the value or variable itself. Variables can change types at runtime quite easily, because there is no type information tied to that variable. Proponents of dynamic typing advocate the flexibility and speed that it takes to develop; there's nowhere near as much fighting with compilers.

Python is a dynamically typed language. As you saw during the discussion about mechanical representation, there was type information embedded inside the values of a variable. Python has no qualms about changing the type of a variable at runtime:

```
>>> a = 5
>>> a = "string"
>>> a
"string"

>>> a = tuple()
>>> a
()
```

Unfortunately, the ability to change types at runtime is a hindrance to robust code in many cases. You cannot make strong assumptions about a variable throughout its lifetime. As assumptions are broken, it's easy to write unstable assumptions on top of them, leading to a ticking logic bomb in your code.

Are Dynamically Typed Languages Inherently Not Robust?

Just like weakly typed languages, it is still absolutely possible to write robust code in a dynamically typed language. You just have to work a little harder for it. You will have to make more deliberate decisions to make your codebase more maintainable. On the flip side, being statically typed doesn't guarantee robustness either; one can do the bare minimum with types and see little benefit.

To make things worse, the type annotations I showed earlier have no effect on this behavior at runtime:

```
>>> a: int = 5
>>> a = "string"
>>> a
"string"
```

No errors, no warnings, no anything. But hope is not lost, and you have plenty of strategies to make code more robust (otherwise, this would be quite the short book). We will discuss one last thing as a contributor to robust code, and then start diving into the meat of improving our codebase.

Duck Typing

It is perhaps an unwritten law that whenever someone mentions duck typing, someone must reply with:

> If it walks like a duck and it quacks like a duck, then it must be a duck.

My problem with this saying is that I find it completely unhelpful for explaining what duck typing actually is. It's catchy, concise, and, crucially, only comprehensible to those who already understand duck typing. When I was younger, I just nodded politely, afraid that I was missing something profound in this simple phrase. It wasn't until later on that I truly understood the power of duck typing.

Duck typing is the ability to use objects and entities in a programming language as long as they adhere to some interface. It is a wonderful thing in Python, and most people use it without even knowing it. Let's look at a simple example to illustrate what I'm talking about:

```
from typing import Iterable
def print_items(items: Iterable):
    for item in items:
        print(item)

print_items([1,2,3])
print_items({4, 5, 6})
print_items({"A": 1, "B": 2, "C": 3})
```

In all three invocations of print_items, we loop through the collection and print each item. Think about how this works. print_items has absolutely no knowledge of what type it will receive. It just receives a type at runtime and operates upon it. It's not introspecting each argument and deciding to do different things based on the type. The truth is much simpler. Instead, all print_items is doing is checking that whatever is passed in can be iterated upon (by calling an __iter__ method). If the attribute __iter__ exists, it's called and the returned iterator is looped over.

We can verify this with a simple code example:

```
>>> print_items(5)

Traceback (most recent call last):
  File "<stdin>", line 1, in <module>
  File "<stdin>", line 2, in print_items
TypeError: 'int' object is not iterable

>>> '__iter__' in dir(int)
False
>>> '__iter__' in dir(list)
True
```

Duck typing is what makes this possible. As long as a type supports the variables and methods used by a function, you can use that type in that function freely.

Here's another example:

```
>>>def double_value(value):
>>>    return value + value

>>>double_value(5)
10

>>>double_value("abc")
"abcabc"
```

It doesn't matter that we're passing an integer in one place or a string in another; both support the + operator, so either will work just fine. Any object that supports the + operator can be passed in. We can even do it with a list:

```
>>>double_value([1, 2, 3])
[1, 2, 3, 1, 2, 3]
```

So how does this play into robustness? It turns out that duck typing is a double-edged sword. It can increase robustness because it increases composability (we'll learn more about composability in Chapter 17). Building up a library of solid abstractions able to handle a multitude of types lessens the need for complex special cases. However, if duck typing is overused, you start to break down assumptions that a developer can rely upon. When updating code, it's not simple enough to just make the changes; you must look at all calling code and make sure that the types passed into your function satisfy your new changes as well.

With all this in mind, it might be best to reword the idiom earlier in this section as such:

> If it walks like a duck and quacks like a duck, and you are looking for things that walk and quack like ducks, then you can treat it as if it were a duck.

Doesn't roll off the tongue as well, does it?

Discussion Topic

Do you use duck typing in your codebase? Are there places where you can pass in types that don't match what the code is looking for, but things still work? Do you think these increase or decrease robustness for your use cases?

Closing Thoughts

Types are a pillar of clean, maintainable code and serve as a communication tool to other developers. If you take care with types, you communicate a great deal, creating less burden for future maintainers. The rest of Part I will show you how to use types to enhance a codebase's robustness.

Remember, Python is dynamically and strongly typed. The strongly typed nature will be a boon for us; Python will notify us about errors when we use incompatible types. But its dynamically typed nature is something we will have to overcome in order to write better code. These language choices shape how Python code is written and you should keep them in mind as you write your code.

In the next chapter, we're going to talk about type annotations, which is how we can be explicit about the type we use. Type annotations serve a crucial role: our primary communication method of behaviors to future developers. They help overcome the limitations of a dynamically typed language and allow you to enforce intentions throughout a codebase.

Type Annotations

Python is a dynamically typed language; types aren't known until runtime. This is an obstacle when trying to write robust code. Since types are embedded in the value itself, developers have a very tough time knowing what type they are working with. Sure, that name looks likes a `str` today, but what happens if someone makes it `bytes`? Assumptions about types are built on shaky ground with dynamically typed languages. Hope is not lost, though. In Python 3.5, a brand-new feature was introduced: type annotations.

Type annotations bring your ability to write robust code to a whole new level. Guido van Rossum, creator of Python, says it best:

> I've learned a painful lesson that for small programs dynamic typing is great. For large programs you have to have a more disciplined approach and it helps if the language actually gives you that discipline, rather than telling you "Well, you can do whatever you want."[1]

Type annotations are the more disciplined approach, the extra bit of care you need to wrangle larger codebases. In this chapter, you'll learn how to use type annotations, why they are so important, and how to utilize a tool called a typechecker to enforce your intentions throughout your codebase.

---

1 Guido van Rossum. "A Language Creators' Conversation." PuPPy (Puget Sound Programming Python) Annual Benefit 2019. *https://oreil.ly/1xf01*.

What Are Type Annotations?

In Chapter 2, you got your first glance at a type annotation:

```
def close_kitchen_if_past_close(point_in_time: datetime.datetime): ❶
    if point_in_time >= closing_time():
        close_kitchen()
        log_time_closed(point_in_time)
```

❶ The type annotation here is : `datetime.datetime`

Type annotations are an additional syntax notifying the user of an expected type of your variables. These annotations serve as *type hints*; they provide hints to the reader, but they are not actually used by the Python language at runtime. In fact, you are completely free to ignore the hints. Consider the following snippet of code, along with a comment written by the developer.

```
# CustomDateTime offers all the same functionality with
# datetime.datetime. I'm using it here for its better
# logging facilities.
close_kitchen_if_past_close(CustomDateTime("now")) # no error
```

 It should be a rare case where you go against a type hint. The author very clearly intended a specific use case. If you aren't going to follow the type annotation, you are setting yourself up for problems if the original code changes in a way that is incompatible with the types that you are using (such as expecting a certain function to work with that type).

Python will not throw any error at runtime in this scenario. As a matter of fact, it won't use the type annotations at all during runtime. There is no checking or cost for using these when Python executes. These type annotations still serve a crucial purpose: informing your readers of the expected type. Maintainers of code will know what types they are allowed to use when changing your implementation. Calling code will also benefit, as developers will know exactly what type to pass in. By implementing type annotations, you reduce friction.

Put yourself in your future maintainer's shoes. Wouldn't it be nice to come across code that is intuitive to use? You wouldn't have to dig through function after function to determine usage. You wouldn't assume a wrong type and then need to deal with the fallout of exceptions and wrong behavior.

Consider another piece of code that takes in employees' availability and a restaurant's opening time, and then schedules available workers for that day. You want to use this piece of code and you see the following:

```
def schedule_restaurant_open(open_time, workers_needed):
```

Let's ignore the implementation for a minute, because I want to focus on first impressions. What do you think can get passed into this? Stop, close your eyes, and ask yourself what are reasonable types that can be passed in before reading on. Is open_time a datetime, the number of seconds since epoch, or maybe a string containing an hour? Is workers_needed a list of names, a list of Worker objects, or something else? If you guess wrong, or aren't sure, you need to go look at either the implementation or calling code, which I've established takes time and is frustrating.

Let me provide an implementation and you can see how close you were.

```
import datetime
import random

def schedule_restaurant_open(open_time: datetime.datetime,
                             workers_needed: int):
    workers = find_workers_available_for_time(open_time)
    # Use random.sample to pick X available workers
    # where X is the number of workers needed.
    for worker in random.sample(workers, workers_needed):
        worker.schedule(open_time)
```

You probably guessed that open_time is a datetime, but did you consider that workers_needed could have been an int? As soon as you see the type annotations, you get a much better picture of what's happening. This reduces cognitive overhead and reduces friction for maintainers.

 This is certainly a step in the right direction, but don't stop here. If you see code like this, consider renaming the variable to number_of_workers_needed to reflect just what the integer means. In the next chapter, I'll also explore type aliases, which provide an alternate way of expressing yourself.

So far, all the examples I've shown have focused on parameters, but you're also allowed to annotate *return types*.

Consider the schedule_restaurant_open function. In the middle of that snippet, I called find_workers_available_for_time. This returns to a variable named workers. Suppose you want to change the code to pick workers who have gone the longest without working, rather than random sampling? Do you have any indication what type workers is?

If you were to just look at the function signature, you would see the following:

```
def find_workers_available_for_time(open_time: datetime.datetime):
```

Nothing in here helps us do your job more quickly. You could guess and the tests would tell us, right? Maybe it's a list of names? Instead of letting the tests fail, maybe you should go look through the implementation.

```
def find_workers_available_for_time(open_time: datetime.datetime):
    workers = worker_database.get_all_workers()
    available_workers = [worker for worker in workers
                            if is_available(worker)]
    if available_workers:
        return available_workers

    # fall back to workers who listed they are available
    # in an emergency
    emergency_workers = [worker for worker in get_emergency_workers()
                            if is_available(worker)]

    if emergency_workers:
        return emergency_workers

    # Schedule the owner to open, they will find someone else
    return [OWNER]
```

Oh no, there's nothing in here that tells you what type you should be expecting. There are three different return statements throughout this code, and you hope that they all return the same type. (Surely every `if` statement is tested through unit tests to make sure they are consistent, right? Right?) You need to dig deeper. You need to look at `worker_database`. You need to look at `is_available` and `get_emergency_workers`. You need to look at the `OWNER` variable. Every one of these needs to be consistent, or else you'll need to handle special cases in your original code.

And what if these functions also don't tell you exactly what you need? What if you have to go deeper through multiple function calls? Every layer you have to go through is another layer of abstraction you need to keep in your brain. Every piece of information contributes to cognitive overload. The more cognitive overload you are burdened with, the more likely it is that a mistake will happen.

All of this is avoided by annotating a return type. Return types are annotated by putting `-> <type>` at the end of the function declaration. Suppose you came across this function signature:

```
def find_workers_available_for_time(open_time: datetime.datetime) -> list[str]:
```

You now know that you should indeed treat workers as a list of strings. No digging through databases, function calls, or modules needed.

In Python 3.8 and earlier, built-in collection types such as `list`, `dict`, and `set` did not allow bracket syntax such as `list[Cookbook]` or `dict[str,int]`. Instead, you needed to use type annotations from the typing module:

```python
from typing import Dict,List
AuthorToCountMapping = Dict[str, int]
def count_authors(
                cookbooks: List[Cookbook]
            ) -> AuthorToCountMapping:
        # ...
```

You can also annotate variables when needed:

```python
workers: list[str] = find_workers_available_for_time(open_time)
numbers: list[int] = []
ratio: float = get_ratio(5,3)
```

While I will annotate all of my functions, I typically don't bother annotating variables unless there is something specific I want to convey in my code (such as a type that is different than expected). I don't want to get too into the realm of putting type annotations on literally everything—the lack of verbosity is what drew many developers to Python in the first place. The types can clutter your code, especially when it is blindingly obvious what the type is.

```python
number: int = 0
text: str = "useless"
values: list[float] = [1.2, 3.4, 6.0]
worker: Worker = Worker()
```

None of these type annotations provide more value than what is already provided by Python itself. Readers of this code know that `"useless"` is a `str`. Remember, type annotations are used for type hinting; you are providing notes for the future to improve communication. You don't need to state the obvious everywhere.

Type Annotations Before Python 3.5

If you have the misfortune of not being able to use a later version of Python, hope is not lost. There is an alternative syntax for type annotations, even for Python 2.7.

To write the annotations, you need to do so in a comment:

```python
ratio = get_ratio(5,3) # type: float
def get_workers(open): # type: (datetime.datetime) -> List[str]
```

This is easier to miss, as the types are not visually close to the variable itself. If you have the ability to upgrade to Python 3.5, consider doing so and using the newer method of type annotations.

Benefits of Type Annotations

As with every decision you make, you need to weigh the costs and benefits. Thinking about types up front helps your deliberate design process, but do type annotations provide other benefits? I'll show you how type annotations really pull their weight through tooling.

Autocomplete

I've mainly talked about communication to other developers, but your Python environment benefits from type annotations as well. Since Python is dynamically typed, it is difficult to know what operations are available. With type annotations, many Python-aware code editors will autocomplete your variable's operations.

In Figure 3-1, you'll see a screenshot that illustrates a popular code editor, VS Code, detecting a `datetime` and offering to autocomplete my variables.

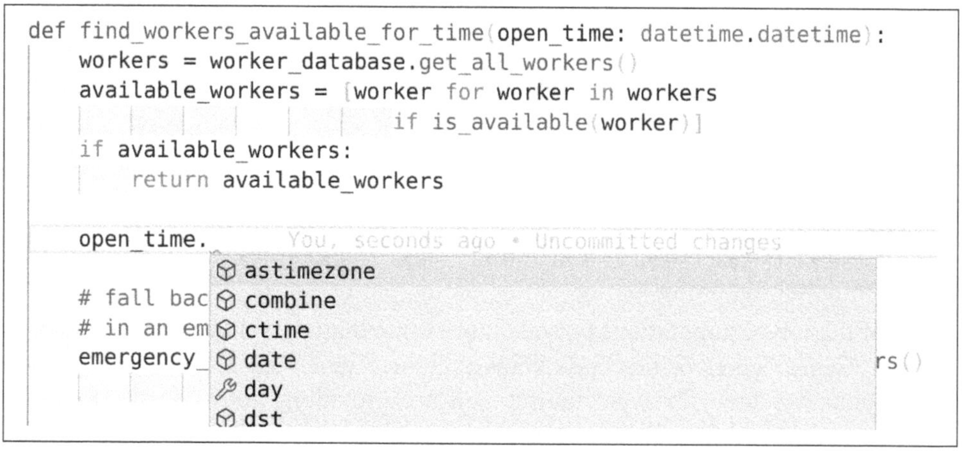

```
def find_workers_available_for_time(open_time: datetime.datetime):
    workers = worker_database.get_all_workers()
    available_workers = [worker for worker in workers
                         if is_available(worker)]
    if available_workers:
        return available_workers

    open_time.        You, seconds ago • Uncommitted changes
              ⊙ astimezone
    # fall bac ⊙ combine
    # in an em ⊙ ctime
    emergency_ ⊙ date                                          rs()
              ⌀ day
              ⊙ dst
```

Figure 3-1. VS Code showing autocompletion

Typecheckers

Throughout this book, I've been talking about how types communicate intent, but have been leaving out one key detail: no programmer has to honor these type annotations if they don't want to. If your code contradicts a type annotation, it is probably an error and you're still relying on humans to catch bugs. I want to do better. I want a computer to find these sorts of bugs for me.

I showed this snippet when talking about dynamic typing back in Chapter 2:

```
>>> a: int = 5
>>> a = "string"
>>> a
"string"
```

Herein lies the challenge: how do type annotations make your codebase robust, when you can't trust that developers will follow their guidance? In order to be robust, you want your code to stand the test of time. To do that, you need some sort of tool that can check all your type annotations and flag if anything is amiss. That tool is called a typechecker.

Typecheckers are what allow the type annotations to transcend from communication method to a safety net. It is a form of static analysis. *Static analysis tools* are tools that run on your source code, and don't impact your runtime at all. You'll learn more about static analysis tools in Chapter 20, but for now, I will just explain typecheckers.

First, I need to install one. I'll use mypy, a very popular typechecker.

```
pip install mypy
```

Now I'll create a file named *invalid_type.py* with incorrect behavior:

```
a: int = 5
a = "string"
```

If I run mypy on the command line against that file, I will get an error:

```
mypy invalid_type.py

chapter3/invalid_type.py:2: error: Incompatible types in assignment
                          (expression has type "str", variable has type
                          "int")
Found 1 error in 1 file (checked 1 source file)
```

And just like that, my type annotations become a first line of defense against errors. Anytime you make a mistake and go against the author's intent, a type checker will find out and alert you. In fact, in most development environments, it's possible to get this analysis in real time, notifying you of errors as you type. (Without reading your mind, this is about as early as a tool can catch errors, which is pretty great.)

Exercise: Spot the Bug

Here are some more examples of mypy catching errors in my code. I want you to look for the error in each code snippet and time how long it takes you to find the bug or give up, and then check the output listed below the snippet to see if you got it right.

```
def read_file_and_reverse_it(filename: str) -> str:
    with open(filename) as f:
        # Convert bytes back into str
        return f.read().encode("utf-8")[::-1]
```

Here's the mypy output showing the error:

```
mypy chapter3/invalid_example1.py
chapter3/invalid_example1.py:3: error: Incompatible return value type
                                       (got "bytes", expected "str")
Found 1 error in 1 file (checked 1 source file)
```

Whoops, I'm returning bytes, not a str. I made a call to encode instead of decode, and got my return type all mixed up. I can't even tell you how many times I made this mistake moving Python 2.7 code to Python 3. Thank goodness for typecheckers.

Here's another example:

```
# takes a list and adds the doubled values
# to the end
# [1,2,3] => [1,2,3,2,4,6]
def add_doubled_values(my_list: list[int]):
    my_list.update([x*2 for x in my_list])

add_doubled_values([1,2,3])
```

The mypy error is as follows:

```
mypy chapter3/invalid_example2.py
chapter3/invalid_example2.py:6: error: "list[int]" has no attribute "update"
Found 1 error in 1 file (checked 1 source file)
```

Another innocent mistake I made by calling update on a list instead of extend. These sorts of mistakes can happen quite easily when moving between collection types (in this case from a set, which does offer an update method, to a list, which doesn't).

One more example to wrap it up:

```
# The restaurant is named differently
# in different parts of the world
def get_restaurant_name(city: str) -> str:
    if city in ITALY_CITIES:
            return "Trattoria Viafore"
    if city in GERMANY_CITIES:
            return "Pat's Kantine"
    if city in US_CITIES:
            return "Pat's Place"
    return None


if get_restaurant_name('Boston'):
    print("Location Found")
```

The mypy error is as follows:

```
chapter3/invalid_example3.py:14: error: Incompatible return value type
                                        (got "None", expected "str")
Found 1 error in 1 file (checked 1 source file)
```

This one is subtle. I'm returning None when a string value is expected. If all the code is just checking conditionally for the restaurant name to make decisions, like I do above, tests will pass, and nothing will be amiss. This is true even for the negative case, because None is absolutely fine to check for in if statements (it is false-y). This is an example of Python's dynamic typing coming back to bite us.

However, a few months from now, some developer will start trying to use this return value as a string, and as soon as a new city needs to be added, the code starts trying to operate on None values, which causes exceptions to be raised. This is not very robust; there is a latent code bug just waiting to happen. But with typecheckers, you can stop worrying about this and catch these mistakes early.

 With typecheckers available, do you even need tests? You certainly do. Typecheckers catch a specific class of errors: those of incompatible types. There are plenty of other classes of errors that you still need to test for. Treat typecheckers as just one tool in your arsenal of bug identification.

In all of these examples, typecheckers found a bug just waiting to happen. It doesn't matter if the bug would have been caught by tests, or by code review, or by customers; typecheckers catch it earlier, which saves time and money. Typecheckers start giving us the benefit of a statically typed language, while still allowing the Python runtime to remain dynamically typed. This truly is the best of both worlds.

At the beginning of the chapter, you'll find a quote from Guido van Rossum. While working at Dropbox, he found that large codebases struggled without having a safety net. He became a huge proponent for driving type hinting into the language. If you want your code to communicate intent and catch errors, start adopting type annotations and typechecking today.

Discussion Topic

Has your codebase had an error slip through that could have been caught by typecheckers? How much do those errors cost you? How many times has it been a code review or an integration test that caught the bug? How about bugs that made it to production?

When to Use Type Annotations

Now, before you go adding types to everything, I need to talk about the cost. Adding types is simple, but can be overdone. As users try to test and play around with code, they may start fighting the typechecker because they feel bogged down when writing all the type annotations. There is an adoption cost for users who are just getting started with type hinting. I also mentioned that I don't type annotate everything. I won't annotate all my variables, especially if the type is obvious. I also won't typically type annotate parameters for every small private method in a class.

When should you use typecheckers?

- With functions that you expect other modules or users to call (e.g., public APIs, library entry points, etc.)
- When you want to highlight where a type is complicated (e.g., a dictionary of strings mapped to lists of objects) or unintuitive
- Areas where mypy complains that you need a type (typically when assigning to an empty collection—it's easier to go along with the tool than against it)

A typechecker will infer types for any value that it can, so even if you don't fill in all types, you still reap the benefits. I will cover configuring typecheckers in Chapter 6.

Closing Thoughts

There was consternation in the Python community when type hinting was introduced. Developers were afraid that Python was becoming a statically typed language like Java or C++. They worried that adding types everywhere would slow them down and destroy the benefits of the dynamically typed language they fell in love with.

However, type hints are just that: hints. They are completely optional. I don't recommend them for small scripts, or any piece of code that isn't going to live a very long time. But if your code needs to be maintainable for the long term, type hints are invaluable. They serve as a communication method, make your environment smarter, and detect errors when combined with typecheckers. They protect the original author's intent. When annotating types, you decrease the burden a reader has in understanding your code. You reduce the need to read the implementation of a function to know what its doing. Code is complicated, and you should be minimizing how much code a developer needs to read. By using well-thought-out types, you reduce surprise and increase reading comprehension.

The typechecker is also a confidence builder. Remember, in order for your code to be robust, it has to be easy to change, rewrite, and delete if needed. The typechecker can allow developers to do that with less trepidation. If something was relying on a type or field that got changed or deleted, the typechecker will flag the offending code as incompatible. Automated tooling makes you and your future collaborators' jobs simpler; fewer bugs will make it to production and features will get delivered quicker.

In the next chapter, you're going to go beyond basic type annotations and learn how to build a vocabulary of all new types. These types will help you constrain behavior in your codebase, limiting the ways things can go wrong. I've only scratched the surface of how useful type annotations can be.

## CHAPTER 4

Constraining Types

Many developers learn the basic type annotations and call it a day. But we're far from done. There is a wealth of advanced type annotations that are invaluable. These advanced type annotations allow you to constrain types, further restricting what they can represent. Your goal is to make illegal states unrepresentable. Developers should physically not be able to create types that are contradictory or otherwise invalid in your system. You can't have errors in your code if it's impossible to create the error in the first place. You can use type annotations to achieve this very goal, saving time and money. In this chapter I'll teach you six different techniques:

Optional
> Use to replace None references in your codebase.

Union
> Use to present a selection of types.

Literal
> Use to restrict developers to very specific values.

Annotated
> Use to provide additional description of your types.

NewType
> Use to restrict a type to a specific context.

Final
> Use to prevent variables from being rebound to a new value.

Let's start with handling None references with Optional types.

Optional Type

Null references are often referred to as the "billion-dollar mistake," coined by C.A.R. Hoare:

> I call it my billion-dollar mistake. It was the invention of the null reference in 1965. At that time, I was designing the first comprehensive type system for references in an object oriented language. My goal was to ensure that all use of references should be absolutely safe, with checking performed automatically by the compiler. But I couldn't resist the temptation to put in a null reference, simply because it was so easy to implement. This has led to innumerable errors, vulnerabilities, and system crashes, which have probably caused a billion dollars of pain and damage in the last forty years.[1]

While null references started in Algol, they would pervade countless other languages. C and C++ are often derided for null pointer dereference (which produces a segmentation fault or other program-halting crash). Java was well-known for requiring the user to catch `NullPointerException` throughout their code. It's not a stretch to say that these sorts of bugs have a price tag measured in the billions. Think of the developer time, customer loss, and system failures due to accidental null pointers or references.

So, why does this matter in Python? Hoare's quote is about object-oriented compiled languages back in the 60s; Python must be better by now, right? I regret to inform you that this billion-dollar mistake is in Python as well. It appears to us under a different name: None. I will show you a way to avoid the costly None mistake, but first, let's talk about why None is so bad.

It is especially illuminating that Hoare admits that null references were born out of convenience. It goes to show you how taking the quicker path can lead to all sorts of pain later in your development life cycle. Think how your short-term decisions today will adversely affect your maintenance tomorrow.

Let's consider some code that runs an automated hot dog stand. I want my system to take a bun, put a frank in the bun, and then squirt ketchup and mustard through automated dispensers, as described in Figure 4-1. What could go wrong?

Figure 4-1. Workflow for the automated hot dog stand

---

1 C.A.R. Hoare. "Null References: The Billion Dollar Mistake." *Historically Bad Ideas*. Presented at Qcon London 2009, n.d.

```
def create_hot_dog():
    bun = dispense_bun()
    frank = dispense_frank()
    hot_dog = bun.add_frank(frank)
    ketchup = dispense_ketchup()
    mustard = dispense_mustard()
    hot_dog.add_condiments(ketchup, mustard)
    dispense_hot_dog_to_customer(hot_dog)
```

Pretty straightforward, no? Unfortunately, there's no way to really tell. It's easy to think through the happy path, or the control flow of the program when everything goes right, but when talking about robust code, you need to consider error conditions. If this were an automated stand with no manual intervention, what errors can you think of?

Here's a noncomprehensive list of errors I can think of:

- Out of ingredients (buns, hot dogs, or ketchup/mustard).
- Order cancelled midprocess.
- Condiments get jammed.
- Power is interrupted.
- Customer doesn't want ketchup or mustard and tries to move the bun midprocess.
- Rival vendor switches the ketchup out with catsup; chaos ensues.

Now, your system is state of the art and will detect all of these conditions, but it does so by returning None when any one step fails. What does this mean for this code? You start seeing errors like the following:

```
Traceback (most recent call last):
  File "<stdin>", line 4, in <module>
AttributeError: 'NoneType' object has no attribute 'add_frank'

Traceback (most recent call last):
  File "<stdin>", line 7, in <module>
AttributeError: 'NoneType' object has no attribute 'add_condiments'
```

It would be catastrophic if these errors bubbled up to your customers; you pride yourself on a clean UI and don't want ugly tracebacks defiling your interface. To address this, you start to code *defensively*, or coding in such a way that you try to foresee every possible error case and account for it. Defensive programming is a good thing, but it leads to code like this:

```
def create_hot_dog():
    bun = dispense_bun()
    if bun is None:
        print_error_code("Bun unavailable. Check for bun")
        return

    frank = dispense_frank()
    if frank is None:
        print_error_code("Frank was not properly dispensed")
        return

    hot_dog = bun.add_frank(frank)
    if hot_dog is None:
        print_error_code("Hot Dog unavailable. Check for Hot Dog")
        return

    ketchup = dispense_ketchup()
    mustard = dispense_mustard()
    if ketchup is None or mustard is None:
        print_error_code("Check for invalid catsup")
        return

    hot_dog.add_condiments(ketchup, mustard)
    dispense_hot_dog_to_customer(hot_dog)
```

This feels, well, tedious. Because any value can be None in Python, it seems like you need to engage in defensive programming and do an is None check before every dereference. This is overkill; most developers will trace through the call stack and ensure that no None values are returned to the caller. That leaves calls to external systems and maybe a scant few calls in your codebase that you always have to wrap with None checking. This is error prone; you cannot expect every developer who ever touches your codebase to know instinctively where to check for None. Furthermore, the original assumptions you've made when writing (e.g., this function will never return None) can be broken in the future, and now your code has a bug. And herein lies your problem: counting on manual intervention to catch error cases is unreliable.

Exceptions

A valiant attempt at solving the billion-dollar problem is exceptions. Anytime something goes wrong in your system, throw an exception! When an exception is thrown, that function stops executing and the exception gets passed up the call chain, until either a) some code catches it in an appropriate except block, or b) nobody catches it and it terminates the program. This will not help your robustness problems. You still rely on manual intervention to catch errors (by someone writing an appropriate except block). If that manual intervention isn't applied, the program crashes and the user will have a bad time.

This should not come as a surprise; dereferencing None values throws an exception, so it's the exact same behavior. In order to be able to detect exceptions through static analysis, you typically need support in the language for checked exceptions: exceptions that are part of your type signature that tell your static analysis tools what exceptions to expect. Python does not support any sort of checked exception at the time of this writing and I am doubtful it ever will, due to the verbosity and viral nature of checked exceptions.

This isn't to say don't use exceptions. Use them for exceptional use cases that you don't expect to happen, but still wish to guard against, such as the network going down. Don't use exceptions for normal behavior, such as not finding an element when searching through a list. Remember, the return value can be enforced through typing, but exceptions cannot.

The reason this is so tricky (and so costly) is that None is treated as a special case. It exists outside the normal type hierarchy. Every variable can be assigned to None. In order to combat this, you need to find a way of representing None inside your type hierarchy. You need Optional types.

Optional types offer you two choices: either you have a value or you don't. In other words, it is optional to set the variable to a value.

```
from typing import Optional
maybe_a_string: Optional[str] = "abcdef" # This has a value
maybe_a_string: Optional[str] = None     # This is the absence of a value
```

This code indicates that the variable maybe_a_string may optionally contain a string. That code typechecks just fine, whether maybe_a_string contains "abcdef" or None.

At first glance, it's not apparent what this buys you. You still need to use None to represent the absence of a value. I have good news for you, though. There are three benefits I associate with Optional types.

First, you communicate your intent more clearly. If a developer sees an Optional type in a type signature, they view that as a big red flag that they should expect None as a possibility.

```
def dispense_bun() -> Optional[Bun]:
    # ...
```

If you notice a function returning an Optional value, take heed and check for None values.

Second, you are able to further distinguish the absence of value from an empty value. Consider the innocuous list. What happens if you make a function call and receive an empty list? Was it just that no results were provided back to you? Or was it that an error occurred and you need to take explicit action? If you are receiving a raw list, you don't know without trawling through source code. However, if you use an Optional, you are conveying one of three possibilities:

A list with elements
   Valid data to be operated on

A list with no elements
   No error occurred, but no data was available (provided that no data is not an error condition)

None
   An error occurred that you need to handle

Finally, typecheckers can detect Optional types and make sure that you aren't letting None values slip through.

Consider:

```
def dispense_bun() -> Bun:
    return Bun('Wheat')
```

Let's add some error cases to this code:

```
def dispense_bun() -> Bun:
    if not are_buns_available():
        return None
    return Bun('Wheat')
```

When run with a typechecker, you get the following error:

```
code_examples/chapter4/invalid/dispense_bun.py:12:
    error: Incompatible return value type (got "None", expected "Bun")
```

Excellent! The typechecker will not allow you to return a None value by default. By changing the return type from Bun to Optional[Bun], the code will typecheck successfully. This will give developers hints that they should not return None without encoding information in the return type. You can catch a common mistake and make this code more robust. But what about the calling code?

It turns out that the calling code benefits from this as well. Consider:

```
def create_hot_dog():
    bun = dispense_bun()
    frank = dispense_frank()
    hot_dog = bun.add_frank(frank)
    ketchup = dispense_ketchup()
    mustard = dispense_mustard()
    hot_dog.add_condiments(ketchup, mustard)
    dispense_hot_dog_to_customer(hot_dog)
```

If dispense_bun returns an Optional, this code will not typecheck. It will complain with the following error:

```
code_examples/chapter4/invalid/hotdog_invalid.py:27:
    error: Item "None" of "Optional[Bun]" has no attribute "add_frank"
```

Depending on your typechecker, you may need to specifically enable an option to catch these sorts of errors. Always look through your typechecker's documentation to learn what options are available. If there is an error you absolutely want to catch, you should test that your typechecker does indeed catch the error. I highly recommend testing out Optional behavior specifically. For the version of mypy I am running (0.800), I have to use --strict-optional as a command-line flag to catch this error.

If you are interested in silencing the typechecker, you need to check for None explicitly and handle the None value, or assert that the value cannot be None. The following code typechecks successfully:

```python
def create_hot_dog():
    bun = dispense_bun()
    if bun is None:
        print_error_code("Bun could not be dispensed")
        return

    frank = dispense_frank()
    hot_dog = bun.add_frank(frank)
    ketchup = dispense_ketchup()
    mustard = dispense_mustard()
    hot_dog.add_condiments(ketchup, mustard)
    dispense_hot_dog_to_customer(hot_dog)
```

None values truly are a billion-dollar mistake. If they slip through, programs can crash, users are frustrated, and money is lost. Use Optional types to tell other developers to beware of None, and benefit from the automated checking of your tools.

Discussion Topic

How often do you deal with None in your codebase? How confident are you that every possible None value is handled correctly? Look through bugs and failing tests to see how many times you've been bitten by incorrect None handling. Discuss how Optional types will help your codebase.

Union Types

A Union type is a type that indicates that multiple disparate types may be used with the same variable. A Union[int,str] means that either an int *or* a str can be used for a variable. For instance, consider the following code:

```
def dispense_snack() -> HotDog:
    if not are_ingredients_available():
        raise RuntimeError("Not all ingredients available")
    if order_interrupted():
        raise RuntimeError("Order interrupted")
    return create_hot_dog()
```

I now want my hot dog stand to break into the lucrative pretzel business. Instead of trying to deal with weird class inheritance (we'll cover more about inheritance in Part II) that doesn't belong between hot dogs and pretzels, you simply can return a Union of the two.

```
from typing import Union
def dispense_snack(user_input: str) -> Union[HotDog, Pretzel]:
    if user_input == "Hot Dog":
        return dispense_hot_dog()
    elif user_input == "Pretzel":
        return dispense_pretzel()
    raise RuntimeError("Should never reach this code,"
                       "as an invalid input has been entered")
```

 Optional is just a specialized version of a Union. Optional[int] is the same exact thing as Union[int, None].

Using a Union offers much the same benefit as an Optional. First, you reap the same communication advantages. A developer encountering a Union knows that they must be able to handle more than one type in their calling code. Furthermore, a type-checker is just as aware of Union as it is of Optional.

You will find Unions useful in a variety of applications:

- Handling disparate types returned based on user input (as above)
- Handling error return types a la Optionals, but with more information, such as a string or error code
- Handling different user input (such as if a user is able to supply a list or a string)
- Returning different types, say for backward compatibility (returning an old version of an object or a new version of an object depending on requested operation)
- And any other case where you may legitimately have more than one value represented

Suppose you had code that called the dispense_snack function but was only expecting a HotDog (or None) to be returned:

```
from typing import Optional
def place_order() -> Optional[HotDog]:
    order = get_order()
    result = dispense_snack(order.name)
    if result is None
        print_error_code("An error occurred" + result)
        return None
    # Return our HotDog
    return result
```

As soon as `dispense_snack` starts returning `Pretzels`, this code fails to typecheck.

```
code_examples/chapter4/invalid/union_hotdog.py:22:
    error: Incompatible return value type (got "Union[HotDog, Pretzel]",
                                          expected "Optional[HotDog]")
```

The fact that the typechecker errors out in this case is fantastic. If any function you depend on changes to return a new type, its return signature must be updated to Union a new type, which forces you to update your code to handle the new type. This means that your code will be flagged when your dependencies change in a way that contradicts your assumptions. With the decisions you make today, you can catch errors in the future. This is the mark of robust code; you are making it increasingly harder for developers to make mistakes, which reduces their error rates, which reduces the number of bugs users will experience.

There is one more fundamental benefit of using a Union, but to explain it, I need to teach you a smidge of *type theory*, which is a branch of mathematics around type systems.

Product and Sum Types

Unions are beneficial because they help constrain representable state space. *Representable state space* is the set of all possible combinations an object can take.

Take this `dataclass`:

```
from dataclasses import dataclass
# If you aren't familiar with data classes, you'll learn more in chapter 10
# but for now, treat this as four fields grouped together and what types they are
@dataclass
class Snack:
    name: str
    condiments: set[str]
    error_code: int
    disposed_of: bool


Snack("Hotdog", {"Mustard", "Ketchup"}, 5, False)
```

I have a name, the condiments that can go on top, an error code in case something goes wrong, and if something does go wrong, a boolean to track whether I have disposed of the item correctly or not. How many different combinations of values can be put into this dictionary? A potentially infinite number, right? The `name` alone could be anything from valid values ("hotdog" or "pretzel") to invalid values ("samosa", "kimchi", or "poutine") to absurd ("12345", "", or "(ノ °□°)ノ ︵ ┻━┻"). `condiments` has a similar problem. As it stands, there is no way to compute the possible options.

For the sake of simplicity, I will artificially constrain this type:

- The name can be one of three values: hotdog, pretzel, or veggie burger
- The condiments can be empty, mustard, ketchup, or both.
- There are six error codes (0–5; 0 indicates success).
- `disposed_of` is only `True` or `False`.

Now how many different values can be represented in this combination of fields? The answer is 144, which is a grossly large number. I achieve this by the following:

> 3 possible types for name × 4 possible types for condiments × 6 error codes × 2 boolean values for if the entry has been disposed of = 3×4×6×2 = 144.

If you were to accept that any of these values could be `None`, the total balloons to 420. While you should always think about `None` while coding (see earlier in this chapter about `Optional`), for this thought exercise, I'm going to ignore `None values`.

This sort of operation is known as a *product type*; the number of representable states is determined by the product of possible values. The problem is, not all of these states are valid. The variable `disposed_of` should only be set to `True` if an error code is set to nonzero. Developers will make this assumption, and trust that the illegal state never shows up. However, one innocent mistake can bring your whole system crashing to a halt. Consider the following code:

```
def serve(snack):
    # if something went wrong, return early
    if snack.disposed_of:
        return
    # ...
```

In this case, a developer is checking `disposed_of` without checking for the nonzero error code first. This is a logic bomb waiting to happen. This code will work completely fine as long as `disposed_of` is `True` *and* the error code is nonzero. If a valid snack ever sets the `disposed_of` flag to `True` erroneously, this code will start producing invalid results. This can be hard to find, as there's no reason for a developer who is creating the snack to check this code. As it stands, you have no way of catching this sort of error other than manually inspecting every use case, which is intractable for large code bases. By allowing an illegal state to be representable, you open the door to fragile code.

To remedy this, I need to make this illegal state unrepresentable. To do that, I'll rework my example and use a Union:

```python
from dataclasses import dataclass
from typing import Union
@dataclass
class Error:
    error_code: int
    disposed_of: bool

@dataclass
class Snack:
    name: str
    condiments: set[str]

snack: Union[Snack, Error] = Snack("Hotdog", {"Mustard", "Ketchup"})

snack = Error(5, True)
```

In this case, snack can be either a Snack (which is just a name and condiments) or an Error (which is just a number and a boolean). With the use of a Union, how many representable states are there now?

For Snack, there are 3 names and 4 possible list values, which is a total of 12 representable states. For ErrorCode, I can remove the 0 error code (since that was only for success), which gives me 5 values for the error code and 2 values for the boolean for a total of 10 representable states. Since the Union is an either/or construct, I can either have 12 representable states in one case or 10 in the other, for a total of 22. This is an example of a *sum type*, since I'm adding the number of representable states together rather than multiplying.

That's 22 total representable states. Compare that with the 144 states when all the fields were lumped in a single entity. I've reduced my representable state space by almost 85%. I've made it impossible to mix and match fields that are incompatible with one another. It becomes much harder to make a mistake, and there are far fewer combinations to test. Anytime you use a sum type, such as a Union, you are dramatically decreasing the number of possible representable states.

Literal Types

When calculating the number of representable states, I made some assumptions in the last section. I limited the number of values that were possible, but that's a bit of a cheat, isn't it? As I said before, there is almost an infinite number of values possible.

Fortunately, there is a way to limit the values through Python: Literals. Literal types allow you to restrict the variable to a very specific set of values.

I'll change my earlier Snack class to employ Literal values:

```python
from typing import Literal
@dataclass
class Error:
    error_code: Literal[1,2,3,4,5]
    disposed_of: bool

@dataclass
class Snack:
    name: Literal["Pretzel", "Hot Dog", "Veggie Burger"]
    condiments: set[Literal["Mustard", "Ketchup"]]
```

Now, if I try to instantiate these data classes with wrong values:

```python
Error(0, False)
Snack("Invalid", set())
Snack("Pretzel", {"Mustard", "Relish"})
```

I receive the following typechecker errors:

```
code_examples/chapter4/invalid/literals.py:14: error: Argument 1 to "Error" has
    incompatible type "Literal[0]";
                    expected "Union[Literal[1], Literal[2], Literal[3],
                            Literal[4], Literal[5]]"

code_examples/chapter4/invalid/literals.py:15: error: Argument 1 to "Snack" has
    incompatible type "Literal['Invalid']";
                    expected "Union[Literal['Pretzel'], Literal['Hotdog'],
                            Literal['Veggie Burger']]"

code_examples/chapter4/invalid/literals.py:16: error: Argument 2 to <set> has
    incompatible type "Literal['Relish']";
                    expected "Union[Literal['Mustard'], Literal['Ketchup']]"
```

Literals were introduced in Python 3.8, and they are an invaluable way of restricting possible values of a variable. They are a little more lightweight than Python enumerations (which I'll cover in Chapter 8).

Annotated Types

What if I wanted to get even deeper and specify more complex constraints? It would be tedious to write hundreds of literals, and some constraints aren't able to be modeled by Literal types. There's no way with a Literal to constrain a string to a certain size or to match a specific regular expression. This is where Annotated comes in. With Annotated, you can specify arbitrary metadata alongside your type annotation.

```python
x: Annotated[int, ValueRange(3,5)]
y: Annotated[str, MatchesRegex('[0-9]{4}')]
```

Unfortunately, the above code will not run, as `ValueRange` and `MatchesRegex` are not built-in types; they are arbitrary expressions. You will need to write your own metadata as part of an `Annotated` variable. Secondly, there are no tools that will typecheck this for you. The best you can do until such a tool exists is write dummy annotations or use strings to describe your constraints. At this point, `Annotated` is best served as a communication method.

NewType

While waiting for tooling to support `Annotated`, there is another way to represent more complicated constraints: `NewType`. `NewType` allows you to, well, create a new type.

Suppose I want to separate my hot dog stand code to handle two separate cases: a hot dog in its unservable form (no plate, no napkins) and a hot dog that is ready to serve (plated, with napkins). In my code, there exist some functions that should only be operating on the hot dog in one case or the other. For example, an unservable hot dog should never be dispensed to the customer.

```
class HotDog:
    # ... snip hot dog class implementation ...

def dispense_to_customer(hot_dog: HotDog):
    # note, this should only accept ready-to-serve hot dogs.
    # ...
```

However, nothing prevents someone from passing in an unservable hot dog. If a developer makes a mistake and passes an unservable hot dog to this function, customers will be quite surprised to see just their order with no plate or napkins come out of the machine.

Rather than relying on developers to catch these errors whenever they happen, you need a way for your typechecker to catch this. To do that, you can use `NewType`:

```
from typing import NewType

class HotDog:
    ''' Used to represent an unservable hot dog'''
    # ... snip hot dog class implementation ...

ReadyToServeHotDog = NewType("ReadyToServeHotDog", HotDog)

def dispense_to_customer(hot_dog: ReadyToServeHotDog):
    # ...
```

A `NewType` takes an existing type and creates a brand new type that has all the same fields and methods as the existing type. In this case, I am creating a type `ReadyToServeHotDog` that is distinct from `HotDog`; they are not interchangeable. What's beautiful about this is that this type restricts implicit type conversions. You cannot use a HotDog anywhere you are expecting a ReadyToServeHotDog (you can use a ReadyToServe HotDog in place of HotDog, though). In the previous example, I am restricting dispense_to_customer to only take ReadyToServeHotDog values as an argument. This prevents developers from invalidating assumptions. If a developer were to pass a HotDog to this method, the typechecker will yell at them:

```
code_examples/chapter4/invalid/newtype.py:10: error:
        Argument 1 to "dispense_to_customer"
        has incompatible type "HotDog";
        expected "ReadyToServeHotDog"
```

It is important to stress the one-way nature of this type conversion. As a developer, you can control when your old type becomes your new type.

For example, I'll create a function that takes a unservable HotDog and makes it ready to serve:

```python
def prepare_for_serving(hot_dog: HotDog) -> ReadyToServeHotDog:
    assert not hot_dog.is_plated(), "Hot dog should not already be plated"
    hot_dog.put_on_plate()
    hot_dog.add_napkins()
    return ReadyToServeHotDog(hot_dog)
```

Notice how I'm explicitly returning a ReadyToServeHotDog instead of a normal Hot Dog. This acts as a "blessed" function; it is the only sanctioned way that I want developers to create a ReadyToServeHotDog. Any user trying to use a method that takes a ReadyToServeHotDog needs to create it using prepare_for_serving first.

It is important to notify users that the only way to create your new type is through a set of "blessed" functions. You don't want users creating your new type in any circumstance other than a predetermined method, as that defeats the purpose.

```python
def make_snack():
    serve_to_customer(ReadyToServeHotDog(HotDog()))
```

Unfortunately, Python has no great way of telling users this, other than a comment.

```python
from typing import NewType
# NOTE: Only create ReadyToServeHotDog using prepare_for_serving method.
ReadyToServeHotDog = NewType("ReadyToServeHotDog", HotDog)
```

Still, NewType is applicable to many real-world scenarios. For example, these are all scenarios that I've run into that a NewType would solve:

- Separating a str from a SanitizedString, to catch bugs like SQL injection vulnerabilities. By making SanitizedString a NewType, I made sure that only properly sanitized strings were operated upon, eliminating the chance of SQL injection.

- Tracking a `User` object and `LoggedInUser` separately. By restricting `Users` with `NewType` from `LoggedInUser`, I wrote functions that were only applicable to users that were logged in.
- Tracking an integer that should represent a valid User ID. By restricting the User ID to a `NewType`, I could make sure that some functions were only operating on IDs that were valid, without having to check `if` statements.

In Chapter 10, you'll see how you can use classes and invariants to do something very similar, with a much stronger guarantee of avoiding illegal states. However, `NewType` is still a useful pattern to be aware of, and is much more lightweight than a full-blown class.

Type Aliases

`NewType` is not the same as a type alias. A type alias just provides another name for a type and is completely interchangeable with the old type.

For example:

```
IdOrName = Union[str, int]
```

If a function expects `IDOrName`, it can take either an `IDOrName` or a `Union[str,int]` and it will typecheck just fine, where a `NewType` will only work if an `IDOrName` is passed in.

I have found type aliases to be very helpful when I start nesting complex types, such as `Union[dict[int, User], list[dict[str, User]]]`. It's much easier to give it a conceptual name, such as `IDOrNameLookup`, to simplify types.

Final Types

Finally (pun intended), you may want to restrict a type from changing its value. That's where `Final` comes in. `Final`, introduced in Python 3.8, indicates to a typechecker that a variable cannot be bound to another value. For instance, I want to start franchising out my hot dog stand, but I don't want the name to be changed by accident.

```
VENDOR_NAME: Final = "Viafore's Auto-Dog"
```

If a developer accidentally changed the name later on, they would see an error.

```
def display_vendor_information():
    vendor_info = "Auto-Dog v1.0"
    # whoops, copy-paste error, this code should be vendor_info += VENDOR_NAME
    VENDOR_NAME += VENDOR_NAME
    print(vendor_info)
```

```
code_examples/chapter4/invalid/final.py:3: error:
        Cannot assign to final name "VENDOR_NAME"
Found 1 error in 1 file (checked 1 source file)
```

In general, Final is best used when the variable's scope spans a large amount of code, such as a module. It is difficult for developers to keep track of all the uses of a variable in such large scopes; letting the typechecker catch immutability guarantees is a boon in these cases.

 Final will not error out when mutating an object through a function. It only prevents the variable from being rebound (set to a new value).

Closing Thoughts

You've learned about many different ways to constrain your types in this chapter. All of them serve a specific purpose, from handling None with Optional to restricting to specific values with Literal to preventing a variable from being rebound with Final. By using these techniques, you'll be able to encode assumptions and restrictions directly into your codebase, preventing future readers from needing to guess about your logic. Typecheckers will use these advanced type annotations to provide you with stricter guarantees about your code, which will give maintainers confidence when working in your codebase. With this confidence, they will make fewer mistakes, and your codebase will become more robust because of it.

In the next chapter, you'll move on from type annotating single values, and learn how to properly annotate collection types. Collection types pervade most of Python; you must take care to express your intentions for them as well. You need to be well-versed in all the ways you can represent a collection, including in cases where you must create your own.

## CHAPTER 5

Collection Types

You can't go very far in Python without encountering *collection types*. Collection types store a grouping of data, such as a list of users or a lookup between restaurant or address. Whereas other types (e.g., `int`, `float`, `bool`, etc.) may focus on a single value, collections may store any arbitrary amount of data. In Python, you will encounter common collection types such as dictionaries, lists, and sets (oh, my!). Even a string is a type of collection; it contains a sequence of characters. However, collections can be difficult to reason about when reading new code. Different collection types have different behaviors.

Back in Chapter 1, I went over some of the differences between the collections, where I talked about mutability, iterability, and indexing requirements. However, picking the right collection is just the first step. You must understand the implications of your collection and ensure that users can reason about it. You also need to recognize when the standard collection types aren't cutting it and you need to roll your own. But the first step is knowing how to communicate your collection choices to the future. For that, we'll turn to an old friend: type annotations.

Annotating Collections

I've covered type annotations for non–collection types, and now you need to know how to annotate collection types. Fortunately, these annotations don't differ too much from the annotations you've already learned.

To illustrate this, suppose I'm building a digital cookbook app. I want to organize all my cookbooks digitally so I can search them by cuisine, ingredient, or author. One of the questions I might have about a cookbook collection is how many books from each author I have:

```
def create_author_count_mapping(cookbooks: list) -> dict:
    counter = defaultdict(lambda: 0)
    for book in cookbooks:
        counter[book.author] += 1
    return counter
```

This function has been annotated; it takes in a list of cookbooks and will return a dictionary. Unfortunately, while this tells me what collections to expect, it doesn't tell me how to use the collections at all. There is nothing telling me what the elements inside the collection are. For instance, how do I know what type the cookbook is? If you were reviewing this code, how do you know that the use of book.author is legitimate? Even if you do the digging to make sure book.author is right, this code is not future-proof. If the underlying type changes, such as removing the author field, this code will break. I need a way to catch this with my typechecker.

I'll do this by encoding more information with my types by using bracket syntax to indicate information about the types *inside* the collection:

```
AuthorToCountMapping = dict[str, int]
def create_author_count_mapping(
                              cookbooks: list[Cookbook]
                              ) -> AuthorToCountMapping:
    counter = defaultdict(lambda: 0)
    for book in cookbooks:
        counter[book.author] += 1
    return counter
```

I used an alias, AuthorToCountMapping, to represent a dict[str, int]. I do this because I find it difficult sometimes to remember what the str and the int are supposed to represent. However, I do concede that this loses some information (readers of the code will have to find out what AuthorToCountMapping is an alias to). Ideally, your code editor can display what the underlying type is without you needing to look it up.

I can indicate the exact types expected in the collection. The cookbooks list contains Cookbook objects, and the return value of the function is returning a dictionary mapping strings (keys) to integers (values). Note that I'm using a type alias to give more meaning to my return value. Mapping from a str to an int does not tell the user the context of the type. Instead, I create a type alias named AuthorToCountMapping to make it clear how this dictionary relates to the problem domain.

You need to think through what types are contained in the collection in order to be effective in type-hinting it. In order to do that, you need to think about homogeneous and heterogeneous collections.

Homogeneous Versus Heterogeneous Collections

Homogeneous collections are collections in which every value has the same type. In contrast, values in *heterogeneous collections* may have different types within them. From a usability standpoint, your lists, sets, and dictionaries should nearly always be homogenous. Users need a way to reason about your collections, and they can't if they don't have the guarantee that every value is the same type. If you make a list, set, or dictionary a heterogeneous collection, you are indicating to the user that they need to take care to handle special cases. Suppose I want to resurrect an example from Chapter 1 for adjusting recipes for my cookbook app:

```
def adjust_recipe(recipe, servings):
    """
    Take a meal recipe and change the number of servings
    :param recipe: A list, where the first element is the number of servings,
                   and the remainder of elements follow the (name, amount, unit)
                   format, such as ("flour", 1.5, "cup")
    :param servings: the number of servings
    :return list: a new list of ingredients, where the first element is the
                  number of servings
    """
    new_recipe = [servings]
    old_servings = recipe[0]
    factor = servings / old_servings
    recipe.pop(0)
    while recipe:
            ingredient, amount, unit = recipe.pop(0)
            # please only use numbers that will be easily measurable
            new_recipe.append((ingredient, amount * factor, unit))
    return new_recipe
```

At the time, I mentioned how parts of this code were ugly; one confounding factor was the fact that the first element of the recipe list was a special case: an integer representing the servings. This contrasts with the rest of the list elements, which are tuples representing actual ingredients, such as ("flour", 1.5, "cup"). This highlights the troubles of a heterogeneous collection. For every use of your collection, the user needs to remember to handle the special case. This is predicated on the assumption that the developer even knew about the special case in the first place. There's no way as it stands to represent that a specific element needs to be handled differently. Therefore, a typechecker will not catch when a developer forgets. This leads to brittle code down the road.

When talking about homogeneity, it's important to talk about what a *single type* means. When I mention a single type, I'm not necessarily referring to a concrete type in Python; rather, I'm referring to a set of behaviors that define that type. A single type indicates that a consumer must operate on every value of that type in the exact same way. For the cookbook list, the single type is a Cookbook. For the dictionary example, the key's single type is a string and the value's single type is an integer. For heterogeneous collections, this will not always be the case. What do you do if you must have different types in your collection and there is no relation between them?

Consider what my ugly code from Chapter 1 communicates:

```
def adjust_recipe(recipe, servings):
    """
    Take a meal recipe and change the number of servings
    :param recipe: A list, where the first element is the number of servings,
                   and the remainder of elements follow the (name, amount, unit)
                   format, such as ("flour", 1.5, "cup")
    :param servings: the number of servings
    :return list: a new list of ingredients, where the first element is the
                  number of servings
    """
    # ...
```

There is a lot of information in the docstring, but docstrings have no guarantee of being correct. They also won't protect developers if they accidentally break assumptions. This code does not communicate intention adequately to future collaborators. Those future collaborators won't be able to reason about your code. The last thing you want to burden them with is having to go through the codebase, looking for invocations and implementations to work out how to use your collection. Ultimately, you need a way to reconcile the first element (an integer) with the remaining elements in the list (which are tuples). To solve this, I'll use a Union (and some type aliases to make the code more readable):

```
Ingredient = tuple[str, int, str] # (name, quantity, units)
Recipe = list[Union[int, Ingredient]] # the list can be servings or ingredients
def adjust_recipe(recipe: Recipe, servings):
    # ...
```

This takes a heterogeneous collection (items could be an integer or an ingredient) and allows developers to reason about the collection as if it were homogeneous. The developer needs to treat every single value as the same—it is either an integer or an Ingredient—before operating on it. While more code is needed to handle the type-checks, you can rest easier knowing that your typechecker will catch users not checking for special cases. Bear in mind, this is not perfect by any means; it'd be better if there was no special case in the first place and servings was passed to the function another way. But for the cases where you absolutely must handle special cases, represent them as a type so that the typechecker benefits you.

 When heterogeneous collections are complex enough that they involve lots of validation logic strewn about your codebase, consider making them a user-defined type, such as a data class or class. Consult Part II for more information on creating user-defined types.

You can add too many types in a Union, though. The more special cases of types you handle, the more code a developer has to write every time they use that type, and the more unwieldy the codebase becomes.

At the far end of the spectrum lies the Any type. Any can be used to indicate that all types are valid in this context. This sounds appealing to get around special cases, but it also means that the consumers of your collection have no clue what to do with the values in the collection, defeating the purpose of type annotations in the first place.

 Developers working in a statically typed language don't need to put in as much care to ensure collections are homogeneous; the static type system does that for them already. The challenge in Python is due to Python's dynamically typed nature. It is much easier for a developer to create a heterogeneous collection without any warnings from the language itself.

Heterogeneous collection types still have a lot of uses; don't assume that you should use homogeneity for every collection type because it is easier to reason about. Tuples, for example, are often heterogeneous.

Suppose a tuple containing a name and page count represents a Cookbook:

```
Cookbook = tuple[str, int] # name, page count
```

I am describing specific fields for this tuple: name and page count. This is a prime example of an heterogeneous collection:

- Each field (name and page count) will always be in the same order.
- All names are strings; all page counts are integers.
- Iterating over the tuple is rare, since I won't treat both types the same.
- Name and page count are fundamentally different types, and should not be treated as equivalent.

When accessing a tuple, you will typically index to the specific field you want:

```
food_lab: Cookbook = ("The Food Lab", 958)
odd_bits: Cookbook = ("Odd Bits", 248)

print(food_lab[0])
>>> "The Food Lab"

print(odd_bits[1])
>>> 248
```

However, in many codebases, tuples like these soon become burdensome. Developers tire of writing cookbook[0] whenever they want a name. A better thing to do would be to find some way to name these fields. A first choice might be a dictionary:

```
food_lab = {
    "name": "The Food Lab",
    "page_count": 958
}
```

Now, they can refer to fields as `food_lab['name']` and `food_lab['page_count']`. The problem is, dictionaries are typically meant to be a homogeneous mapping from a key to a value. However, when dictionaries are used to represent data that is heterogeneous, you run into similar problems as above when writing a valid type annotation. If I want to try to use a type system to represent this dictionary, I end up with the following:

```
def print_cookbook(cookbook: dict[str, Union[str,int]])
    # ...
```

This approach has the following problems:

- Large dictionaries may have many different types of values. Writing a `Union` is quite cumbersome.

- It is tedious for a user to handle every case for every dictionary access. (Since I indicate that the dictionary is homogeneous, I convey to developers that they need to treat every value as the same type, meaning typechecks for every value access. *I* know that the `name` is always a `str` and the `page_count` is always an `int`, but a consumer of this type would not know that.)

- Developers do not have any indication what keys are available in the dictionary. They must search all the code from dictionary creation time to the current access to see what fields have been added.

- As the dictionary grows, developers have a tendency to use `Any` as the type of the value. Using `Any` defeats the purpose of the typechecker in this case.

 Any can be used for valid type annotations; it merely indicates that you are making zero assumptions about what the type is. For instance, if you wanted to copy a list, the type signature would be `def copy(coll: list[Any]) -> list[Any]`. Of course, you could also do `def copy(coll: list) -> list`, and it would mean the same thing.

These problems all stem from heterogeneous data in homogeneous data collections. You either pass the burden onto the caller or abandon type annotations completely. In some cases, you want the caller to explicitly check each type on each value access, but in other cases, this is overcomplicated and tedious. So, how can you explain your reasoning with heterogeneous types, especially in cases where keeping data in a

---

dictionary is natural, such as API interactions or user-configurable data? For these cases, you should use a TypedDict.

TypedDict

TypedDict, introduced in Python 3.8, is for the scenarios where you absolutely must store heterogeneous data in a dictionary. These are typically situations where you can't avoid heterogeneous data. JSON APIs, YAML, TOML, XML, and CSVs all have easy-to-use Python modules that convert these data formats into a dictionary and are naturally hetereogeneous. This means the data that gets returned has all the same problems as listed in the previous section. Your typechecker won't help out much and users won't know what keys and values are available.

 If you have full control of the dictionary, meaning you create it in code you own and handle it in code you own, you should consider using a dataclass (see Chapter 9) or a class (see Chapter 10) instead.

For example, suppose I want to augment my digital cookbook app to provide nutritional information for the recipes listed. I decide to use the Spoonacular API (*https://oreil.ly/joTNh*) and write some code to get nutritional information:

```
nutrition_information = get_nutrition_from_spoonacular(recipe_name)
# print grams of fat in recipe
print(nutrition_information["fat"]["value"])
```

If you were reviewing the code, how would you know that this code is right? If you wanted to also print out the calories, how do you access the data? What guarantees do you have about the fields inside of this dictionary? To answer these questions, you have two options:

- Look up the API documentation (if any) and confirm that the right fields are being used. In this scenario, you hope that the documentation is actually complete and correct.
- Run the code and print out the returned dictionary. In this situation, you hope that test responses are pretty identical to production responses.

The problem is that you are requiring every reader, reviewer, and maintainer to do one of these two steps in order to understand the code. If they don't, you will not get good code review feedback and developers will run the risk of using the response incorrectly. This leads to incorrect assumptions and brittle code. TypedDict allows you to encode what you've learned about that API directly into your type system.

```
from typing import TypedDict
class Range(TypedDict):
    min: float
    max: float

class NutritionInformation(TypedDict):
    value: int
    unit: str
    confidenceRange95Percent: Range
    standardDeviation: float

class RecipeNutritionInformation(TypedDict):
    recipes_used: int
    calories: NutritionInformation
    fat: NutritionInformation
    protein: NutritionInformation
    carbs: NutritionInformation

nutrition_information:RecipeNutritionInformation = \
        get_nutrition_from_spoonacular(recipe_name)
```

Now it is incredibly apparent exactly what data types you can rely upon. If the API ever changes, a developer can update all the TypedDict classes and let the typechecker catch any incongruities. Your typechecker now completely understands your dictionary, and readers of your code can reason about responses without having to do any external searching.

Even better, these TypedDict collections can be as arbitrarily complex as you need them to be. You'll see that I nested TypedDict instances for reusability purposes, but you can also embed your own custom types, Unions, and Optionals to reflect the possibilities that an API can return. And while I've mostly been talking about API, remember that these benefits apply to any heterogeneous dictionary, such as when reading JSON or YAML.

 TypedDict is only for the typechecker's benefit. There is no runtime validation at all; the runtime type is just a dictionary.

So far, I've been teaching you how to deal with built-in collection types: lists/sets/dictionaries for homogeneous collections and tuples/TypedDict for heterogenous collections. What if these types don't do *everything* that you want? What if you want to create new collections that are easy to use? To do that, you'll need a new set of tools.

Creating New Collections

When writing a new collection, you should ask yourself: am I trying to write a new collection that isn't representable by another collection type, or am I trying to modify an existing collection to provide some new behavior? Depending on the answer, you may need to employ different techniques to achieve your goal.

If you write a collection type that isn't representable by another collection type, you are bound to come across *generics* at some point.

Generics

A generic type indicates that you don't care what type you are using. However, it helps restrict users from mixing types where inappropriate.

Consider the innocuous reverse list function:

```
def reverse(coll: list) -> list:
    return coll[::-1]
```

How do I indicate that the returned list should contain the same type as the passed-in list? To achieve this, I use a generic, which is done with a TypeVar in Python:

```
from typing import TypeVar
T = TypeVar('T')
def reverse(coll: list[T]) -> list[T]:
    return coll[::-1]
```

This says that for a type T, reverse takes in a list of elements of type T and returns a list of elements of type T. I can't mix types: a list of integers will never be able to become a list of strings if those lists aren't using the same TypeVar.

I can use this sort of pattern to define entire classes. Suppose I want to integrate a cookbook recommender service into the cookbook collection app. I want to be able to recommend cookbooks or recipes based on a customer's ratings. To do this, I want to store each of these pieces of rating information in a *graph*. A graph is a data structure that contains a series of entities known as *nodes* and that tracks *edges* (relationships between those nodes). However, I don't want to write separate code for a cookbook graph and a recipe graph. So I define a Graph class that can be used for generic types:

```
from collections import defaultdict
from typing import Generic, TypeVar

Node = TypeVar("Node")
Edge = TypeVar("Edge")

# directed graph
class Graph(Generic[Node, Edge]):
    def __init__(self):
        self.edges: dict[Node, list[Edge]] = defaultdict(list)
```

```
    def add_relation(self, node: Node, to: Edge):
        self.edges[node].append(to)

    def get_relations(self, node: Node) -> list[Edge]:
        return self.edges[node]
```

With this code, I can define all sorts of graphs and still have them typecheck successfully:

```
cookbooks: Graph[Cookbook, Cookbook] = Graph()
recipes: Graph[Recipe, Recipe] = Graph()

cookbook_recipes: Graph[Cookbook, Recipe] = Graph()

recipes.add_relation(Recipe('Pasta Bolognese'),
                     Recipe('Pasta with Sausage and Basil'))

cookbook_recipes.add_relation(Cookbook('The Food Lab'),
                              Recipe('Pasta Bolognese'))
```

Whereas this code does not typecheck:

```
cookbooks.add_relation(Recipe('Cheeseburger'), Recipe('Hamburger'))

code_examples/chapter5/invalid/graph.py:25:
    error: Argument 1 to "add_relation" of "Graph" has
           incompatible type "Recipe"; expected "Cookbook"
```

Using generics can help you write collections that use types consistently throughout their lifetime. This reduces the amount of duplication in your codebase, which minimizes the chances of bugs and reduces cognitive burden.

Other Uses for Generics

While generics are often used for collections, you can technically use them for any type. For example, suppose you want to simplify your API error handling. You've already forced your code to return a Union of the response type and an error type like so:

```
def get_nutrition_info(recipe: str) -> Union[NutritionInfo, APIError]:
    # ...

def get_ingredients(recipe: str) -> Union[list[Ingredient], APIError]:
    #...

def get_restaurants_serving(recipe: str) -> Union[list[Restaurant], APIError]:
    # ...
```

But this is unneccessarily duplicated code. You have to specify a Union[X, APIError] each time, where only X changes. What if you wanted to change the error response

---

class, or force users to handle different types of errors separately? Generics can help with deduplicating these types:

```
T = TypeVar("T")
APIResponse = Union[T, APIError]

def get_nutrition_info(recipe: str) -> APIResponse[NutritionInfo]:
    # ...

def get_ingredients(recipe: str) -> APIResponse[list[Ingredient]]:
    #...

def get_restaurants_serving(recipe: str) -> APIResponse[list[Restaurant]]:
    # ...
```

Now you have a single place to control all of your API error handling. If you were to change it, you can rely on your typechecker to catch all the places needing changes.

Modifying Existing Types

Generics are nice for creating your own collection types, but what if you just want to tweak some behavior of an existing collection type, such as a list or dictionary? Having to completely rewrite all the semantics of a collection would be tedious and error-prone. Thankfully, methods exist to make this a snap. Let's go back to our cookbook app. I've written code earlier that grabs nutrition information, but now I want to store all that nutrition information in a dictionary.

However, I hit a problem: the same ingredient has very different names depending on where you're from. Take a dark leafy green, common in salads. While an American chef might call it "arugula," a European might call it "rocket." This doesn't even begin to cover the names in languages other than English. To combat this, I want to create a dictionary-like object that automatically handles these aliases:

```
>>> nutrition = NutritionalInformation()
>>> nutrition["arugula"] = get_nutrition_information("arugula")
>>> print(nutrition["rocket"]) # arugula is the same as rocket
{
    "name": "arugula",
    "calories_per_serving": 5,
    # ... snip ...
}
```

So how can I write NutritionalInformation to act like a dict?

A lot of a developer's first instinct is to subclass dictionaries. No worries if you aren't awesome at subclassing; I'll be going much more in depth in Chapter 12. For now, just treat subclassing as a way of saying, "I want my subclass to behave exactly like the parent class." However, you'll learn that subclassing a dictionary may not always be what you want. Consider the following code:

```
class NutritionalInformation(dict): ❶
    def __getitem__(self, key): ❷
        try:
            return super().__getitem__(key) ❸
        except KeyError:
            pass
        for alias in get_aliases(key):
            try: ❹
                return super().__getitem__(alias)
            except KeyError:
                pass
        raise KeyError(f"Could not find {key} or any of its aliases") ❺
```

❶ The (dict) syntax indicates that we are subclassing from dictionaries.

❷ __getitem__ is what gets called when you use brackets to check a key in a dictionary: (nutrition["rocket"]) calls __getitem__(nutrition, "rocket").

❸ If a key is found, use the parent dictionary's key check.

❹ For every alias, check if it is in the dictionary.

❺ Throw a KeyError if no key is found, either with what's passed in or any of its aliases.

We are overriding the __getitem__ function, and this works!

If I try to access nutrition["rocket"] in that snippet above, I get the same nutritional information as nutrition["arugula"]. Huzzah! So you deploy it in production and call it a day.

But (and there's always a but), as time goes on, a developer comes to you and complains that sometimes the dictionary doesn't work. You spend some time debugging, and it always works for you. You look for race conditions, threading, API tomfoolery, or any other nondeterminism, and come up with absolutely zero potential bugs. Finally, you get some time where you can sit with the other developer and see what they are doing.

And sitting at their terminal are the following lines:

```
# arugula is the same as rocket
>>> nutrition = NutritionalInformation()
>>> nutrition["arugula"] = get_nutrition_information("arugula")
>>> print(nutrition.get("rocket", "No Ingredient Found"))
"No Ingredient Found"
```

The get function on a dictionary tries to get the key, and if not found, will return the second argument (in this case "No Ingredient Found"). Herein lies the problem: when subclassing from a dictionary and overriding methods, you have no guarantee that those methods are called from every other method in the dictionary. Built-in collection types are built with performance in mind; many methods use inlined code to go fast. This means that overriding one method, such as __getitem__, will not be used in most dictionary methods. This certainly violates the Law of Least Surprise, which we talked about in Chapter 1.

 It is OK to subclass from the built-in collection if you are only adding methods, but because future modifications may make this same mistake, I still prefer to use one of the other methods of building custom collections.

So overriding dict is out. Instead I'll use types from the collections module. For this case, there is a handy type called collections.UserDict. UserDict fits the exact use case that I need: I can subclass from UserDict, override key methods, and get the behavior I expect.

```python
from collections import UserDict
class NutritionalInformation(UserDict):
    def __getitem__(self, key):
        try:
            return self.data[key]
        except KeyError:
            pass
        for alias in get_aliases(key):
            try:
                return self.data[alias]
            except KeyError:
                pass
        raise KeyError(f"Could not find {key} or any of its aliases")
```

This fits your use case exactly. You subclass from UserDict instead of dict, and then use self.data to access the underlying dictionary.

You go run your teammate's code again:

```python
# arugula is the same as rocket
>>> print(nutrition.get("rocket", "No Ingredient Found"))
{
    "name": "arugula",
    "calories_per_serving": 5,
    # ... snip ...
}
```

And you get the nutrition information for arugula.

UserDict isn't the only collection type that you can override in this case. There also is a UserString and a UserList in the collections model. Anytime you want to tweak a dictionary, string, or list, these are the collections you want to use.

Inheriting from these classes does incur a performance cost. Built-in collections make some assumptions in order to achieve performance. With `UserDict`, `UserString`, and `UserList`, methods can't be inlined, since you might override them. If you need to use these constructs in performance-critical code, make sure you benchmark and measure your code to find potential problems.

You'll notice that I talked about dictionaries, lists, and strings above, but left out one big built-in: sets. There exists no `UserSet` in the `collections` module. I'll have to select a different abstraction from the `collections` module. More specifically, I need abstract base classes, which are found in `collections.abc`.

As Easy as ABC

Abstract base classes (ABCs) in the `collections.abc` module provide another grouping of classes that you can override to create your own collections. ABCs are classes intended to be subclassed, and require the subclass to implement very specific functions. For the `collections.abc`, these ABCs are all centered on custom collections. In order to create a custom collection, you must override specific functions, depending on the type you want to emulate. Once you implement these required functions, though, the ABC fills in other functions automatically. You can find a full list of required functions to implement at the `collections.abc`'s module documentation (*https://oreil.ly/kb8j3*).

In contrast to the `User*` classes, there is no built-in storage, such as `self.data`, inside the `collections.abc` classes. You must provide your own storage.

Let's look at a `collections.abc.Set`, since there is no `UserSet` elsewhere in collections. I want to create a custom set that automatically handles aliases of ingredients (such as rocket and arugula). In order to create this custom set, I need to implement three methods, as required by `collections.abc.Set`:

`__contains__`
    This is for membership checks: `"arugula" in ingredients`.

`__iter__`
    This is for iterating: `for ingredient in ingredients`.

`__len__`
    This is for checking the length: `len(ingredients)`.

Once these three methods are defined, methods like relational operations, equality operations, and set operations (union, intersection, difference, disjoint) will just work. That's the beauty of collections.abc. Once you define a select few methods, the rest come for free. Here it is in action:

```
import collections
class AliasedIngredients(collections.abc.Set):
    def __init__(self, ingredients: set[str]):
        self.ingredients = ingredients

    def __contains__(self, value: str):
        return value in self.ingredients or any(alias in self.ingredients
                                                for alias in get_aliases(value))

    def __iter__(self):
        return iter(self.ingredients)

    def __len__(self):
        return len(self.ingredients)

>>> ingredients = AliasedIngredients({'arugula', 'eggplant', 'pepper'})
>>> for ingredient in ingredients:
>>>     print(ingredient)
'arugula'
'eggplant'
'pepper'

>>> print(len(ingredients))
3

>>> print('arugula' in ingredients)
True

>>> print('rocket' in ingredients)
True

>>> list(ingredients | AliasedIngredients({'garlic'}))
['pepper', 'arugula', 'eggplant', 'garlic']
```

That's not the only cool thing about collections.abc, though. Using it in type annotations can help you write more generic code. Take this code from all the way back in Chapter 2:

```
def print_items(items):
    for item in items:
        print(item)

print_items([1,2,3])
print_items({4, 5, 6})
print_items({"A": 1, "B": 2, "C": 3})
```

I talked about how duck typing can be both a boon and a curse for robst code. It's great that I can write a single function that can take so many different types, but communicating intent through type annotations becomes challenging. Fortunately, I can use the `collections.abc` classes to provide type hints:

```
def print_items(items: collections.abc.Iterable):
    for item in items:
        print(item)
```

In this case, I am indicating that items are simply iterable through the `Iterable` ABC. As long as the parameter supports an `__iter__` method (and most collections do), this code will typecheck.

As of Python 3.9, there are 25 different ABCs for you to use. Check them all out in the Python documentation (*https://oreil.ly/lDeak*).

Closing Thoughts

You can't go far without running into collections in Python. Lists, dictionaries, and sets are commonplace, and it's imperative that you provide hints to the future about what collection types you're working with. Consider whether your collections are homogeneous or heterogeneous and what that tells future readers. For the cases where you do use heterogeneous collections, provide enough information for other developers to reason about them, such as a `TypedDict`. Once you learn the techniques to allow other developers to reason about your collections, your codebase becomes so much more understandable.

Always think through your options when creating new collections:

- If you are just extending a type, such as adding new methods, you can subclass directly from collections such as a list or dictionary. However, beware the rough edges, as there is some surprising Python behavior if a user ever overrides a built-in method.

- If you are looking to change out a small part of a list, dictionary or string, use `collections.UserList`, `collections.UserDict`, or `collections.UserString`, respectively. Remember to reference `self.data` to access the storage of the respective type.

- If you need to write a more complicated class with the interface of another collection type, use `collections.abc`. You will need to provide your own storage for the data inside the class and implement all required methods, but once you do, you can customize that collection to your heart's content.

Discussion Topic

Look through the uses of collections and generics in your codebase, and assess how much information is conveyed to future developers. How many custom collection types are in your codebase? What can a new developer tell about the collection types by just looking at type signatures and names? Are there collections you could be defining more generically? What about other types using generics?

Now, type annotations don't reach their full potential without the aid of a type-checker. In the next chapter, I'm going to focus on the typechecker itself. You'll learn how to effectively configure a typechecker, generate reports, and evaluate different checkers. The more you know about a tool, the more effectively you can wield it. This is especially true for your typechecker.

## CHAPTER 6

Customizing Your Typechecker

Typecheckers are one of your best resources for building robust codebases. Jukka Lehtosalo, the lead developer of mypy, offers a beautifully concise definition of type-checkers: "In essence, [a typechecker] provides verified documentation."[1] Type annotations provide documentation about your codebase, allowing other developers the ability to reason about your intentions. Typecheckers use those annotations to verify that the documentation matches the behavior.

As such, a typechecker is invaluable. Confucius once said, "The mechanic, who wishes to do his work well, must first sharpen his tools."[2] This chapter is all about sharpening your typechecker. Great coding techniques can get you far, but it's your surrounding tooling that takes you to the next level. Don't stop with just learning your editor, compiler, or operating system. Learn your typechecker too. I will show you some of the more useful options to get the most out of your tools.

Configuring Your Typechecker

I will focus on one of the most popular typecheckers out there: mypy. When you run a typechecker in an IDE (such as PyCharm), it typically runs mypy underneath the hood (although many IDEs will allow you to change the default typechecker). Anytime you configure mypy (or whatever your default typechecker is), your IDE will use that configuration as well.

---

1 Jukka Lehtosalo. "Our Journey to Type Checking 4 Million Lines of Python." *Dropbox.Tech* (blog). Dropbox, September 5, 2019. *https://oreil.ly/4BK3k*.

2 Confucius and Arthur Waley. *The Analects of Confucius*. New York, NY: Random House, 1938.

Mypy offers quite a few configuration options to control the typechecker's *strictness*, or the amount of errors reported. The stricter you make your typechecker, the more type annotations you need to write, which provides better documentation and creates fewer bugs. However, make the typechecker too strict, and you will find the minimum bar for developing code too high, incurring high costs to make changes. Mypy configuration options control these strictness levels. I'll go through the different options available to you, and you can decide where that bar lies for you and your codebase.

First, you need to install mypy (if you haven't already). The easiest way is through `pip` on the command line:

```
pip install mypy
```

Once you have mypy installed, you you can control configuration in one of three ways:

Command line
> When instantiating mypy from a terminal, you can pass various options to configure behavior. This is great for exploring new checks in your codebase.

Inline configuration
> You can specify configuration values at the top of a file to indicate any options you may want to set. For example:
>
> ```
> # mypy: disallow-any-generics
> ```
>
> Putting this line at the top of your file will tell mypy to explicitly fail if it finds any generic type annotated with Any.

Configuration file
> You can set up a configuration file to use the same options every time mypy runs. This is extremely useful when needing to share the same options across a team. This file is typically stored in version control alongside the code.

Configuring mypy

When running mypy, it looks in your current directory for a configuration file named *mypy.ini*. This file will define which options you have set up for the project. Some options will be global, applied to every file, and other options will be per-module. A sample *mypy.ini* file might look as follows:

```
# Global options:

[mypy]
python_version = 3.9
warn_return_any = True

# Per-module options:
```

```
[mypy-mycode.foo.*]
disallow_untyped_defs = True

[mypy-mycode.bar]
warn_return_any = False

[mypy-somelibrary]
ignore_missing_imports = True
```

 You can use the --config-file command-line option to specify
config files in different places. Also, mypy will look for configuration files in specific home directories if it can't find a local config
file, in case you want the same settings across multiple projects. For
more information, check out the mypy documentation (*https://
oreil.ly/U1JO9*).

As a note, I won't cover too much more about the configuration file. Most options
that I'll talk about work in both a configuration file and on the command line, and for
the sake of simplicity, I'll show you how to run the commands on mypy invocations.

In the following pages, I will cover a multitude of typechcecker configurations; you
do not need to apply every single one of them to see value in a typechecker. Most
typecheckers provide immense value right out of the box. However, feel free to consider the following options to improve a typechecker's likelihood of finding errors.

Catching dynamic behavior

As mentioned before, Python's dynamically typed nature will make maintenance hard
on codebases that last a long time. Variables are free to be rebound to values with different types at any time. When this happens, the variable is essentially an Any type.
Any types indicate that you should make no assumptions about what type that variable is. This makes it tricky to reason about: your typechecker won't be of much use
in preventing errors and you aren't communicating anything special to future
developers.

Mypy comes with a set of flags that you can turn on to flag instances of the Any type.

For instance, you can turn on the --disallow-any-expr option to flag any expression that has an Any type. The following code will fail with that option turned on:

```
from typing import Any
x: Any = 1
y = x + 1

test.py:4: error: Expression has type "Any"
Found 1 error in 1 file (checked 1 source file)
```

Another option I like for disallowing Any in type declarations (such as in collections) is --disallow-any-generics. This catches the use of Any for anything using a generic (such as collection types). The following code fails to typecheck with this option turned on:

```
x: list = [1,2,3,4]
```

You would need to use list[int] explicitly to get this code to work.

You can check out all the ways to disable the use of Any in the mypy dynamic typing documentation (*https://oreil.ly/Fmspo*).

Be careful with disabling Any too broadly, though. There is a valid use case of Any that you don't want to flag erroneously. Any should be reserved for when you absolutely don't care what type something is and that it is up to the caller to verify the type. A prime example is a heterogeneous key-value store (perhaps a general-purpose cache).

Requiring types

An expression is *untyped* if there is no type annotation. In these cases, mypy treats the result of that expression as an Any type if it can't otherwise infer the type. However, the previous checks for disallowing Any will not catch where a function is left untyped. There is a separate set of flags for checking for untyped functions.

This code will not error out in a typechecker unless the --disallow-untyped-defs option is set:

```
def plus_four(x):
    return x + 4
```

With that option set, you receive the following error:

```
test.py:4: error: Function is missing a type annotation
```

If this is too severe for you, you might want to check out --disallow-incomplete-defs, which only flags functions if they only have some variables/return values annotated (but not all), or --disallow-untyped-calls, which only flags calls from annotated functions to unannotated functions. You'll find all the different options concerning untyped functions in the mypy documentation (*https://oreil.ly/pOvWs*).

Handling None/Optional

In Chapter 4, you learned how easy it was to make the "billion-dollar mistake" when using None values. If you turn on no other options, make sure that you have --strict-optional turned on in your typechecker to catch these costly errors. You absolutely want to be checking that your use of None is not hiding any latent bugs.

When using --strict-optional, you must explicitly perform is None checks; otherwise, your code will fail typechecking.

If `--strict-optional` is set (the default is different depending on the mypy version, so be sure to double-check), this code should fail:

```
from typing import Optional
x: Optional[int] = None
print(x + 5)

test.py:3: error: Unsupported operand types for + ("None" and "int")
test.py:3: note: Left operand is of type "Optional[int]"
```

It's worth noting that mypy also treats None values as Optionals implicitly. I recommend turning this off, so that you are being more explicit in your code. For example:

```
def foo(x: int = None) -> None:
    print(x)
```

The parameter x is implicitly converted to an Optional[int], since None is a valid value for it. If you were to do any integer operations on x, the typechecker would flag it. However, it's better to be more explicit and express that a value can be None (to disambiguate for future readers).

You can set `--no-implicit-optional` in order to get an error, forcing you to specify Optional. If you were to typecheck the above code with this option set, you would see:

```
test.py:2: error: Incompatible default for argument "x"
             (default has type "None", argument has type "int")
```

Mypy Reporting

If a typechecker fails in the forest and nobody is around to see it, does it print an error message? How do you know that mypy is actually checking your files, and that it will actually catch errors? Use mypy's built-in reporting techniques to better visualize results.

First, you can get an HTML report about how many lines of code mypy was able to check by passing in `--html-report` to mypy. This produces a HTML file that will provide a table similar to the one pictured in Figure 6-1.

mypy.sharedparse	0.00% imprecise	114 LOC
mypy.sitepkgs	3.13% imprecise	32 LOC
mypy.solve	3.90% imprecise	77 LOC
mypy.split_namespace	38.24% imprecise	34 LOC
mypy.state	0.00% imprecise	18 LOC

Figure 6-1. HTML report from running mypy on the mypy source code

If you want a plain-text file, you can use --linecount-report instead.

Mypy also allows you to track explicit Any expressions to understand how you are doing on a line-by-line basis. When using the --any-exprs-report command-line option, mypy will create a text file enumerating per-module statistics for how many times you use Any. This is very useful for seeing how explicit your type annotations are across a codebase. Here are the first few lines from running the --any-exprs-report option on the mypy codebase itself:

```
                Name   Anys   Exprs   Coverage
------------------------------------------------
       mypy.__main__      0      29    100.00%
           mypy.api       0      57    100.00%
     mypy.applytype       0     169    100.00%
       mypy.argmap        0     394    100.00%
       mypy.binder        0     817    100.00%
    mypy.bogus_type       0      10    100.00%
        mypy.build       97    6257     98.45%
      mypy.checker       10   12914     99.92%
     mypy.checkexpr      18   10646     99.83%
   mypy.checkmember       6    2274     99.74%
mypy.checkstrformat      53    2271     97.67%
   mypy.config_parser    16     737     97.83%
```

If you'd like more machine-readable formats, you can use the --junit-xml option to create an XML file in the JUnit format. Most continuous integration systems can parse this format, making it ideal for automated report generation as part of your build system. To learn about all the different reporting options, check out the mypy report-generation documentation (*https://oreil.ly/vVRsm*).

Speeding Up mypy

One of the common complaints about mypy is the time it takes to typecheck large codebases. By default, mypy *incrementally* checks files. That is, it uses a cache (typically a *.mypy_cache* folder, but the location is also configurable) to check only what has changed since last typecheck. This does speed up typechecking, but as your codebase gets larger, your typechecker will take longer to run, no matter what. This is detrimental for fast feedback during development cycles. The longer a tool takes to provide useful feedback to developers, the less often developers will run the tool, thus defeating the purpose. It is in everyone's interest for typecheckers to run as fast as possible, so that developers are getting type errors at near real time.

In order to speed up mypy even more, you may want to consider a *remote cache*. A remote cache provides a way of caching your mypy typechecks somewhere accessible to your entire team. This way, you can cache results based on specific commit IDs in your version control and share typechecker information. Building this system is outside the scope of this book, but the remote cache documentation (*https://oreil.ly/5gO9N*) in mypy will provide a solid start.

You also should consider mypy in daemon mode. Daemon mode is when mypy runs as a standalone process, and keeps the previous mypy state in memory rather than on a file system (or across a network link). You can start a mypy daemon by running `dmypy run -- mypy-flags <mypy-files>`. Once the daemon is running, you can run the exact same command to check the files again.

For instance, I ran mypy on the mypy source code itself. My initial run took 23 seconds. Subsequent typechecks on my system took between 16 and 18 seconds. This is *technically* faster, but I would not consider it fast. When I use the mypy daemon, though, my subsequent runs ended up being under half a second. With times like that, I can run my typechecker much more often to get feedback faster. Check out more about dmypy in the mypy daemon mode documentation (*https://oreil.ly/6Coxe*).

Alternative Typecheckers

Mypy is highly configurable, and its wealth of options will let you decide on the exact behavior you are looking for, but it won't meet all of your needs all of the time. It isn't the only typechecker out there. I'd like to introduce two other typecheckers: Pyre (written by Facebook) and Pyright (written by Microsoft).

Pyre

You can install Pyre with `pip`:

```
pip install pyre-check
```

Pyre (*https://pyre-check.org*) runs very similarly to mypy's daemon mode. A separate process will run, from which you can ask for typechecking results. To typecheck your code, you need to set up Pyre (by running `pyre init`) in your project directory, and then run `pyre` to start the daemon. From here, the information you receive is pretty similar to mypy. However, there are two features that set Pyre apart from other typecheckers: codebase querying and the Python Static Analyzer (Pysa) framework.

Codebase querying

Once the pyre daemon is running, there are a lot of cool queries you can make to inspect your codebase. I'll use the mypy codebase as an example codebase for all of the following queries.

For instance, I can learn about the attributes of any class in my codebase:

```
pyre query "attributes(mypy.errors.CompileError)" ❶

{
    "response": {
        "attributes": [
            {
                "name": "__init__", ❷
                "annotation": "BoundMethod[
                                typing.Callable(
                                    mypy.errors.CompileError.__init__)
                                [[Named(self, mypy.errors.CompileError),
                                Named(messages, typing.list[str]),
                                Named(use_stdout, bool, default),
                                Named(module_with_blocker,
                                typing.Optional[str], default)], None],
                                mypy.errors.CompileError]",
                "kind": "regular",
                "final": false
            },
            {
                "name": "messages", ❸
                "annotation": "typing.list[str]",
                "kind": "regular",
                "final": false
            },
            {
                "name": "module_with_blocker", ❹
                "annotation": "typing.Optional[str]",
                "kind": "regular",
                "final": false
            },
            {
                "name": "use_stdout", ❺
                "annotation": "bool",
                "kind": "regular",
                "final": false
            }
        ]
    }
}
```

❶ Pyre query for attributes

❷ A description of the __init__ method

❸ A list of strings for messages

❹ An `Optional` string describing a module with blocker

❺ A flag indicating printing to a screen

Look at all this information I can find out about the attributes in a class! I can see their type annotations to understand how the tool sees these attributes. This is incredibly handy in exploring classes as well.

Another cool query is the `callees` of any function:

```
pyre query "callees(mypy.errors.remove_path_prefix)"

{
    "response": {
        "callees": [
            {
                "kind": "function", ❶
                "target": "len"
            },
            {
                "kind": "method", ❷
                "is_optional_class_attribute": false,
                "direct_target": "str.__getitem__",
                "class_name": "str",
                "dispatch": "dynamic"
            },
            {
                "kind": "method", ❸
                "is_optional_class_attribute": false,
                "direct_target": "str.startswith",
                "class_name": "str",
                "dispatch": "dynamic"
            },
            {
                "kind": "method", ❹
                "is_optional_class_attribute": false,
                "direct_target": "slice.__init__",
                "class_name": "slice",
                "dispatch": "static"
            }
        ]
    }
}
```

❶ Calls the length function

❷ Calls the string.*getitem* function (such as `str[0]`)

❸ Calls the startswith function on a string

❹ Initializes a list slice (such as str[3:8])

The typechecker needs to store all this information to do its job. It's a huge bonus that you can query the information as well. I could write a whole extra book on what you can do with this information, but for now, check out the Pyre query documentation (*https://oreil.ly/X4h0h*). You will learn about different queries you can execute, such as observing class hierarchies, call graphs, and more. These queries allow you to learn more about your codebase or to build new tools to better understand your codebase (and catch other types of errors that a typechecker can't, such as temporal dependencies, which I'll cover in Part III).

Python Static Analyzer (Pysa)

Pysa (pronounced like the Leaning Tower of Pisa) is a static code analyzer built into Pyre. Pysa specializes in a type of security static analysis known as *taint analysis*. Taint analysis is the tracking of potentially tainted data, such as user-supplied input. The tainted data is tracked for the entire life cycle of the data; Pyre makes sure that any tainted data cannot propagate to a system in an insecure fashion.

Let me walk you through the process to catch a simple security flaw (modified from the Pyre documentation (*https://oreil.ly/l8gK8*)). Consider the case where a user creates a new recipe in a filesystem:

```python
import os

def create_recipe():
    recipe = input("Enter in recipe")
    create_recipe_on_disk(recipe)

def create_recipe_on_disk(recipe):
    command = "touch ~/food_data/{}.json".format(recipe)
    return os.system(command)
```

This looks pretty innocuous. A user can enter in carrots to create the file *~/food_data/carrots.json*. But what if a user enters in carrots; ls ~;? If this were entered, it would print out the entire home directory (the command becomes touch ~/food_data/carrots; ls ~;.json). Based on input, a malicious user could enter in arbitrary commands on your server (this is known as remote code execution [RCE]), which is a huge security risk.

Pysa provides tools to check this. I can specify that anything coming from input() is potentially tainted data (known as a *taint source*), and anything passed to os.system should not be tainted (known as a *taint sink*). With this information, I need to build a *taint model*, which is a set of rules for detecting potential security holes. First, I must specify a *taint.config* file:

```
{
  sources: [
    {
      name: "UserControlled", ❶
      comment: "use to annotate user input"
    }
  ],

  sinks: [
    {
      name: "RemoteCodeExecution", ❷
      comment: "use to annotate execution of code"
    }
  ],

  features: [],

  rules: [
    {
      name: "Possible shell injection", ❸
      code: 5001,
      sources: [ "UserControlled" ],
      sinks: [ "RemoteCodeExecution" ],
      message_format: "Data from [{$sources}] source(s) may reach " +
                      "[{$sinks}] sink(s)"
    }
  ]
}
```

❶ Specify an annotation for user-controlled input.

❷ Specify an annotation for RCE flaws.

❸ Specify a rule that makes any tainted data from UserControlled sources an error
    if it ends up in a RemoteCodeExecution sink.

From there, I must specify a taint model to annotate these sources as tainted:

```
# stubs/taint/general.pysa

 # model for raw_input
def input(__prompt = ...) -> TaintSource[UserControlled]: ...

# model for os.system
def os.system(command: TaintSink[RemoteCodeExecution]): ...
```

These stubs tell Pysa through type annotations about where your taint sources and
sinks are in your system.

Finally, you need to tell Pyre to detect tainted information by modifying the `.pyre_configuration` to add in your directory:

```
"source_directories": ["."],
"taint_models_path": ["stubs/taint"]
```

Now, when I run `pyre analyze` on that code, Pysa flags an error.

```
[
    {
        "line": 9,
        "column": 26,
        "stop_line": 9,
        "stop_column": 32,
        "path": "insecure.py",
        "code": 5001,
        "name": "Possible shell injection",
        "description":
            "Possible shell injection [5001]: " +
            "Data from [UserControlled] source(s) may reach " +
            "[RemoteCodeExecution] sink(s)",
        "long_description":
            "Possible shell injection [5001]: " +
            "Data from [UserControlled] source(s) may reach " +
            "[RemoteCodeExecution] sink(s)",
        "concise_description":
            "Possible shell injection [5001]: " +
            "Data from [UserControlled] source(s) may reach " + "
            "[RemoteCodeExecution] sink(s)",
        "inference": null,
        "define": "insecure.create_recipe"
    }
]
```

In order to fix this, I either need to make this data flow impossible or run tainted data through a *sanitizer* function. Sanitizer functions take untrusted data and inspect/modify it so that it can be trusted. Pysa allows you decorate functions with `@sanitize` to specify your sanitizers.[3]

This was admittedly a simple example, but Pysa allows you to annotate your codebase to catch more complicated problems (such as SQL injection and cookie mismanagement). To learn everything that Pysa can do (including built-in common security flaw checking), check out the complete documentation (*https://oreil.ly/lw7BP*).

---

3 You can learn more about sanitizers at *https://oreil.ly/AghGg*.

Pyright

Pyright (*https://oreil.ly/VhZBj*) is a typechecker designed by Microsoft. I have found it to be the most configurable of the typecheckers I've come across. If you would like more control than your current typechecker, explore the Pyright configuration documentation (*https://oreil.ly/nwkne*) for all that you can do. However, Pyright has an additional awesome feature: VS Code integration.

VS Code (also built by Microsoft) is an immensely popular code editor for developers. Microsoft leveraged the ownership of both tools to create a VS Code extension called Pylance (*https://oreil.ly/Y6WAC*). You can install Pylance from your VS Code extensions browser. Pylance is built upon Pyright and uses type annotations to provide a better code-editing experience. Before, I mentioned that autocomplete was a benefit of type annotations in IDEs, but Pylance takes it to the next level. Pylance offers the following features:

- Automatic insertion of imports based on your types
- Tooltips with full type annotations based on signatures
- Codebase browsing such as finding references or browsing a call graph
- Real-time diagnostic checking

It's this last feature that sells Pylance/Pyright for me. Pylance has a setting that allows you to constantly run diagnostics in your whole workspace. This means that every time you edit a file, `pyright` will run across your entire workspace (and it runs fast, too) to look for additional areas that you broke. You don't need to manually run any commands; it happens automatically. As someone who likes to refactor often, I find this tool invaluable for finding breakages early. Remember, you want to find your errors in as close to real time as possible.

I've pulled up the mypy source codebase again and have Pylance enabled and in workplace diagnostics mode. I want to change one type on line 19 from a `sequence` to a `tuple` and see how Pylance handles the change. The code snippet I'm changing is shown in Figure 6-2.

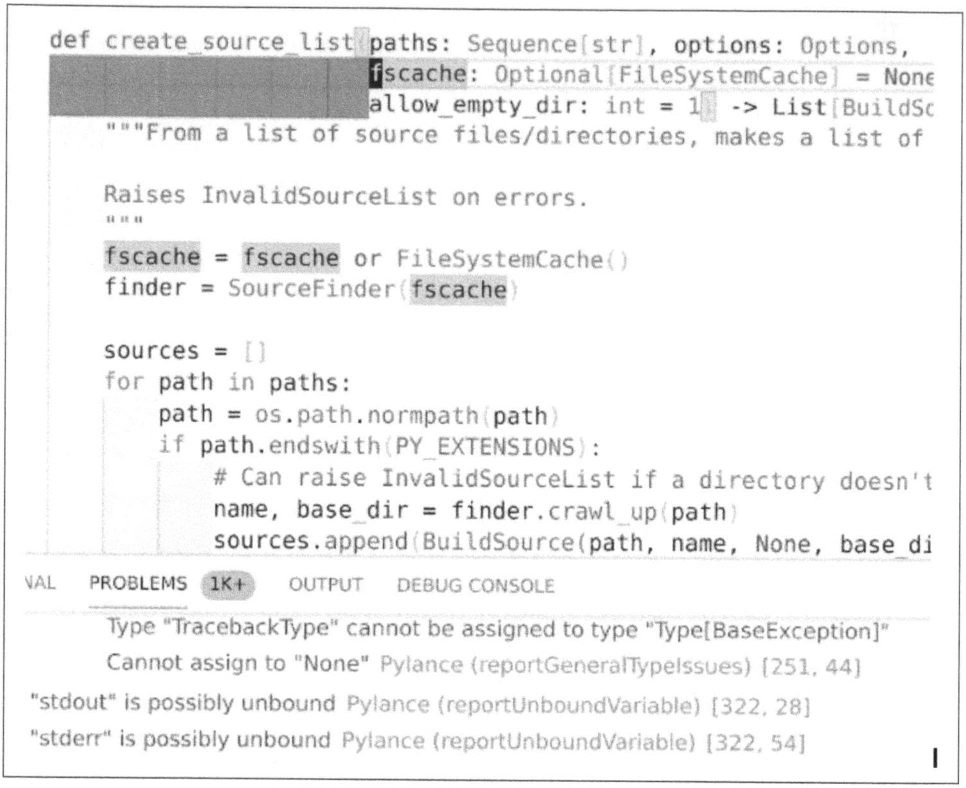

```
def create_source_list paths: Sequence[str], options: Options,
                        fscache: Optional[FileSystemCache] = None
                        allow_empty_dir: int = 1  -> List[BuildSc
    """From a list of source files/directories, makes a list of

    Raises InvalidSourceList on errors.
    """
    fscache = fscache or FileSystemCache()
    finder = SourceFinder(fscache)

    sources = []
    for path in paths:
        path = os.path.normpath(path)
        if path.endswith(PY_EXTENSIONS):
            # Can raise InvalidSourceList if a directory doesn't
            name, base_dir = finder.crawl_up(path)
            sources.append(BuildSource(path, name, None, base_di
```

VAL   PROBLEMS 1K+   OUTPUT   DEBUG CONSOLE

Type "TracebackType" cannot be assigned to type "Type[BaseException]"
Cannot assign to "None" Pylance (reportGeneralTypeIssues) [251, 44]

"stdout" is possibly unbound Pylance (reportUnboundVariable) [322, 28]

"stderr" is possibly unbound Pylance (reportUnboundVariable) [322, 54]

Figure 6-2. Problems in VS Code before editing

Notice at the bottom where my "Problems" are listed. The current view is showing issues in another file that imports and uses the current function I'm editing. Once I change the `paths` parameter from `sequence` to a `tuple`, see how the "Problems" change in Figure 6-3.

Within half a second of saving my file, new errors have shown up in my "Problems" pane, telling me that I've just broken assumptions in calling code. I don't have to wait to run a typechecker manually, or wait for a continuous integration (CI) process to yell at me; my errors show up right in my editor. If that doesn't lead me to finding errors earlier, I don't know what will.

```
def create_source_list(paths: Tuple[str], options: Options,
                        fscache: Optional[FileSystemCache] = None,
                        allow_empty_dir: int = 1) -> List[BuildSou
    """From a list of source files/directories, makes a list of E

    Raises InvalidSourceList on errors.
    """
    fscache = fscache or FileSystemCache()
    finder = SourceFinder(fscache)

    sources = []
    for path in paths:
        path = os.path.normpath(path)
        if path.endswith(PY_EXTENSIONS):
            # Can raise InvalidSourceList if a directory doesn't
            name, base_dir = finder.crawl_up(path)
```

NAL   PROBLEMS 1K+   OUTPUT   DEBUG CONSOLE

Type "TracebackType" cannot be assigned to type "Type[BaseException]"
Cannot assign to "None" Pylance (reportGeneralTypeIssues) [251, 44]

"stdout" is possibly unbound Pylance (reportUnboundVariable) [322, 28]

"stderr" is possibly unbound Pylance (reportUnboundVariable) [322, 54]

∧ Argument of type "Sequence[str]" cannot be assigned to parameter "paths" of typ
      "Sequence[str]" is incompatible with "Tuple[str]" Pylance (reportGeneralTypeIssu

∧ Argument of type "List[str]" cannot be assigned to parameter "paths" of type "Tu
      "List[str]" is incompatible with "Tuple[str]" Pylance (reportGeneralTypeIssues) [3

Figure 6-3. Problems in VS Code after editing

Closing Thoughts

Python typecheckers put a wealth of options at your disposal, and you need to be comfortable with advanced configuration to get the most out of your tooling. You can control severity options and reporting, or even use different typecheckers to reap benefits. As you evaluate tools and options, ask yourself how strict you want your typecheckers to be. As you increase the scope of errors that can be caught, you will increase the amount of time and effort needed to make your codebase compliant. However, the more informative you can make your code, the more robust it will be in its lifetime.

In the next chapter, I will talk about how to assess the trade-offs between benefits and costs associated with typechecking. You'll learn how to identify important areas to typecheck and use strategies to mitigate your pain.

## CHAPTER 7

Adopting Typechecking Practically

Many developers dream of the days when they'll finally work in a completely *green-field* project. A green-field project is one that is brand-new, where you have a blank slate with your code's architecture, design, and modularity. However, most projects soon become *brown-field*, or legacy code. These projects have been around the block a bit; much of the architecture and design has been solidified. Making big, sweeping changes will impact real users. The term *brown-field* is often seen as derogatory, especially when it feels like you are slogging through a big ball of mud.

However, not all brown-field projects are a punishment to work in. Michael Feathers, author of *Working Effectively With Legacy Code* (Pearson), has this to say:

> In a well-maintained system, it might take a while to figure out how to make a change, but once you do, the change is usually easy and you feel much more comfortable with the system. In a legacy system, it can take a long time to figure out what to do, and the change is difficult also.[1]

Feathers defines legacy code as "code without tests." I prefer an alternate definition: legacy code is simply code where you can no longer discuss the code with the developers who wrote it. In lieu of that communication, you rely on the codebase itself to describe its behavior. If the codebase clearly communicates its intentions, it is a well-maintained system that is easy to work in. It may take a little bit of time to understand it all, but once you do, you are able to add features and evolve the system. However, if that codebase is difficult to understand, you will face an uphill battle. That code becomes unmaintainable. This is why robustness is paramount. Writing robust code eases the transition from green-field to brown-field by making the code more maintainable.

---

1 Michael C. Feathers. *Working Effectively with Legacy Code*. Upper Saddle River, NJ: Pearson, 2013.

Most of the type annotation strategies that I've shown in the first part of this book are easier to adopt when a project is new. Adopting these practices in a mature project is more challenging. It is not impossible, but the cost may be higher. This is the heart of engineering: making smart decisions about trade-offs.

Trade-offs

Every decision you make involves a trade-off. Lots of developers focus on the classic time versus space trade-off in algorithms. But there are plenty of other trade-offs, often involving intangible qualities. I've already covered the benefits of a typechecker quite extensively throughout this first part of the book:

- A typechecker increases communication and reduces the chances of bugs.
- A typechecker provides a safety net for making changes and increases the robustness of your codebase.
- A typechecker allows you to deliver functionality faster.

But what are the costs? Adopting type annotations is not free, and they only get worse the larger your codebase is. These costs include:

- The need for buy-in. Depending on culture, it might take some time convincing an organization to adopt typechecking.
- Once you have buy-in, there is an initial cost of adoption. Developers don't start type annotating their code overnight, and it takes time before they grok it. They need to learn it and experiment before they are on board.
- It takes time and effort to adopt tooling. You need centralized checking of some fashion, and developers need to familiarize themselves with running the tooling as part of their workflows.
- It will take time to write type annotations in your codebase.
- As type annotations are checked, developers will have to get used to the slow-down in fighting the typechecker. There is additional cognitive overload in thinking about types.

Developer time is expensive, and it is easy to focus on what else those developers could be doing. Adopting type annotations is not free. Worse, with a large enough codebase, these costs can easily dwarf the initial benefit you get from typechecking. The problem is fundamentally a chicken-and-egg conundrum. You won't see benefits for annotating types until you have written enough types in your codebase. However, it is tough to get buy-in for writing types when the benefit isn't there early on. You can model your value as such:

Value = (Total Benefits) − (Total Costs)

Your benefits and costs will follow a curve; they are not linear functions. I've outlined the basic shapes of the curves in Figure 7-1.

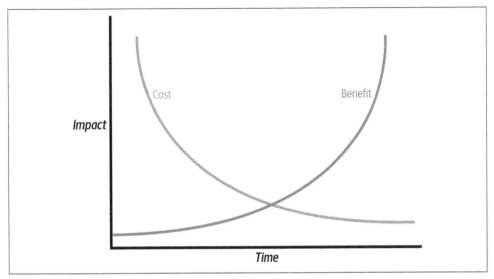

Figure 7-1. Cost and benefit curves over time

I've purposely left off the range, because the scale will change depending on the size of your codebase, but the shapes remain the same. Your costs will start out high, but get easier as adoption increases. Your benefits will start off low, but as you annotate your codebase, you will see more value. You won't see a return on investment until these two curves meet. To maximize value, you need to reach that intersection as early as possible.

Breaking Even Earlier

To maximize the benefits of type annotations, you need to either get value earlier or decrease your costs earlier. The intersection of these two curves is a break-even point; this is where the amount of effort that you're expending is paid back by the value you are receiving. You want to reach this point as fast as sustainably possible so that your type annotations have a positive impact. Here are some strategies to do that.

Find Your Pain Points

One of the best ways to produce value is to reduce the pain you are currently experiencing. Ask yourself: where do I currently lose time in my process? Where do I lose money? Take a look at your test failures and customer bugs. These error cases incur real costs; you should be doing root cause analysis. If you find that a common root cause can be fixed by type annotations, you have a solid case for type annotation adoption. Here are specific bug classes you need to keep an eye out for:

- Any error surrounding None
- Invalid attribute access, such as trying to access variables of functions on the wrong type
- Errors surrounding type conversions such as integers versus strings, bytes versus strings, or lists versus tuples

Also, talk to the people who have to work in the codebase itself. Root out the areas that are a constant source of confusion. If developers have trouble with certain parts of the codebase today, it's likely that future developers will struggle too.

Don't forget to talk to those who are invested in your codebase but maybe don't directly work in it, such as your tech support, product management, and QA. They often have a unique perspective on painful areas of the codebase that might not be apparent when looking through the code. Try to put these costs into concrete terms, such as time or money. This will be invaluable in evaluating where type annotations will be of benefit.

Target Code Strategically

You may want to focus on trying to receive value earlier. Type annotations do not appear overnight in a large codebase. Instead, you will need to identify specific and strategic areas of code to target for type annotations. The beauty of type annotations is that they are completely optional. By typechecking just these areas, you very quickly see benefits without a huge up-front investment. Here are some strategies that you might employ to selectively type annotate your code.

Type annotate new code only

Consider leaving your current unannotated code the way it is and annotate code based on these two rules:

- Annotate any new code that you write.
- Annotate any old code that you change.

Throughout time, you'll build out your type annotations in all code except code that hasn't been changed in a long time. Code that hasn't been changing is relatively stable, and is probably not read too often. Type annotating it is not likely to gain you much benefit.

Type annotate from the bottom up

Your codebase may depend on common areas of code. These are your core libraries and utilities that serve as a foundation upon which everything else is built. Type annotating these parts of your codebase makes your benefit less about depth and more about breadth. Because so many other pieces sit atop this foundation, they will all reap the benefits of typechecking. New code will quite often depend on these utilities as well, so your new code will have an extra layer of protection.

Type annotate your moneymakers

In some codebases, there is a clear separation between the core business logic and all the rest of the code that supports your business logic. Your *business logic* is the area of your system that is most responsible for delivering value. It might be the core reservation system for a travel agency, an ordering system in a restaurant, or a recommendation system for media services. All of the rest of the code (such as logging, messaging, database drivers, and user interface) exists to support your business logic. By type annotating your business logic, you are protecting a core part of your codebase. This code is often long-lived, making it an easy win for long-lasting value.

Type annotate the churners

Some parts of your codebase change way more often than the others. Every time a piece of code changes, you run the risk of an incorrect assumption introducing a bug. The whole point of robust code is to lessen the chance of introducing errors, so what better place to protect than the code that changes the most often? Look for your code that has many different commits in version control, or analyze which files have the most lines of code changed over a time period. Also take a look at which files have the most committers; this is a great indication that this is an area where you can shore up type annotations for communication purposes.

Type annotate the complex

If you come across some complex code, it will take some time to understand. After understanding that code, the best thing you can do is reduce the complexity for the next developer who reads the code. Refactoring the code, improving naming, and adding comments are all fantastic ways to improve comprehension, but consider also adding more type annotations. Type annotations will help developers understand what types are used, how to call functions, and how to deal with return values. Type annotations provide additional documentation for complex code.

Discussion Topic

Which of these strategies would benefit your codebase the most? Why does that strategy work best for you? What would the cost be to implement that strategy?

Lean on Your Tooling

There are things that computers do well, and there are things that humans do well. This section is about the former. When trying to adopt type annotations, there are some fantastic things that automated tooling can assist with. First, let's talk about the most common typechecker out there: mypy.

I've covered the configuration of mypy quite extensively in Chapter 6, but there are a few more options I'd like to delve into that will help you adopt typechecking. One of the biggest problems you will run into is the sheer number of errors that mypy will report the first time you run it on a larger codebase. The biggest mistake you can make in this situation is to keep the hundreds (or thousands) of errors turned on and hope that developers whittle away at the errors over time.

These errors will not get fixed in any quick fashion. If these errors are always turned on, you will not see the benefits of a typechecker, because it will be nearly impossible to detect new errors. Any new issue will simply be lost in the noise of the multitude of other issues.

With mypy, you can tell the typechecker to ignore certain classes of errors or modules through configuration. Here's a sample mypy file, which globally warns if Any types are returned, and sets config options on a per-module basis:

```
# Global options:

[mypy]
python_version = 3.9
warn_return_any = True

# Per-module options:

[mypy-mycode.foo.*]
disallow_untyped_defs = True

[mypy-mycode.bar]
warn_return_any = False

[mypy-somelibrary]
ignore_missing_imports = True
```

Using this format, you can pick and choose which errors your typechecker tracks. You can mask all of your existing errors, while focusing on fixing new errors. Be as specific as possible in defining which errors get ignored; you don't want to mask new errors that show up in unrelated parts of the code.

To be even more specific, mypy will ignore any line commented with # type: ignore.

```
# typechecks just fine
a: int = "not an int" # type: ignore
```

`# type: ignore` should not be an excuse to be lazy! When writing new code, don't ignore type errors—fix them as you go.

Your first goal for adopting type annotations is to get a completely clean run of your typechecker. If there are errors, you either need to fix them with annotations (recommended) or accept that not all errors can be fixed soon and ignore them.

Over time, make sure the number of ignored sections of code decreases. You can track the number of lines containing `# type : ignore` or the number of configuration file sections that you are using; no matter what, strive to ignore as few sections as you can (within reasonable limits, of course—there is a law of diminishing returns).

I also recommend turning the `warn_unused_ignores` flag on in your mypy configuration, which will warn when an ignore directive is no longer required.

Now, none of this helps you get any closer to actually annotating your codebase; it just gives you a starting point. To help annotate your codebase with tooling, you will need something that can automatically insert annotations.

MonkeyType

MonkeyType (*https://github.com/Instagram/MonkeyType*) is a tool that will automatically annotate your Python code. This is a great way to typecheck a large amount of code without a lot of effort.

First install MonkeyType with `pip`:

```
pip install monkeytype
```

Suppose your codebase controls an automatic chef with robotic arms that is capable of cooking perfect food every time. You want to program the chef with my family's favorite recipe, Pasta with Italian Sausage:

```
# Pasta with Sausage Automated Maker  ❶
italian_sausage = Ingredient('Italian Sausage', 4, 'links')
olive_oil = Ingredient('Olive Oil', 1, 'tablespoon')
plum_tomato = Ingredient('Plum Tomato', 6, '')
garlic = Ingredient('Garlic', 4, 'cloves')
black_pepper = Ingredient('Black Pepper', 2, 'teaspoons')
basil = Ingredient('Basil Leaves', 1, 'cup')
pasta = Ingredient('Rigatoni', 1, 'pound')
salt = Ingredient('Salt', 1, 'tablespoon')
water = Ingredient('Water', 6, 'quarts')
cheese = Ingredient('Pecorino Romano', 2, "ounces")
pasta_with_sausage = Recipe(6, [italian_sausage,
                                olive_oil,
                                plum_tomato,
```

```
                              garlic,
                              black_pepper,
                              pasta,
                              salt,
                              water,
                              cheese,
                              basil])

    def make_pasta_with_sausage(servings):  ❷
        sauté_pan = Receptacle('Sauté Pan')
        pasta_pot = Receptacle('Stock Pot')
        adjusted_recipe = adjust_recipe(pasta_with_sausage, servings)

        print("Prepping ingredients")  ❸

        adjusted_tomatoes = adjusted_recipe.get_ingredient('Plum Tomato')
        adjusted_garlic = adjusted_recipe.get_ingredient('Garlic')
        adjusted_cheese = adjusted_recipe.get_ingredient('Pecorino Romano')
        adjusted_basil = adjusted_recipe.get_ingredient('Basil Leaves')

        garlic_and_tomatoes = recipe_maker.dice(adjusted_tomatoes,
                                                adjusted_garlic)
        grated_cheese = recipe_maker.grate(adjusted_cheese)
        sliced_basil = recipe_maker.chiffonade(adjusted_basil)

        print("Cooking Pasta")  ❹
        pasta_pot.add(adjusted_recipe.get_ingredient('Water'))
        pasta_pot.add(adjusted_recipe.get_ingredient('Salt'))
        recipe_maker.put_receptacle_on_stovetop(pasta_pot, heat_level=10)

        pasta_pot.add(adjusted_recipe.get_ingredient('Rigatoni'))
        recipe_maker.set_stir_mode(pasta_pot, ('every minute'))

        print("Cooking Sausage")
        sauté_pan.add(adjusted_recipe.get_ingredient('Olive Oil'))
        heat_level = recipe_maker.HeatLevel.MEDIUM
        recipe_maker.put_receptacle_on_stovetop(sauté_pan, heat_level)
        sauté_pan.add(adjusted_recipe.get_ingredient('Italian Sausage'))
        recipe_maker.brown_on_all_sides('Italian Sausage')
        cooked_sausage = sauté_pan.remove_ingredients(to_ignore=['Olive Oil'])

        sliced_sausage = recipe_maker.slice(cooked_sausage, thickness_in_inches=.25)

        print("Making Sauce")
        sauté_pan.add(garlic_and_tomatoes)
        recipe_maker.set_stir_mode(sauté_pan, ('every minute'))
        while recipe_maker.is_not_cooked('Rigatoni'):
            time.sleep(30)
        cooked_pasta = pasta_pot.remove_ingredients(to_ignore=['Water', 'Salt'])

        sauté_pan.add(sliced_sausage)
        while recipe_maker.is_not_cooked('Italian Sausage'):
```

```
        time.sleep(30)

    print("Mixing ingredients together")
    sauté_pan.add(sliced_basil)
    sauté_pan.add(cooked_pasta)
    recipe_maker.set_stir_mode(sauté_pan, "once")

    print("Serving") ❺
    dishes = recipe_maker.divide(sauté_pan, servings)

    recipe_maker.garnish(dishes, grated_cheese)
    return dishes
```

❶ Definition of all ingredients

❷ Function to make pasta with sausage

❸ Prepping instructions

❹ Cooking instructions

❺ Serving instructions

I've left out a lot of the helper functions to save space, but this gives you an idea of what I'm trying to achieve. You can see the full example in the GitHub repo (*https://github.com/pviafore/RobustPython*) that accompanies this book.

Throughout the entire example, I have zero type annotations. I don't want to write all the type annotations by hand, so I'll use MonkeyType. To help, I can generate *stub files* to create type annotations. Stub files are files that just contain function signatures.

In order to generate the stub files, you have to run your code. This is an important detail; MonkeyType will only annotate code that you run first. You can run specific scripts like so:

```
monkeytype run code_examples/chapter7/main.py
```

This will generate a `SQLite` database that stores all the function calls made throughout the execution of that program. You should try to run as many parts of your system as you can in order to populate this database. Unit tests, integration tests, and test programs all contribute to populating the database.

 Because MonkeyType works by instrumenting your code using `sys.setprofile`, other instrumentation such as code coverage and profiling will not work at the same time. Any tool that uses instrumentation will need to be run separately.

Once you have run through as many paths of your code as you want, you can generate the stub files:

```
monkeytype stub code_examples.chapter7.pasta_with_sausage
```

This will output the stub file for this specific module:

```
def adjust_recipe(
    recipe: Recipe,
    servings: int
) -> Recipe: ...


class Receptacle:
    def __init__(self, name: str) -> None: ...
    def add(self, ingredient: Ingredient) -> None: ...


class Recipe:
    def clear_ingredients(self) -> None: ...
    def get_ingredient(self, name: str) -> Ingredient: ...
```

It won't annotate everything, but it will certainly give you more than enough of a head start in your codebase. Once you are comfortable with the suggestions, you can apply them with `monkeytype apply <module-name>`. Once these annotations have been generated, search through the codebase for any use of `Union`. A `Union` tells you that more than one type has been passed to that function as part of the execution of your code. This is a *code smell*, or something that looks a little funny, even if it's not totally wrong (yet). In this case, the use of a `Union` may indicate unmaintainable code; your code is receiving different types and might not be equipped to handle them. If wrong types are passed as a parameter, that's a likely sign that assumptions have been invalidated somewhere along the way.

To illustrate, the stubs for my `recipe_maker` contain a `Union` in one of my function signatures:

```
def put_receptacle_on_stovetop(
    receptacle: Receptacle,
    heat_level: Union[HeatLevel, int]
) -> None: ...
```

The parameter `heat_level` has taken a `HeatLevel` in some cases and an integer in other cases. Looking back at my recipe, I see the following lines of code:

```
recipe_maker.put_receptacle_on_stovetop(pasta_pot, heat_level=10)
# ...
heat_level = recipe_maker.HeatLevel.MEDIUM
recipe_maker.put_receptacle_on_stovetop(sauté_pan, heat_level)
```

Whether this is an error or not depends on the implementation of the function. In my case, I want to be consistent, so I would change the integer usage to Enum usage. For your codebase, you will need to determine what is acceptable and what is not.

Pytype

One of the problems with MonkeyType is that it only annotates code it sees at runtime. If there are branches of your code that are costly or unable to be run, Monkey-Type will not help you that much. Fortunately, a tool exists to fill in this gap: Pytype (*https://github.com/google/pytype*), written by Google. Pytype adds type annotations through static analysis, which means it does not need to run your code to figure out types.

To run Pytype, install it with `pip`:

```
pip install pytype
```

Then, run Pytype against your code folder (e.g., *code_examples/chapter7*):

```
pytype code_examples/chapter7
```

This will generate a set of *.pyi* files in a *.pytype* folder. These are very similar to the stub files that MonkeyType created. They contain annotated function signatures and variables that you can then copy into your source files.

Pytype offers other intriguing benefits as well. Pytype is not just a type annotator; it is a full linter and typechecker. It has a different typechecking philosophy than other typecheckers such as mypy, Pyright, and Pyre.

Pytype will use inference to do its typechecking, which means it will typecheck your code even in the absence of type annotations. This is a great way to get the benefit of a typechecker without having to write types throughout your codebase.

Pytype is also a little more lenient on types changing in the middle of their lifetime. This is a boon for those who fully embrace Python's dynamically typed nature. As long as code will work at runtime, Pytype is happy. For instance:

```
# Run in Python 3.6
def get_pasta_dish_ingredients(ingredients: list[Ingredient]
                               ) -> list[str]:
    names = ingredients
    # make sure there is water to boil the pasta in
    if does_not_contain_water(ingredients)
        names.append("water")
    return [str(i) for i in names]
```

In this case, names will start off as a list of `Ingredients`. If water is not among the ingredients, I add the string "water" to the list. At this point, the list is heterogeneous; it contains both ingredients and strings. If you were to annotate names as a `list[Ingredient]`, mypy would error out in this case. I would typically throw a red flag here as well; heterogeneous collections are harder to reason about in the absence of good type annotations. However, the next line renders both mypy and my objections moot. Everything is getting converted to a string when returned, which fulfills the annotation of the expected return type. Pytype is intelligent enough to detect this and consider this code to have no issues.

Pytype's leniency and approach to typechecking make it very forgiving for adopting into existing codebases. You don't need any type annotations in order to see the value. This means you get all the benefits of a typechecker with very minimal work. High value, but low cost? Yes, please.

However, Pytype is a double-edged sword in this case. Make sure you don't use Pytype as a crutch; you should still be writing type annotations. It becomes incredibly easy with Pytype to think that you don't need type annotations at all. However, you should still write them for two reasons. Firstly, type annotations provide a documentation benefit, which helps your code's readability. Secondly, Pytype will be able to make even more intelligent decisions if type annotations are present.

Closing Thoughts

Type annotations are incredibly useful, but there is no denying their cost. The larger the codebase, the higher the cost will be for practically adopting type annotations. Every codebase is different; you need to evaluate the value and cost of type annotations for your specific scenario. If type annotations are too costly to adopt, consider three strategies to get past that hurdle:

Find pain points
> If you can eliminate entire classes of pain points through type annotations, such as errors, broken tests, or unclear code, you will save time and money. You target the areas that hurt the most, and by lessening that pain you are making it easier for developers to deliver value over time (which is a sure sign of maintainable code).

Target code strategically
> Pick your spots wisely. In a large codebase, it will be near impossible to annotate every meaningful part of your code. Instead, focus on smaller sections that would see a huge benefit.

Lean on your tooling
> Use mypy to help you selectively ignore files (and make sure that you are ignoring fewer lines of code over time). Use type annotators such as MonkeyType and Pytype to quickly generate types throughout your code. Don't discount Pytype as a typechecker either, as it can find bugs lurking in your code with minimal setup.

This wraps up Part I of the book. It has focused exclusively on type annotations and typechecking. Feel free to mix and match the strategies and tools I've discussed. You don't need to type annotate absolutely everything, as type annotations can constrain expressiveness if too strictly applied. But you should strive to clarify code and make it harder for bugs to crop up. You will find the balance over time, but you need to start thinking about types in Python and how you can express them to other developers. Remember, the goal is a maintainable codebase. People need to understand as much of your intentions as they can from the code alone.

In Part II, I'm going to focus on creating your own types. You've seen a little of this with building your own collection types, but you can go so much further. You'll learn about enumerations, data classes, and classes, and learn why you should pick one over the other. You'll learn how to craft an API and subclass types and model your data. You'll continue to build a vocabulary that improves readability in your codebase.

## PART II

Defining Your Own Types

Welcome to Part II, where you'll learn all about *user-defined types*. User-defined types are types that you, as a developer, create. In the first part of this book, I primarily focused on types that Python provides. However, these types are built for general use cases. They don't tell you anything about the specific domain that you are operating in. In contrast, user-defined types serve as a conduit in which you express domain concepts in your codebase.

You need to build types that represent your domain. Python provides a few different ways to define your own data types, but you should take care with which one you choose. In this part of the book, we'll go over three different user-defined types:

*Enumerations (*Enums*)*
Enumerations provide a developer with a restricted set of values.

Data classes
Data classes represent a relationship between different concepts.

Classes
Classes represent a relationship between different concepts, with an invariant that needs to be preserved.

You'll learn all about using these types in a natural way and how they relate to one another. At the end of Part II, we'll walk through modeling your domain data in a more natural way. The choices you make when designing your types are crucial. By learning the principles behind user-defined types, you will more effectively communicate to future developers.

## CHAPTER 8

User-Defined Types: Enums

In this chapter, I'm going to focus on what a user-defined type is and cover the simplest user-defined data type: enumerations. I'll discuss how to create an enumeration that will protect your code from common programming mistakes. I'll then go over advanced features that allow you to express your ideas more clearly, such as creating aliases, making enumerations unique, or providing automatically generated values.

User-Defined Types

A user-defined type is a type that you, as a developer, create. You define what data is associated with the type and what behaviors are associated with your type. Each of these types should tie to a singular concept. This will help other developers build mental models about your codebase.

For instance, if I am writing restaurant point-of-sale systems, I would expect to come across concepts about the restaurant domain in your codebase. Concepts like restaurants, menu items, and tax calculations should all be naturally represented in code. If I were to use lists, dictionaries, and tuples instead, I'd force my readers to constantly reinterpret the meaning of variables to their more natural mappings.

Consider a simple function that calculates a total with tax. Which function would you rather work with?

```python
def calculate_total_with_tax(restaurant: tuple[str, str, str, int],
                             subtotal: float) -> float:
    return subtotal * (1 + tax_lookup[restaurant[2]])
```

or

```python
def calculate_total_with_tax(restaurant: Restaurant,
                             subtotal: decimal.Decimal) -> decimal.Decimal:
    return subtotal * (1 + tax_lookup[restaurant.zip_code])
```

By using the custom type `Restaurant`, you give readers crucial knowledge about the behavior of your code. Simple as it may be, it is incredibly powerful to build out these domain concepts. Eric Evans, author of *Domain-Driven Design*, wrote, "The heart of software is its ability to solve domain-related problems for its user."[1] If the heart of software is the ability to solve domain-related problems, domain-specific abstractions are the blood vessels. They are the support system, the network that flows through your codebase, all tying back to the central life giver that is the reason your code exists. By building up great domain-related types, you build a healthier system.

The most readable codebases are those that can be reasoned about, and it's easiest to reason about the concepts that you encounter in your day to day. Newcomers to the codebase will already have a leg up if they are familiar with the core business concepts. You've spent the first part of this book focusing on expressing intent through annotations; this next part will focus on communicating intentions by building a shared vocabulary and making that vocabulary available to every developer working in the codebase.

The first way you'll learn how to map a domain concept to a type is through Python's enumeration type: `Enum`.

Enumerations

In some scenarios, you want a developer to pick one value from a list. Colors of a traffic light, pricing plans of a web service, and HTTP methods are all great examples of this type of relationship. To express that relationship in Python, you should use *enumerations*. Enumerations are a construct that let you define the list of values, and developers pick the specific value they want. Python first supported enumerations in Python 3.4.

To illustrate what makes enumerations so special, let's suppose you are developing an application that makes French cooking more accessible by providing a home-delivery network, from baguettes to beignets. It features a menu from which hungry users can select and then receive all the ingredients and cooking instructions by mail.

One of the most popular offerings in this app is the customization. Users can pick which meat they want, which side, and which sauce to prepare. One of the most essential parts of French cooking is its *mother sauces*. These five well-known sauces are building blocks for countless other sauces, and I want to programmatically add new ingredients to these, creating what's known as *daughter sauces*. This way, users can learn how French sauces are categorized when they order their food.

---

1 Eric Evans. *Domain-Driven Design: Tackling Complexity in the Heart of Software*. Upper Saddle River, NJ: Addison-Wesley Professional, 2003.

Let's suppose I represent the mother sauces as a Python tuple:

```
# Note: use UPPER_CASE variable names to denote constant/immutable values
MOTHER_SAUCES = ("Béchamel", "Velouté", "Espagnole", "Tomato", "Hollandaise")
```

What does this tuple communicate to other developers?

- This collection is immutable.
- They can iterate over this collection to get all the sauces.
- They can retrieve a specific element through static indexing.

The immutability and retrieval properties are important for my application. I don't want to add or subtract any mother sauces at runtime (such would be culinary blasphemy). Using a tuple makes it clear to future developers that they should not change these values. Retrieval lets me choose just one sauce, although it is a bit clunky. Every time I need to reference an element, I can do so through static indexing:

```
MOTHER_SAUCES[2]
```

This unfortunately does not communicate intent. Every time a developer sees this, they must remember that 2 means "Espagnole". Constantly correlating numbers to sauces wastes time. This is fragile and will invariably cause mistakes. Should somebody alphabetically sort the sauces, the indices will change, breaking the code. Statically indexing into this tuple will not help the robustness of this code.

To combat this, I'll make aliases for each of these:

```
BÉCHAMEL = "Béchamel"
VELOUTÉ = "Velouté"
ESPAGNOLE = "Espagnole"
TOMATO = "Tomato"
HOLLANDAISE = "Hollandaise"
MOTHER_SAUCES = (BÉCHAMEL, VELOUTÉ, ESPAGNOLE, TOMATO, HOLLANDAISE)
```

That's a bit more code, and still doesn't make it any easier to index into that tuple. Furthermore, there is still a lingering issue in calling code.

Consider a function that creates a daughter sauce:

```
def create_daughter_sauce(mother_sauce: str,
                          extra_ingredients: list[str]):
    # ...
```

I want you to pause a moment and consider what this function tells future developers. I'm purposely leaving out the implementation, because I want to talk about first impressions; the function signature is the first thing a developer will see. Based on the function signature alone, does this function properly convey what is allowed?

Future developers would come across code like this:

```
create_daughter_sauce(MOTHER_SAUCES[0], ["Onions"]) # not super helpful
create_daughter_sauce(BÉCHAMEL, ["Onions"]) # Better
```

Or:

```
create_daughter_sauce("Hollandaise", ["Horseradish"])
create_daughter_sauce("Veloute", ["Mustard"])


# Definitely wrong
create_daughter_sauce("Alabama White BBQ Sauce", [])
```

And here lies the crux of the problem. On the happy path, a developer can use the predefined variables. But if somebody accidentally were to use the wrong sauce (after all, `create_daughter_sauce` expects a string, which could be anything), you soon get unwanted behavior. Remember, I am talking about developers looking at this months (or potentially years) later. They have been tasked to add a feature to the codebase, even though they are not familiar with it. By choosing a string type, I'm just inviting the wrong values to be supplied later.

 Even honest mistakes have ramifications. Did you catch that I left an accent off of the "e" in Veloute? Have fun debugging that in production.

Instead, you want to find a way to communicate that you want a very specific, restricted set of values in specific locations. Since you're in a chapter about "enumerations" and I haven't shown them yet, I'm sure you can guess what the solution is.

Enum

Here's an example of Python's enumeration, Enum, in action:

```
from enum import Enum
class MotherSauce(Enum):
    BÉCHAMEL = "Béchamel"
    VELOUTÉ = "Velouté"
    ESPAGNOLE = "Espagnole"
    TOMATO = "Tomato"
    HOLLANDAISE = "Hollandaise"
```

To access specific instances, you can just do:

```
MotherSauce.BÉCHAMEL
MotherSauce.HOLLANDAISE
```

This is near identical to the string aliases, but there are a few extra benefits.

You cannot accidentally create a MotherSauce with an unexpected value:

```
>>>MotherSauce("Hollandaise") # OKAY

>>>MotherSauce("Alabama White BBQ Sauce")
ValueError: 'Alabama White BBQ Sauce' is not a valid MotherSauce
```

That will certainly limit errors (either with invalid sauces or innocent typos).

If you wanted to print out all the values of the enumeration, you can simply iterate over the enumeration (no need to create a separate list).

```
>>>for option_number, sauce in enumerate(MotherSauce, start=1):
>>>    print(f"Option {option_number}: {sauce.value}")

Option 1: Béchamel
Option 2: Velouté
Option 3: Espagnole
Option 4: Tomato
Option 5: Hollandaise
```

Finally, and crucially, you can communicate your intent in functions that use this Enum:

```
def create_daughter_sauce(mother_sauce: MotherSauce,
                          extra_ingredients: list[str]):
    # ...
```

This tells all the developers looking at this function that they should be passing in a MotherSauce enumeration, and not just any old string. It becomes much harder to introduce typos or incorrect values. (A user can still pass wrong values if they really want to, but they would be in direct violation of what's expected, which is easier to catch—I covered how to catch these errors in Part I.)

Discussion Topic

What sets of data in your codebase would benefit from an Enum? Do you have areas of code where developers pass in the wrong value, even though it is the right type? Discuss where enumerations would improve your codebase.

When Not to Use

Enumerations are great for communicating a static set of choices for users. You don't want to use them where your options are determined at runtime, as you lose a lot of their benefits around communicating intent and tooling (it is much tougher for a reader of code to know what values are possible if they can change in every run-through). If you find yourself in this situation, I recommend a dictionary, which offers a natural mapping between two values that can be changed at runtime. You will need to perform membership checks if you need to restrict what values a user can select, though.

Advanced Usage

Once you master the basics of enumerations, there are quite a few things you can do to even further refine your usage. Remember, the more specific type you choose, the more specific information you convey.

Automatic Values

For some enumerations, you might want to explicitly specify that you don't care about the value that the enumeration is tied to. This tells users that they should not rely on these values. For this, you can use the `auto()` function.

```
from enum import auto, Enum
class MotherSauce(Enum):
    BÉCHAMEL = auto()
    VELOUTÉ = auto()
    ESPAGNOLE = auto()
    TOMATO = auto()
    HOLLANDAISE = auto()

>>>list(MotherSauce)
[<MotherSauce.BÉCHAMEL: 1>, <MotherSauce.VELOUTÉ: 2>, <MotherSauce.ESPAGNOLE: 3>,
 <MotherSauce.TOMATO: 4>, <MotherSauce.HOLLANDAISE: 5>]
```

By default, `auto()` will select monotonically increasing values (1, 2, 3, 4, 5...). If you would like to control what values are set, you should implement a _gener ate_next_value_() function:

```
from enum import auto, Enum
class MotherSauce(Enum):
    def _generate_next_value_(name, start, count, last_values):
        return name.capitalize()
    BÉCHAMEL = auto()
    VELOUTÉ = auto()
    ESPAGNOLE = auto()
    TOMATO = auto()
    HOLLANDAISE = auto()

>>>list(MotherSauce)
[<MotherSauce.BÉCHAMEL: 'Béchamel'>, <MotherSauce.VELOUTÉ: 'Velouté'>,
 <MotherSauce.ESPAGNOLE: 'Espagnole'>, <MotherSauce.TOMATO: 'Tomato'>,
 <MotherSauce.HOLLANDAISE: 'Hollandaise'>]
```

Very rarely will you see _generate_next_value_ defined like this, right inside of an enumeration with values. If auto is used to indicate that the value doesn't matter, then _generate_next_value_ indicates that you want very specific values for auto. It feels contradictory. This is why you typically use _generate_next_value_ in base Enum classes, which are enumerations that are meant to be subtyped and don't include any values. The Flag class, which you'll see next, is a good example of a base class.

Enums Versus Literals

Python's Literal (introduced in Python 3.8) has many of the same benefits as an Enum with automatically set values (assuming there is no _generate_next_value_). In both cases, you are restricting your variables to a very specific set of values.

From a typechecker's perspective, there is very little difference between this:

```
sauce: Literal['Béchamel', 'Velouté', 'Espagnole',
              'Tomato', 'Hollandaise'] = 'Hollandaise'
```

and this:

```
sauce: MotherSauce = MotherSauce.HOLLANDAISE
```

If you just need a simple restriction, reach for Literal first. However, if you want iteration, runtime checking, or different values mapped from name to value, use an Enum.

Flags

Now that you have the mother sauces represented in an Enum, you decide that you are ready to start serving meals with those sauces. But before you begin, you want to be conscious of your customers' allergies, so you decide to represent allergy information for each dish. With your newfound knowledge of auto(), setting up the Allergen enumeration is a piece of cake:

```
from enum import auto, Enum
from typing import Set
class Allergen(Enum):
    FISH = auto()
    SHELLFISH = auto()
    TREE_NUTS = auto()
    PEANUTS = auto()
    GLUTEN = auto()
    SOY = auto()
    DAIRY = auto()
```

And for a recipe, you might track a list of allergens as such:

```
allergens: Set[Allergen] = {Allergen.FISH, Allergen.SOY}
```

This tells readers that a collection of allergens will be unique, and that there might be zero, one, or many allergens. This is exactly what you want. But what if I wanted all allergen information in the system to be tracked like this? I don't want to rely on every developer remembering to use a set (just one use of a list or dictionary can invite wrong behavior). I want some way to represent a grouping of unique enumeration values universally.

The enum module gives you a handy base class to use—Flag:

```
from enum import Flag
class Allergen(Flag):
    FISH = auto()
    SHELLFISH = auto()
    TREE_NUTS = auto()
    PEANUTS = auto()
    GLUTEN = auto()
    SOY = auto()
    DAIRY = auto()
```

This lets you perform bitwise operations to combine allergens or check if certain allergens are present.

```
>>>allergens = Allergen.FISH | Allergen.SHELLFISH
>>>allergens
<Allergen.SHELLFISH|FISH: 3>

>>>if allergens & Allergen.FISH:
>>>    print("This recipe contains fish.")
This recipe contains fish.
```

This is great when you want to represent a selection of values (say, something that was set through a multi–drop down or a bitmask). There are some limitations, though. The values must support the bitwise operations (|, &, etc.). Strings would be an example of types that don't, while integers do. Furthermore, the values cannot overlap when bitwise operations are performed. For example, you cannot use the values 1 through 3 (inclusive) for your Flag, because if you set the Flag to be value 3, performing a "bitwise and" (&) of 1,2, or 3 will all evaluate to True when converted to a boolean value, which makes it difficult to use the Flag effectively. auto() takes care of this for you because the _generate_next_value_ of Flag automatically uses powers of 2.

```
class Allergen(Flag):
    FISH = auto()
    SHELLFISH = auto()
    TREE_NUTS = auto()
    PEANUTS = auto()
    GLUTEN = auto()
    SOY = auto()
    DAIRY = auto()
    SEAFOOD = Allergen.FISH | Allergen.SHELLFISH
    ALL_NUTS = Allergen.TREE_NUTS | Allergen.PEANUTS
```

The use of flags can express what you mean in very specific circumstances, but if you ever want more control of your values, or are enumerating values that don't support bitwise operations, use a nonflag Enum.

As a final note, you are free to create your own aliases for built-in multiple enumeration selections, as I did with SEAFOOD and ALL_NUTS above.

Integer Conversion

There are two more special case enumerations called IntEnum and IntFlag. These map to Enum and Flag, respectively, but allow degradation to raw integers for comparison. I actually do not recommend using these features, and it's important to understand why. First, let's look at the problem they intend to solve.

In French cooking, the measurement of certain ingredients is paramount to success, so you need to make sure you have that covered as well. You create a metric and imperial liquid measure (you want to work internationally, after all) as enumerations, but are dismayed to find that you can't just compare your enumerations to integers.

This code doesn't work:

```
class ImperialLiquidMeasure(Enum):
    CUP = 8
    PINT = 16
    QUART = 32
    GALLON = 128

>>>ImperialLiquidMeasure.CUP == 8
False
```

But, if you were to subclass from IntEnum, it works just fine:

```
class ImperialLiquidMeasure(IntEnum):
    CUP = 8
    PINT = 16
    QUART = 32
    GALLON = 128

>>>ImperialLiquidMeasure.CUP == 8
True
```

An IntFlag performs similarly. You'll see this more when interoperating between systems or possibly hardware. If you were not using an IntEnum, you would need to do something like:

```
>>>ImperialLiquidMeasure.CUP.value == 8
True
```

The convenience of using an IntEnum does not often outweigh the drawback of being a weaker type. Any implicit conversion to integer hides the true intent of the class.

Since implicit integer conversion happens, you might run into a copy/paste mistake (we've all made those, right?) in situations that don't do what you want.

Consider:

```
class Kitchenware(IntEnum):
    # Note to future programmers: these numbers are customer-defined
    # and apt to change
    PLATE = 7
    CUP = 8
    UTENSILS = 9
```

Suppose somebody were to mistakenly do the following:

```
def pour_liquid(volume: ImperialLiquidMeasure):
    if volume == Kitchenware.CUP:
        pour_into_smaller_vessel()
    else:
        pour_into_larger_vessel()
```

If this makes it into production, it will be just fine, no exceptions thrown, all tests pass. However, once the Kitchenware enumeration changes (maybe it adds a BOWL into value 8 and moves CUP to 10), this code will now do the exact opposite of what it was supposed to. Kitchenware.CUP is no longer the same as an ImperialLiquidMeasure.CUP (there's no reason they should be linked); then you'll start pouring into larger vessels instead of smaller vessels, which probably will create an overflow (of your liquid, not of an integer).

This is a textbook example of how unrobust code can lead to subtle mistakes that won't become an issue until much later in the codebase's life. This may be a quick fix, but the bug incurs a very real cost. Tests fail (or worse, a customer complains about pouring the wrong amount of liquid into a vessel), someone has to go crawl through the source code, find the bug, fix it, then take a long coffee break after wondering how this ever worked. All because somebody decided to be lazy and use an IntEnum so that they wouldn't have to type out .value over and over again. So pay your future maintainers a favor: don't use IntEnum unless you absolutely have to for legacy purposes.

Unique

One great feature of enumerations is the ability to alias values. Let's go back to the MotherSauce enumeration. Maybe the codebase developed on French keyboards needs to be adapted to US keyboards, where the keyboard layout is not conducive to adding accent marks over vowels. Removing the accents to anglicize the native French spelling is a nonstarter for many of the developers (they insist we use the original spelling). To avoid an international incident, I will add an alias to some of the sauces.

```
from enum import Enum
class MotherSauce(Enum):
    BÉCHAMEL = "Béchamel"
    BECHAMEL = "Béchamel"
    VELOUTÉ = "Velouté"
    VELOUTE = "Velouté"
    ESPAGNOLE = "Espagnole"
    TOMATO = "Tomato"
    HOLLANDAISE = "Hollandaise"
```

With this, there was much rejoicing from all keyboard owners. Enumerations absolutely allow this sort of behavior; they can have duplicate values as long as the keys are not duplicated.

However, there are cases where you want to force uniqueness on the values. Perhaps you are relying on the enumeration to always contain a set number of values, or perhaps it messes with some of the string representations that are shown to customers. No matter the case, if you want to preserve uniqueness in your Enum, simply add a @unique decorator.

```
from enum import Enum, unique
@unique
class MotherSauce(Enum):
    BÉCHAMEL = "Béchamel"
    VELOUTÉ = "Velouté"
    ESPAGNOLE = "Espagnole"
    TOMATO = "Tomato"
    HOLLANDAISE = "Hollandaise"
```

Creating aliases is more likely than preserving uniqueness in most of the use cases I've come across, so I default to making enumerations nonunique at first, and only adding the unique decorator when needed.

Closing Thoughts

Enumerations are simple, and often overlooked as a powerful communication method. Any time that you want to represent a single value from a static collection of values, an enumeration should be your go-to user-defined type. It's easy to define and use them. They offer a wealth of operations, including iteration, bitwise operations (in the case of Flag enumerations), and control over uniqueness.

Remember these key limitations:

- Enumerations are not meant for dynamic key-value mappings that change at runtime. Use a dictionary for this.

- Flag enumerations only work with values that support bitwise operations with nonoverlapping values.

- Avoid `IntEnum` and `IntFlag` unless absolutely necessary for system interoperability.

Next up, I will explore another user-defined type: a `dataclass`. While enumerations are great at specifying a relationship about a set of values in just one variable, data classes define relationships between multiple variables.

## CHAPTER 9

User-Defined Types: Data Classes

Data classes are user-defined types that let you group related data together. Many types, such as integers, strings, and enumerations, are *scalar*; they represent one and only one value. Other types, such as lists, sets, and dictionaries, represent homogeneous collections. However, you still need to be able to compose multiple fields of data into a single data type. Dictionaries and tuples are OK at this, but they suffer from a few issues. Readability is tricky, as it can be difficult knowing what a dictionary or tuple contains at runtime. This makes them hard to reason about when reading and reviewing code, which is a major blow to robustness.

When your data is hard to understand, readers will make incorrect assumptions and won't be able to spot bugs as easily. Data classes are easier to read and understand, and the typechecker knows how to naturally handle them.

Data Classes in Action

Data classes represent a heterogeneous collection of variables, all rolled into a *composite type*. Composite types are made up of multiple values, and should always represent some sort of relationship or logical grouping. For example, a Fraction is an excellent example of a composite type. It contains two scalar values: a numerator and a denominator.

```
from fraction import Fraction
Fraction(numerator=3, denominator=5)
```

This Fraction represents the relationship between that numerator and denominator. The numerator and denominator are independent of each other; changing one does not change the other. However, by combining them into a single type, they are grouped together to create a logical concept.

Data classes allow you to create these concepts quite easily. To represent a fraction with a `dataclass`, you do the following:

```
from dataclasses import dataclass
@dataclass
class MyFraction:
    numerator: int = 0
    denominator: int = 1
```

Simple, isn't it? The `@dataclass` before the class definition is known as a *decorator*. You'll learn more about decorators in Chapter 17, but for now, all you need to know is that putting `@dataclass` before your class turns it into a `dataclass`. Once you've decorated the class, you need to list out all the fields that you want to represent as a relationship. It is imperative that you provide a default value or a type, so that Python recognizes it as a member of that `dataclass`. In the above case, I am demonstrating both.

By building relationships like this, you are adding to the shared vocabulary in your codebase. Instead of developers always needing to implement each field individually, you instead provide a reusable grouping. Data classes force you to explicitly assign types to your fields, so there's less chance of type confusion among maintainers.

Data classes and other user-defined types can be nested within the `dataclass`. Suppose I'm creating an automated soup maker and I need to group my soup ingredients together. Using `dataclass`, it looks like this:

```
import datetime
from dataclasses import dataclass
from enum import auto, Enum

class ImperialMeasure(Enum):   ❶
    TEASPOON = auto()
    TABLESPOON = auto()
    CUP = auto()

class Broth(Enum):   ❷
    VEGETABLE = auto()
    CHICKEN = auto()
    BEEF = auto()
    FISH = auto()

@dataclass(frozen=True)   ❸
# Ingredients added into the broth
class Ingredient:
    name: str
    amount: float = 1
    units: ImperialMeasure = ImperialMeasure.CUP

@dataclass
class Recipe:   ❹
```

```
    aromatics: set[Ingredient]
    broth: Broth
    vegetables: set[Ingredient]
    meats: set[Ingredient]
    starches: set[Ingredient]
    garnishes: set[Ingredient]
    time_to_cook: datetime.timedelta
```

❶ An enumeration to track different liquid measure sizes

❷ An enumeration to track which broth is used in the soup

❸ A dataclass representing an individual ingredient to be put in the soup. Note that the parameter frozen=True is a special property of data classes to indicate that this dataclass is immutable (more on that later). This does not mean the ingredients come from the freezer section of the supermarket.

❹ A dataclass representing a soup recipe

We're able to take multiple user-defined types (ImperialMeasure, Broth, and Ingredient) to compose them all into the composite type: Recipe. From this Recipe, you can infer multiple concepts:

- A soup recipe is a set of grouped information. Specifically, it can be defined by its ingredients (separated into specific categories), the broth used, and how long it takes to cook.
- Each ingredient has a name and an amount you need for the recipe.
- You have enumerations to tell you about the soup broth and measures. These are not a relationship by themselves, but they do communicate intention to the reader.
- Each grouping of ingredients is a set, rather than a tuple. This means that the user can change these after construction, but still prevent duplicates.

To create the dataclass, I do the following:

```
pepper = Ingredient("Pepper", 1, ImperialMeasure.TABLESPOON)
garlic = Ingredient("Garlic", 2, ImperialMeasure.TEASPOON)
carrots = Ingredient("Carrots", .25, ImperialMeasure.CUP)
celery = Ingredient("Celery", .25, ImperialMeasure.CUP)
onions = Ingredient("Onions", .25, ImperialMeasure.CUP)
parsley = Ingredient("Parsley", 2, ImperialMeasure.TABLESPOON)
noodles = Ingredient("Noodles", 1.5, ImperialMeasure.CUP)
chicken = Ingredient("Chicken", 1.5, ImperialMeasure.CUP)

chicken_noodle_soup = Recipe(
    aromatics={pepper, garlic},
    broth=Broth.CHICKEN,
```

```
        vegetables={celery, onions, carrots},
        meats={chicken},
        starches={noodles},
        garnishes={parsley},
        time_to_cook=datetime.timedelta(minutes=60))
```

You can also get and set individual fields:

```
chicken_noodle_soup.broth
>>> Broth.CHICKEN
chicken_noodle_soup.garnishes.add(pepper)
```

Figure 9-1 shows how this `dataclass` is constructed.

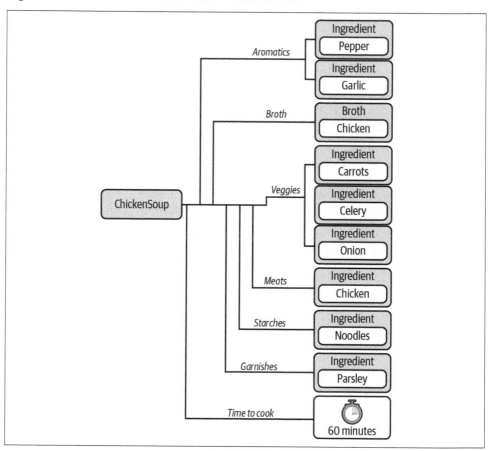

Figure 9-1. Construction of the `dataclass`

Through the use of types, I have made it crystal clear what comprises a recipe. Users cannot leave off fields. Creating composite types is one of the best ways to express relationships through your codebase.

So far, I've just described the fields in a `dataclass`, but you are also able to add in behaviors in the form of methods. Suppose I want to make any soup vegetarian by substituting vegetable broth and removing any meats. I also want to list out all the ingredients so that you can make sure that no meat products snuck in.

I can add methods directly to the `dataclass` like so:

```
@dataclass
class Recipe:
    aromatics: set[Ingredient]
    broth: Broth
    vegetables: set[Ingredient]
    meats: set[Ingredient]
    starches: set[Ingredient]
    garnishes: set[ingredient]
    time_to_cook: datetime.timedelta

    def make_vegetarian(self):
        self.meats.clear()
        self.broth = Broth.VEGETABLE

    def get_ingredient_names(self):
        ingredients = (self.aromatics |
                        self.vegetables |
                        self.meats |
                        self.starches |
                        self.garnishes)

        return ({i.name for i in ingredients} |
                {self.broth.name.capitalize() + " broth"})
```

This is a major improvement over raw dictionaries or tuples. I can embed functionality directly inside my `dataclass`, improving reusability. If a user wants to get all the ingredient names or make a recipe vegetarian, they don't have to remember to do it on their own every time. It's simple enough to call the function. Here's an example of calling a function directly on a `dataclass`.

```
from copy import deepcopy
# make a deep copy so that changing one soup
# does not change the original
noodle_soup = deepcopy(chicken_noodle_soup)
noodle_soup.make_vegetarian()
noodle_soup.get_ingredient_names()
>>> {'Garlic', 'Pepper', 'Carrots', 'Celery', 'Onions',
     'Noodles', 'Parsley', 'Vegetable Broth'}
```

Usage

Data classes have some built-in functions that make them really easy to work with. You've already seen that constructing data classes is a cinch, but what else can you do?

String Conversion

There are two special methods, __str__ and __repr__, used to convert your object to its informal and offical string representation.[1] Note the double underscores surrounding them; they are known as *magic methods*. I'll cover magic methods more in Chapter 11, but for now, you can treat them as functions that get called when you invoke str() or repr() on an object. Data classes define these functions by default:

```
# Both repr() and str() will return the output below
str(chicken_noodle_soup)
>>> Recipe(
    aromatics={
        Ingredient(name='Pepper', amount=1, units=<ImperialMeasure.TABLESPOON: 2>),
        Ingredient(name='Garlic', amount=2, units=<ImperialMeasure.TEASPOON: 1>)},
    broth=<Broth.CHICKEN: 2>,
    vegetables={
        Ingredient(name='Celery', amount=0.25, units=<ImperialMeasure.CUP: 3>),
        Ingredient(name='Onions', amount=0.25, units=<ImperialMeasure.CUP: 3>),
        Ingredient(name='Carrots', amount=0.25, units=<ImperialMeasure.CUP: 3>)},
    meats={
        Ingredient(name='Chicken', amount=1.5, units=<ImperialMeasure.CUP: 3>)},
    starches={
        Ingredient(name='Noodles', amount=1.5, units=<ImperialMeasure.CUP: 3>)},
    garnishes={
        Ingredient(name='Parsley', amount=2,
                   units=<ImperialMeasure.TABLESPOON: 2>)},
    time_to_cook=datetime.timedelta(seconds=3600)
)
```

A bit lengthy, but it means that you won't get something uglier like <__main__.Recipe object at 0x7fef44240730>, which is the default string conversion for other user-defined types.

Equality

If you want to be able to test equality (==, !=) between two data classes, you can specify eq=True when defining your dataclass:

```
from copy import deepcopy
```

---

[1] The informal string representation is useful for printing the object. The official string representation reproduces all information about the object so that it can be reconstructed.

```
@dataclass(eq=True)
class Recipe:
    # ...

chicken_noodle_soup == noodle_soup
>>> False

noodle_soup == deepcopy(noodle_soup)
>>> True
```

By default, equality checks will compare every field across two instances of a data
class. Mechanically, Python invokes a function named __eq__ when doing equality
checks. If you'd like to provide different default functionality for equality checks, you
can write your own __eq__ function.

Relational Comparison

Suppose I want to display nutritional information in my soup app for the health-
conscious. I want to be able to sort the soups by various axes, such as the number of
calories or carbohydrates. Suppose I have a list of dataclass objects called Nutrition
Information, each of which contains the number of calories, grams of fat, and grams
of carbohydrates. I have a list of nutritionals that I ultimately want to sort:

```
nutritionals = [NutritionInformation(calories=100, fat=1, carbohydrates=3),
                NutritionInformation(calories=50, fat=6, carbohydrates=4),
                NutritionInformation(calories=125, fat=12, carbohydrates=3)]
```

By default, data classes do not support relational comparison (<, >, <=, >=), so you
cannot sort the information:

```
>>> sorted(nutritionals)

TypeError: '<' not supported between instances of
           'NutritionInformation' and 'NutritionInformation'
```

If you want to be able to define relational comparison (<, >, <=, >=), you need to set
eq=True and order=True in the dataclass definition. The generated comparison
functions will go through each field, comparing them in the order in which they were
defined.

```
@dataclass(eq=True, order=True)
class NutritionInformation:
    calories: int
    fat: int
    carbohydrates: int
nutritionals = [NutritionInformation(calories=100, fat=1, carbohydrates=3),
                NutritionInformation(calories=50, fat=6, carbohydrates=4),
                NutritionInformation(calories=125, fat=12, carbohydrates=3)]

>>> sorted(nutritionals)
    [NutritionInformation(calories=50, fat=6, carbohydrates=4),
```

```
        NutritionInformation(calories=100, fat=1, carbohydrates=3),
        NutritionInformation(calories=125, fat=12, carbohydrates=3)]
```

If you want to control how comparison is defined, you can write your own __le__, __lt__, __gt__, and __ge__ functions in the dataclass, which map to less-than-or-equals, less-than, greater-than, and greater-than-or-equals, respectively. For instance, if you wanted your NutritionInformation sorted first by fat, then carbohydrates, and then calories by default:

```
@dataclass(eq=True)
class NutritionInformation:
    calories: int
    fat: int
    carbohydrates: int

    def __lt__(self, rhs) -> bool:
        return ((self.fat, self.carbohydrates, self.calories) <
                (rhs.fat, rhs.carbohydrates, rhs.calories))

    def __le__(self, rhs) -> bool:
        return self < rhs or self == rhs

    def __gt__(self, rhs) -> bool:
        return not self <= rhs

    def __ge__(self, rhs) -> bool:
        return not self < rhs

nutritionals = [NutritionInformation(calories=100, fat=1, carbohydrates=3),
                NutritionInformation(calories=50, fat=6, carbohydrates=4),
                NutritionInformation(calories=125, fat=12, carbohydrates=3)]
```

```
>>> sorted(nutritionals)
    [NutritionInformation(calories=100, fat=1, carbohydrates=3),
     NutritionInformation(calories=50, fat=6, carbohydrates=4),
     NutritionInformation(calories=125, fat=12, carbohydrates=3)]
```

If you override comparison functions, do not specify order=True, as that will raise a TypeError.

Immutability

Sometimes, you need to convey that a dataclass should not be able to be changed. In that case, you can specify that a dataclass must be frozen, or unable to change. Anytime you change the state of a dataclass, you introduce entire classes of errors that might happen:

- Callers of your code may be unaware that the fields changed; they could erroneously assume that the fields are static.

- Setting a single field to an incorrect value might be incompatible with how the other fields are set.

- If there are multiple threads modifying the fields, you run the risk of a data race, which means you cannot guarantee in which order the modifications are applied in relation to one another.

None of these error cases occur if your dataclass is frozen. To freeze a dataclass, add a frozen=True to the dataclass decorator:

```
@dataclass(frozen=True)
class Recipe:
    aromatics: Set[Ingredient]
    broth: Broth
    vegetables: Set[Ingredient]
    meats: Set[Ingredient]
    starches: Set[Ingredient]
    garnishes: Set[Ingredient]
    time_to_cook: datetime.timedelta
```

If you want to use your dataclass in a set or as a key in a dictionary it must be *hashable*. This means it must define a __hash__ function that takes your object and distills it down to a number.[2] When you freeze a dataclass, it automatically becomes hashable, as long as you don't explicitly disable equality checking and all fields are hashable.

There are two caveats around this immutability, however. First, when I say immutability, I am referencing the fields in the dataclass, not the variable containing the dataclass itself. For example:

```
# assume that Recipe is immutable because
# frozen was set to true in the decorator
soup = Recipe(
    aromatics={pepper, garlic},
    broth=Broth.CHICKEN,
    vegetables={celery, onions, carrots},
    meats={chicken},
    starches={noodles},
    garnishes={parsley},
    time_to_cook=datetime.timedelta(minutes=60))


# this is an error
soup.broth =  Broth.VEGETABLE
```

---

2 Hashing is a complicated subject, beyond the scope of this book. You can learn more about the hash function in the Python documentation (*https://oreil.ly/JDgLO*).

```
# this is not an error
soup = Recipe(
    aromatics=set(),
    broth=Broth.CHICKEN,
    vegetables=set(),
    meats=set(),
    starches=set(),
    garnishes=set(),
    time_to_cook=datetime.timedelta(seconds=3600))
)
```

If you would like the typechecker to error out if the variable is rebound, you can annotate the variable as Final (see Chapter 4 for more details on Final).

Secondly, a frozen dataclass only prevents its members from being set. If the members are mutable, you are still able to call methods on those members to modify their values. frozen dataclasses do not extend immutability to their attributes.

For example, this code is perfectly fine:

```
soup.aromatics.add(Ingredient("Garlic"))
```

Even though it is modifying the *aromatics* field of a frozen dataclass, no error is raised. When using frozen dataclasses, make the members immutable (such as integers, strings, or other frozen dataclasses) to avoid this pitfall.

Comparison to Other Types

Data classes are relatively new (introduced in Python 3.7); a lot of legacy code will not contain data classes. As you evaluate data class adoption, you need to understand where a data class shines in relation to other constructs.

Data Classes Versus Dictionaries

As discussed in Chapter 5, dictionaries are fantastic for mapping keys to values, but they are most appropriate when they are homogeneous (when all the keys are the same type and all the values are the same type). When used for heterogeneous data, dictionaries are tougher for humans to reason about. Also, typecheckers don't know enough about the dictionary to check for errors.

Data classes, however, are a natural fit for fundamentally heterogeneous data. Readers of the code know the exact fields present in the type and typecheckers can check for correct usage. If you have heterogeneous data, use a data class before you reach for a dictionary.

Data Classes Versus TypedDict

Also discussed in Chapter 5 was the TypedDict type. This is another way to store heterogeneous data that makes sense for readers and typecheckers. At first glance, TypedDict and data classes solve a very similar problem, so it can be tough to decide which one is appropriate. My rule of thumb is to think of a dataclass as the default, as it can have functions defined on it and you can control immutability, comparability, equality, and other operations. However, if you are already working with dictionaries (such as for working with JSON), you should reach for a TypedDict, provided that you don't need any of the benefits of a dataclass.

Data Classes Versus namedtuple

namedtuple is a tuple-like collection type in the collections module. Unlike tuples, it allows for you to name the fields in a tuple like so:

```
>>> from collections import namedtuple
>>> NutritionInformation = namedtuple('NutritionInformation',
                            ['calories', 'fat', 'carbohydrates'])
>>> nutrition = NutritionInformation(calories=100, fat=5, carbohydrates=10)
>>> print(nutrition.calories)

100
```

A namedtuple goes a long way toward making a tuple more readable, but so does using a dataclass in its place. I almost always pick a dataclass instead of a namedtuple. A dataclass, like a namedtuple, provides named fields along with other benefits like:

- Explicitly type annotating your arguments
- Control of immutability, comparability, and equality
- Easier to define functions in the type

In general, I only reach for a namedtuple if I explicitly need compatibility with Python 3.6 or before.

Discussion Topic

What types do you use to represent heterogeneous data in your codebase? If you use dictionaries, how easy is it for developers to know all the key-value pairs in the dictionary? If you use tuples, how easy is it for developers to know what the meaning of individual fields are?

Closing Thoughts

Data classes were a game changer when released in Python 3.7, because they allowed developers to define heterogeneous types that were fully typed while still staying lightweight. As I write code, I find myself reaching for data classes more and more. Whenever you encounter heterogeneous, developer-controlled dictionaries or `namedtuples`, a data class is more suitable. You can find a wealth of additional information in the `dataclass` documentation (*https://oreil.ly/1toSU*).

However, as great as data classes are, they should not be universally used. A data class, at its heart, represents a conceptual relationship, but it really is only appropriate when the members within the data class are independent of one another. If any of the members should be restricted depending on the other members, a data class will make it harder to reason about your code. Any developer could change the fields during your data classes' lifetime, potentially creating an illegal state. In these cases, you need to reach for something a bit heavier. In the next chapter, I'll teach you how to do just that with classes.

## CHAPTER 10

User-Defined Types: Classes

Classes will be the final user-defined type that I'll cover in this book. Many developers learn classes early, and this is both a boon and a bane. Classes are used in many frameworks and codebases, so it pays off to be fluent in class design. However, when developers learn classes too early, they miss the nuance of when and, more importantly, when not to use them.

Think back to your use of classes. Could you represent that data as a `dataclass` instead? What about a set of free functions? I've seen too many codebases that use classes everywhere when they really shouldn't, and maintainability suffers because of it.

However, I've also come across codebases that swing the pendulum the other way: using no classes at all. This also affects maintainability; it is easy to break assumptions and have inconsistent data throughout. In Python, you should strive for a balance. Classes have a place in your codebase, but it is important to recognize their strengths and weaknesses. It's time to really dig deep, cast aside your preconceptions, and learn how classes help you make more robust code.

Class Anatomy

Classes are intended to be another way of grouping related data together. They have decades of history in the object-oriented paradigm and, at first glance, don't differ that much from what you learned about data classes. In fact, you can write a class just like you wrote a `dataclass`:

```
class Person:
    name: str = ""
    years_experience: int = 0
    address: str = ""
```

```
pat = Person()
pat.name = "Pat"
print(f"Hello {pat.name}")
```

Looking at the code above, you could easily write it a different way with a `dict` or dataclass:

```
pat = {
    "name": "",
    "years_experience": 0,
    "address": ""
}

@dataclass
class Person():
    name: str = ""
    years_experience: int = 0
    address: str = ""
```

In Chapter 9, you learned the advantages of data classes over raw dictionaries, and classes offer many of the same benefits. But you might (rightly) wonder why you would ever use a class instead of a data class again?

In fact, given the flexibility and convenvenience of data classes, classes might feel inferior. You don't get the fancy features like `frozen` or `ordered`. You don't get built-in string methods. Why, you can't even instantiate a `Person` as nicely as with data classes.

Try to do something like:

```
pat = Person("Pat", 13, "123 Fake St.")
```

When trying this with a class, you'll be immediately greeted with an error:

```
TypeError: Person() takes no arguments
```

That's really frustrating, at first glance. However, this design decision is intentional. You need to explicitly define how a class gets initialized, which is done through a special method called `__init__`. It may seem like a drawback compared to data classes, but it allows you to have more fine-grained control over the fields in your class. The next few sections will describe how you can use this control to your benefit. First, let's look at what the constructor of a class actually provides you.

Class Initialization

When you construct a new instance of a class, you control how that class is initialized with an `__init__` method:

```
class Person:
    def __init__(self,
                 name: str,
```

```
                years_experience: int,
                address: str):
        self.name = name
        self.years_experience = years_experience
        self.address = address

    pat = Person("Pat", 13, "123 Fake St.")
```

Notice that I tweaked the class a bit. Instead of defining the variables like I did in a dataclass, I am defining all the variables in __init__. This special method gets called when class is instantiated. It takes arguments needed to define your user data type, as well as a special argument called self. The specific name for this parameter is arbitrary, but you'll see most code use self as the convention. Each time you instantiate a class, the self argument refers to that specific instance; one instance's attributes won't conflict with another instance's attributes, even though they are the same class.

So why would you ever write a class? Dictionaries or data classes are simpler to write and involve less ceremony. For something like the Person object listed earlier, I don't disagree. However, a class can convey one key thing that a dictionary or data class can't easily convey: *invariants*.

Invariants

An invariant is a property of an entity that remains unchanged throughout the lifetime of that entity. Invariants are the concepts that hold true about your code. Readers and writers of code will reason about your code and depend upon that reasoning to keep everything straight. Invariants are the building blocks for understanding your codebase. Here are some examples of invariants:

- Every employee has a unique ID; no two employee IDs are duplicated.
- Enemies in a game may only take actions if their health points are above zero.
- Circles may only have a positive radius.
- Pizzas will always have cheese on top of sauce.

Invariants convey immutable properties of objects. They can reflect mathematical properties, business rules, coordination guarantees, or anything else you want to hold true. Invariants do not have to mirror the real world; they just have to be true for *your* system. For instance, Chicago-style deep-dish pizza aficionados may disagree with that last pizza-related bullet, but if your system only handles cheese-on-sauce pizzas, it's OK to encode that as an invariant. The invariant only refers to a specific entity, too. You get to decide the scope of the invariant, whether it is true across your system, or whether it only applies to a specific program, module, or class. This chapter will focus on classes and their role in *preserving* invariants.

So, how does a class help convey invariants? Let's start with the __init__ method. You can put in safeguards and assertions to check that an invariant is satisfied, and from that point on, a user of that class should be able to depend on that invariant being true for the lifetime of the class. Let's see how.

Consider an imaginary automated pizza maker that makes a perfect pizza every time. It will take dough, roll it into a circle, apply sauce and toppings, and then bake the pizza. I will list out some invariants that I want to preserve in my system (these invariants are not universally true about all pizzas in the world, just true for the pizzas I want to create).

I want the following to hold true for the lifetime of the pizza:

- Sauce will never be put on top of toppings (cheese is a topping in this scenario).
- Toppings may go above or below cheese.
- Pizza will have at most only one sauce.
- Dough radius can be only whole numbers.
- The radius of dough may be only between 6 and 12 inches, inclusive (between 15 and 30 centimeters).

Some of these might be for business reasons, some might be for health reasons, and some might be just limitations of machinery, but every one of these is intended to be true for the lifetime of that pizza. I'll check for these invariants during construction of the pizza.

```
from pizza.sauces import is_sauce
class PizzaSpecification:
    def __init__(self,
                    dough_radius_in_inches: int,
                    toppings: list[str]):
        assert 6 <= dough_radius_in_inches <= 12, \
            'Dough must be between 6 and 12 inches'
        sauces = [t for t in toppings if is_sauce(t)]
        assert len(sauces) < 2, \
            'Can only have at most one sauce'

        self.dough_radius_in_inches = dough_radius_in_inches
        sauce = sauces[:1]
        self.toppings = sauce + \
            [t for t in toppings if not is_sauce(t)]
```

Let's break down this invariant checking:

- dough_radius_in_inches is an integer. This doesn't stop callers from passing floats/strings/whatever into the __init__ method, but if used in conjunction with a typechecker (like those you used in Part I), you can detect when callers pass the wrong type. If you aren't using a typechecker, you would have to do an `isinstance()` check (or something similar) instead.

- This code asserts that the dough radius is between 6 and 12 inches (inclusive). If this is not the case, an `AssertionError` is thrown (preventing initialization of the class).

- This code asserts that there is at most one sauce, throwing an `AssertionError` if that does not hold true.

- This code ensures that the sauce is at the beginning of our toppings list (presumably this will be used to tell the pizza maker in what order to lay toppings down).

- Note that I don't explicitly do anything to preserve that toppings can be above or below cheese. This is because the default behavior of the implementation satisfies the invariant. However, you may still choose to communicate the invariant to your callers through documentation.

Assertions Versus Exceptions

Throughout this book, I will use assertions in some cases, and raise exceptions in other cases. When an assertion fails, it raises an `AssertionError`, which is a type of exception. This may make assertions and exceptions seem interchangeable, but I am actually picking one or the other intentionally.

Assertions are not guaranteed to execute at runtime, as your code may be deployed with options that disable assertions. In this case, I use them for things that I always expect to be true, unless a developer in the system messes up. It is intended to catch mistakes during development, and it signals to other developers that it is up to them to not create a situation that fails an assertion.

Exceptions, on the other hand, indicate to a developer that something may be possible due to user error or malicious actors. It is unlikely to happen, but other developers must be prepared to catch the exception if something goes wrong.

If the error is not an exceptional use case, I may choose to return an `Optional` or `Union` instead (see Chapter 4 for more information). Note that this only applies if the function returns a value. The constructors in this chapter do not return any values, so using an `Optional` or `Union` is inappropriate. In these cases, make it crystal clear to future developers that an exception (or assertion) can be thrown, because the typechecker will not be much help.

Avoiding Broken Invariants

It is incredibly important that you never, ever construct this class if the invariants would be broken. You have two avenues that you can choose if the caller ever constructs an object in a way such that invariants would be broken.

Throw an exception
> This prevents the object from being constructed. This is what I did when making sure the dough radius was appropriate and that I had at most one sauce.

Massage the data
> Make the data conform to the invariant. I could have thrown an exception when I didn't get toppings in the right order, but instead, I rearranged them to satisfy the invariant.

What If You Don't Want Exceptions?

If you don't want to use exceptions, you can use a function to create your class instead (also known as a factory method). You can hide your class from help() by preceding the class with an underscore (_), and then create a function in your module that checks invariants and instantiates the class. If the invariants are not satisfiable, you can return None. Make sure you are using Optional types (as covered in Chapter 4) to represent None.

```python
# Note to maintainers, only create this through create_pizza_spec function
class _PizzaSpecification:
    # ... snip class

def create_pizza_spec(dough_radius_in_inches: int,
                      toppings: list[str]) -> Optional[_PizzaSpecification]:
    try:
        return _PizzaSpecification()
    except:
        return None
```

If you really want to, you can move your invariant checking to the function itself, but at that point, you are dealing with an invariant-less type and you should be using a data class. If you are more accustomed to functional programming paradigms, and will be keeping most of your classes immutable, then this is less of an issue.

Why Are Invariants Beneficial?

It is a lot of work to write a class and come up with invariants. But I want you to consciously think about invariants every time you group some data together. Ask yourself:

- Should any of this data be restricted in any form that I can't catch through the type system (such as the order of toppings)?

- Are some fields interdependent (i.e., changing one field may necessitate a change in another field)?

- Are there guarantees I want to provide about the data?

If you answer yes to any of these questions, you have invariants you want to preserve and should write a class. When you choose to write a class and define a set of invariants, you're doing a few things:

1. You're adhering to the Don't Repeat Yourself (DRY) principle.[1] Instead of littering your code with checks before object construction, you put those checks in one place.

2. You're putting more work on the writer to ease the work of the reader/maintainer/caller. Your code will most likely live longer than you work on it. By providing an invariant (and communicating it well—see the next section), you lessen the burden of those who come after you.

3. You're more effectively able to reason about code. There's a reason why languages like Ada (*https://www.adacore.com/about-ada*) and concepts like formal proofs are used in mission-critical environments. They provide developers with comfort; other coders can trust your code to a certain degree.

All of this leads to fewer bugs. You're not running the risk of people misconstructing objects or missing a required check. You're making an easier API for people to think about, and you reduce the risk of people using your objects incorrectly. You will also adhere closer to the Law of Least Surprise. You never want someone to be surprised when using your code (how many times have you heard the phrase, "Wait, *that's* how the class works?"). By defining invariants and sticking to them, there is less chance for someone to be surprised.

A dictionary simply cannot do that.

Consider a pizza specification represented by a dictionary:

```
{
    "dough_radius_in_inches": 7
    "toppings": ["tomato sauce", "mozzarella", "pepperoni"]
}
```

---

1 Andrew Hunt and David Thomas. *The Pragmatic Programmer: From Journeyman to Master.* Reading, MA: Addison-Wesley, 2000.

There is no simple way for you to force a user to construct this dictionary correctly. You would have to rely on callers doing the right thing in every invocation (which will only become more difficult as the codebase grows). There is also no way to prevent users from modifying the dictionary freely and breaking invariants.

 It's true, you could define methods that construct dictionaries after checking invariants, and only mutate the dictionary through functions that also check invariants. Or, you could certainly write a constructor and invariant-checking methods on data classes. But if you go through all that trouble, why not write a class? Be mindful of what your choices communicate to future maintainers. You must be deliberate between your choice of dictionaries, data classes and classes. Each of these abstractions conveys a very specific meaning, and if you choose the wrong one, you'll confuse maintainers.

There's another benefit that I haven't talked about, and it relates to the "S" in SOLID (see the next sidebar): the Single Responsibility Principle. The Single Responsibility Principle states that each object "should have one and only one reason to change."[2] It sounds simple, but in practice it can be a struggle to know exactly how granular *one* reason to change is. My suggestion to you is to define a set of related invariants (such as your dough and toppings) and write a class per set of related invariants. If you ever find yourself writing attributes or methods that do not directly relate to one of those invariants, your class has low *cohesion*, which means it has too many responsibilities.

SOLID Design Principles

The SOLID design principles were first described by Robert C. Martin in his 2000 paper, "Design Principles and Design Patterns" (*https://oreil.ly/GvwUz*). They are five design principles that I have found very useful when developing in larger codebases. The SOLID design principles are as follows:

Single Responsibility Principle
    A principle for reuse and consolidation of code

Open-Closed Principle
    A principle for extensibility

Liskov Substitution Principle
    A principle for subtyping

---

2 Robert C. Martin. "The Single Responsibility Principle." *The Clean Code Blog* (blog), May 8, 2014. *https://oreil.ly/ZOMxb*.

Interface Segregation Principle
    A principle for abstraction

Dependency Inversion Principle
    A principle for decoupling dependencies

Some of these principles will be touched upon throughout the book. Remember that all of these are just principles. Use your best judgment in applying them.

Discussion Topic

Consider some of the most important parts of your codebase. What invariants are true about that system? How well are these invariants enforced, such that developers cannot break them?

Communicating Invariants

Now, you can't realize these benefits unless you can effectively communicate them. Nobody can reason about invariants that they don't know about. So, how do you do that? Well, with any communication, you should consider your audience. You have two types of people with two different use cases:

Consumers of the class
    These are people who are trying to solve their own problems and are looking for tools to help them. They may be trying to debug an issue or find a class in a codebase that helps them out.

Future maintainers of the class
    People will add onto your class, and it's important that they do not break invariants that all your callers have come to depend on.

You will need to keep both in mind when desigining your classes.

Consuming Your Class

First, consumers of your class will typically look at your source code to see how it works and if it meets their needs. Putting assertion statements (or raising other exceptions) in the __init__ method is a great way to tell a user what is and isn't possible with your class. The __init__ method is typically the first place a developer will look (after all, if they can't instantiate your class, how can they use it?). For invariants that you cannot represent in code (yes, those exist), you want to document that in whatever your users use for API reference. The closer to the code your documentation is, the more likely a user will find it when looking at your code.

Knowledge in one's head is not scalable or discoverable. Wikis and/or documentation portals are a decent step, but often are better suited for larger scale ideas that don't go out of date as quickly. A README in the code repository is a better step, but the true best place is a comment or docstring with the class itself.

```
class PizzaSpecification:
    """
    This class represents a Pizza Specification for use in
    Automated Pizza Machines.

    The pizza specification is defined by the size of the dough and
    the toppings. Dough should be a whole number between 6 and 12
    inches (inclusive). If anything else is passed in, an AssertionError
    is thrown. The machinery cannot handle less than 6 inches and the
    business case is too costly for more than 12 inches.

    Toppings may have at most one sauce, but you may pass in toppings
    in any order. If there is more than one sauce, an AssertionError is
    thrown. This is done based on our research telling us that
    consumers find two-sauced pizzas do not taste good.

    This class will make sure that sauce is always the first topping,
    regardless of order passed in.

    Toppings are allowed to go above and below cheese
    (the order of non-sauce toppings matters).

    """
    def __init__(...)
        # ... implementation goes here
```

I've had a bit of a contentious relationship with comments throughout my career. In the beginning, I would comment everything, probably because my university professors required it. A few years later, the pendulum swung too far in the other direction, and I was one to espouse "code shall be self-documenting," meaning that the code should be able to stand on its own. After all, comments could go out of date and, as the common saying goes, "a wrong comment is worse than no comment." The pendulum has since shifted back and I've learned that code should absolutely self-document *what* it's doing (this is just another spin on the Law of Least Surprise), but comments help the human nature of code. Most people simplify this to *why* the code behaves it does, but sometimes that is vague. In the snippet above, I go about it by documenting my invariants (including ones not apparent in code), and backing it up with business reasons. This way, a consumer can ascertain what the class is and isn't used for, as well as whether the class fits into their intended use case.

What About Maintainers?

You will have to deal with the other group, the future maintainers of your code, differently. This is a tricky one. You have a comment that helps define your constraints, but that won't prevent inadvertent changing of invariants. Changing invariants is a delicate thing. People will come to depend on these invariants, even if they aren't reflected in function signatures or type systems. If somebody changes an invariant, every consumer of the class could be affected (sometimes this is inevitable, but be aware of the cost).

To help catch this, I'll lean on an old friend as a safety net—unit tests. Unit tests are snippets of code that will automatically test your own classes and functions. (For more discussion on unit tests, check out Chapter 21.) You should absolutely write unit tests around your expectations and invariants, but there's one additional facet I'd like you to consider: help future test writers know when invariants are broken as well. I like to do this with the help of a context manager—a construct in Python that forces code to run when a with block is exited (if you're not familiar with context managers, you'll learn more in Chapter 11):

```python
import contextlib
from pizza_specification import PizzaSpecification

@contextlib.contextmanager
def create_pizza_specification(dough_radius_in_inches: int,
                              toppings: list[str]):
    pizza_spec = PizzaSpecification(dough_radius_in_inches, toppings)
    yield pizza_spec
    assert 6 <= pizza_spec.dough_radius_in_inches <= 12
    sauces = [t for t in pizza_spec.toppings if is_sauce(t)]
    assert len(sauces) < 2
    if sauces:
        assert pizza_spec.toppings[0] == sauces[0]

    # check that we assert order of all non sauces
    # keep in mind, no invariant is specified that we can't add
    # toppings at a later date, so we only check against what was
    # passed in
    non_sauces = [t for t in pizza_spec.toppings if t not in sauces]
    expected_non_sauces = [t for t in toppings if t not in sauces]
    for expected, actual in zip(expected_non_sauces, non_sauces):
        assert expected == actual


def test_pizza_operations():
    with create_pizza_specification(8, ["Tomato Sauce", "Peppers"]) \
        as pizza_spec:

        # do something with pizza_spec
```

The beauty of using a context manager like this is that every invariant can be checked as a postcondition of the test. This feels like duplication and direct violation of the DRY principle, but in this case, it's warranted. Unit tests are a form of double-entry bookkeeping, and you want them to find errors when one side erroneously changes.

Is Invariant Checking Slow?

There is a runtime cost to checking all these invariants, especially for more complex data types than a pizza. Checking invariants provides a real benefit for making humans go faster, but for an object that is created multiple times in a tight loop, developers may want to eschew conditionals and/or exceptions in favor of code execution performance. If you're in a case where your program is not meeting a benchmark, you've profiled the code, and the invariant checking is the biggest culprit, here's what I want you to do:

Continue to document the invariants the class has, but convey through very explicit means that the onus is on callers to satisfy the invariants, not the class itself. The class should still try to maintain the invariants to help reasonability, but it can't do as much precondition checking as you may like. You are deliberately, in essence, sacrificing maintainability for speed. It will be case by case just how much maintainability suffers and how much of a speedup you will receive. If you do choose this route, supplement other processes in your environment to make up for the decrease of maintainability (more robust linting, more stringent code reviews, etc.).

Encapsulation and Maintaining Invariants

I have a little secret for you. I wasn't completely honest in the last section. I know, I know, shame on me, and I'm sure the eagle-eyed readers have already spotted my deception.

Consider this:

```
pizza_spec = PizzaSpecification(dough_radius_in_inches=8,
                                toppings=['Olive Oil',
                                          'Garlic',
                                          'Sliced Roma Tomatoes',
                                          'Mozzarella'])
```

Nothing at all is preventing a future developer from changing some invariants after the fact.

```
pizza_spec.dough_radius_in_inches = 100  # BAD!
pizza_spec.toppings.append('Tomato Sauce')  # Second sauce, oh no!
```

What was the point of talking about invariants if any developer can immediately invalidate them? Well, it turns out that I have another concept to discuss: *encapsulation*.

Encapsul-what, Now?

Encapsulation. Simply put, it's the ability for an entity to hide properties and the actions that operate upon those properties. Practically speaking, it means that you decide what properties are visible to callers, and restrict how they can access them and/or change data. This is accomplished using an *application programming interface* (API).

When most people think of an API, things like REST or SDKs (software development kits) come to mind. But every class has its own API. It's the cornerstone of how you interact with classes. Every function call, every property access, every initialization is part of an object's API.

So far, I've covered two parts of the API in the `PizzaSpecification`: the initialization and property access. I don't have much more to say about the `__init__` method; its done its job in verifying invariants. Now, I will address how to preserve those invariants as you flesh out the rest of an API (the operations that we wish to bundle with this class).

Protecting Data Access

That leads us back to the problem at the beginning of this section: how do we prevent users of our API (our class) from breaking invariants? By signaling that this data should be *private*.

There are three types of access control in many programming languages:

Public
    Any other piece of code can access this part of the API.

Protected
    Only subclasses (we'll see these more in Chapter 12) should access this part of the API.

Private
    Only this class (and any other instances of this class) should access this part of the API.

Public and protected attributes form your public API, and should be relatively stable before people depend on your class heavily. However, it is a general convention that people should leave your private API alone. This should leave you free to hide things that you feel need to be inaccessible. This is how you can preserve your invariants.

In Python, you signal to other developers that an attribute should be protected by prefixing it with an underscore (_). Private attributes and methods should be prefixed with two underscores (__). (Note that this is not the same as functions *surrounded* by two underscores—those denote special magic methods, which I'll cover in Chapter 11.) In Python, you don't have a compiler that can catch when this access control is broken. There is nothing stopping a developer from reaching in and messing with your protected and private members. Enforcing this becomes an organizational challenge, part of the nature of the beast with a dynamically typed language like Python.

Set up linting, enforce code styles, do thorough code reviews; you should treat your API as a core tenet of your class and not allow it to be broken lightly.

There are a few benefits to making your attributes protected/private. Protected and private attributes don't show up in help() of a class. This will reduce the chance of somebody using these attributes inadvertently. Furthermore, private attributes aren't as easily accessible.

Consider the PizzaSpecification with private members:

```
from pizza.sauces import is_sauce
class PizzaSpecification:
    def __init__(self,
                    dough_radius_in_inches: int,
                    toppings: list[str]):
        assert 6 <= dough_radius_in_inches <= 12, \
        'Dough must be between 6 and 12 inches'
        sauces = [t for t in toppings if is_sauce(t)]
        assert len(sauces) < 2, \
            'Can have at most one sauce'

        self.__dough_radius_in_inches = dough_radius_in_inches ❶
        sauce = sauces[:1]
        self.__toppings = sauce + \
            [t for t in toppings if not is_sauce(t)] ❷

pizza_spec = PizzaSpecification(dough_radius_in_inches=8,
                                toppings=['Olive Oil',
                                          'Garlic',
                                          'Sliced Roma Tomatoes',
                                          'Mozzarella'])

pizza_spec.__toppings.append('Tomato Sauce') # OOPS
>>> AttributeError: type object 'pizza_spec' has no attribute '__toppings'
```

❶ Dough radius in inches is now a private member.

❷ Toppings is now a private member.

Python does something called name mangling when you prefix attributes with two underscores. That is, Python changes the name out from underneath you, making it very obvious when users are abusing your API. I can find out what name mangling is by using the __dict__ attribute of an object:

```
pizza_spec.__dict__
>>> { '_PizzaSpecification__toppings': ['Olive Oil',
                                        'Garlic',
                                        'Sliced Roma Tomatoes',
                                        'Mozzarella'],
      '_PizzaSpecification__dough_radius_in_inches': 8
}
```

```
pizza_spec._PizzaSpecification__dough_radius_in_inches = 100
print(pizza_spec._PizzaSpecification__dough_radius_in_inches)
>>> 100
```

If you see an attribute access like this, you should raise a red flag: developers are messing with class internals and this might break invariants. Fortunately, this is very easy to catch when linting code bases (you'll learn more about linters in Chapter 20). Form a pact with your cocontributors and don't touch anything that is private; otherwise, you'll find yourself in an unmaintainable mess.

Should I Write Getters/Setters for Every Private Member?

It's a common mistake (especially for those just learning about private attributes) to write a getter and setter for every one. If you find your class is almost nothing but getter and setters, you may want to look at a data class instead. You're providing public access, just with more steps.

Even if you do have invariants in your class, beware an abundance of getter methods. You don't want to be returning references to mutable attributes such as lists or dictionaries. In many cases, it may be appropriate to return a copy of that data. If your callers need to mutate that data, try to force them through the API of your choosing (or write a new API, if appropriate, that preserves your invariants).

Operations

So now I have a class whose invariants cannot be (easily) broken. I have a class that is constructible, but I'm not able to change or read any data from it. That's because I've only touched upon one part of encapsulation thus far: the hiding of data. I still need to walk through how to bundle operations with data. Enter methods.

I will trust that you have a good handle on functions that live outside of a class (also known as free functions). What I'll focus on are functions that live inside the class, also known as methods.

Let's say that for my pizza specification, I want to be able to add a topping while the pizza is queued to be made. After all, my pizzas are a huge success (it's my imagination, let me have this one), and there is often a long line of pizzas to be made. But a family just placing their order realizes they missed their son's favorite topping, and in order to prevent a toddler meltdown over melted cheese, they need to modify their order after they've submitted it. I'll define a new function that adds a topping for their convenience.

```
from typing import List
from pizza.exceptions import PizzaException
from pizza.sauces import is_sauce
```

```
class PizzaSpecification:
    def __init__(self,
                    dough_radius_in_inches: int,
                    toppings: list[str]):
        assert 6 <= dough_radius_in_inches <= 12, \
            'Dough must be between 6 and 12 inches'

        self.__dough_radius_in_inches = dough_radius_in_inches
        self.__toppings: list[str] = []
        for topping in toppings:
            self.add_topping(topping) ❶


    def add_topping(self, topping: str): ❷
        '''
        Add a topping to the pizza
        All rules for pizza construction (one sauce, no sauce above
        cheese, etc.) still apply.
        '''
        if (is_sauce(topping) and
                any(t for t in self.__toppings if is_sauce(t))):
            raise PizzaException('Pizza may only have one sauce')

        if is_sauce(topping):
            self.__toppings.insert(0, topping)
        else:
            self.__toppings.append(topping)
```

❶ Use the new add_topping method.

❷ The new add_topping method.

It'd be easy to write a method that merely appends a topping to a list. But that
wouldn't be right. I have an invariant to uphold, and I'm not backing down now. The
code makes sure that we don't add a second sauce, and if the topping is a sauce,
ensures that it is laid down first. Remember, an invariant needs to be true for the lifetime of an object, which extends far past initial construction. Every method you add
should be continuing to preserve that invariant.

Methods are often separated into two categories: accessors and mutators. Some people simplify this to "getters" and "setters," but I feel like that is a bit too narrow. "Getters" and "setters" often describe methods that just return a simple value or set a
member variable. Many methods are much more complicated: setting multiple fields,
performing complex calculations, or manipulating data structures.

Accessors are for retrieving information. If you have invariants that relate to how you
represent data, these are the methods you care about. For example, the pizza specification might include a way to transform its internal data into machine operations

(roll dough, apply sauce, apply toppings, bake). By nature of the invariants, you'd want to make sure you aren't producing invalid machine operations.

Mutators are things that alter the state of your object. If you have mutators, you need to be extra careful that you are preserving any invariants as you change state. Adding new toppings to an existing pizza is a mutator.

This is also a good way to measure whether a function should be inside your class or not. If you have functions that don't concern themselves with invariants, or even worse, don't concern themselves with members of the class, you probably have a free function instead. This function is better served by living at module scope and outside of your class. It may be appealing to jam just one more function into an already bloated class (it often is the easiest), but if you strive for maintainability, having unrelated functions in a class leads to a nightmare. (You set up all sorts of interesting dependency chains; if you've ever asked yourself why one file depends on another file, this is often the reason.) It also may happen that your class has no invariants at all, and you should instead just chain together free functions.

What About @staticmethod and @classmethod?

I do not often use staticmethod and classmethod. For those unfamiliar, these are decorators that allow you to write functions that are bound to a class instead of an instance (classmethod) and functions that live inside a class but aren't bound to it in any way (staticmethod). To me, these are holdovers from an older mentality of programming where there weren't as many robust patterns as there are today.

With staticmethod, I almost always think that it should be a free function at module-level scope rather than tied to a class. With classmethod, there are a few more legitimate use cases (including some around metaprogramming), but in more cases than not, free functions are more robust. Free functions are easier to move around than classes (classes may need to be broken up or joined together), and I don't have to worry about how subtypes override my class methods or static methods (there are some sharp edges with inheritance and class/static methods.)

And that's invariants. It's not something developers talk about enough, but once you start thinking in terms of invariants, you'll see a major boost to class maintainability. Remember, you use invariants to allow users to reason about your objects and reduce cognitive load. It's OK if you take extra time writing code if you will pay off the costs for however many readers after.

Closing Thoughts

I spent a fair amount of time on classes, especially compared to other user-defined data types such as enumerations and data classes. However, this was intentional. Classes are typically taught very early, and rarely revisited. I've found that most developers tend to overuse classes, without considering what they are meant for.

As you decide how to create user-defined types, I offer the following guide for you:

Dictionaries

Dictionaries are meant for mappings from keys to values. If you are using dictionaries but rarely iterating over them or dynamically asking for keys, you aren't using them like an associative mapping and probably need a different type. There is an exception when retrieving data from data sources at runtime (e.g., getting JSON, parsing YAML, retrieving database data, etc.), where a `TypedDict` is appropriate (see Chapter 5). However, if you don't need to use them as dictionaries elsewhere, you should strive to get these into user-defined classes after parsing the data.

Enumerations

Enumerations are great for representing a union of discrete scalar values. You don't necessarily care about what the enumeration values are; you just need separate identifiers to differentiate cases in your code.

Data classes

Data classes are great for bundles of data that are mostly independent. You may have some restrictions on how individual fields can be set, but for the most part, users are free to get and set individual attributes to their heart's content.

Classes

Classes are all about invariants. If you have an invariant you want to preserve, create a class, assert that the preconditions hold when constructing, and don't let any method or user access break that invariant.

Figure 10-1 is a handy flowchart that describes these rules of thumb.

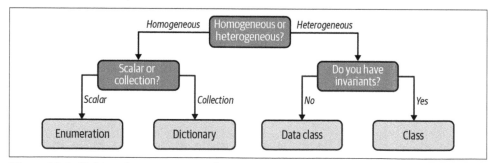

Figure 10-1. Picking the appropriate abstraction

However, knowing which type to pick is only half the battle. Once you've picked the right type, you need to make it seamless to interact with from a consumer's perspective. In the next chapter, you're going to learn how to make your user-defined types more natural to work with by focusing on the type's API.

## CHAPTER 11

Defining Your Interfaces

You have learned how to create your own user-defined types, but creating them is just half the battle. Now developers have to actually use your types. To do this, they use your type's API. This is the set of types and related functions, along with any external functions, that a developer interacts with to use your code.

Once you get your types in front of users, those types will be used (and abused) in ways that you never thought of. And once the developers depend on your types, it will be hard to change their behavior. This gives rise to what I call the *Paradox of Code Interfaces*:

> You have one chance to get your interface right, but you won't know it's right until it's used.

As soon as developers use the types you create, they come to depend on the behavior that those types encompass. If you try to make a backward-incompatible change, you potentially break all calling code. The riskiness in changing your interface is proportional to the amount of outside code depending on it.

This paradox doesn't apply if you control all the code that depends on your type; you can change it. But as soon as that type hits production, and people start using it, you'll find it difficult to change. In a large codebase, where robustness and maintainability matter, coordinating the change and buy-in needed to make a sweeping change is costly. It becomes near impossible if your type is used by entities outside your organizational control, such as open source libraries or platform SDKs. This quickly leads to code that is difficult to work with, and code that is difficult to work with will slow developers down.

What's worse is that you won't truly know if an interface is natural to use until enough people depend on it, giving rise to the paradox. How can you even begin to design an interface if you don't know how it will be used? Sure, you know how *you* would use the interface, and that's a great start, but you have an implicit bias when creating the interface. What feels natural to you won't feel natural to everyone else. Your goal is for your users to do the right things (and avoid the wrong things) with minimal effort. Ideally, the users should not need to do anything extra to use your interface correctly.

I don't have a silver bullet for you; there is no foolproof way of writing an interface that meets everyone's needs on the first try. Instead, I'll talk about some principles you can apply to give you the best chance. For the cases where you need to make changes to an existing API, you'll learn mitigation strategies. Your API is a first impression for other developers; make it count.

Discussion Topic

What interfaces are hard to use in your codebase? Look for common errors that people make when using your types. Also look for parts of your interface that are rarely invoked, especially if you feel like they are useful. Why don't users call these useful functions? Discuss what costs appear when developers encounter these hard-to-use interfaces.

Natural Interface Design

Your goal, tough as it may seem, is to make your interface appear natural to use. In other words, you want to reduce friction for the callers of your code. When code is hard to use, the following happens:

Duplicated functionality

Some developers who find your types hard to use will write their own types, duplicating functionality. It may be healthy for different ideas to compete on a large scale (like competing open source projects), but it is not healthy for that divergence to be present in your codebase. Developers are presented with a multitude of types, not sure which one to use. With their attention split, their wires will get crossed and they will make mistakes, which creates bugs, which costs money. Also, if you want to add anything to one of these types, you need to add them in all the places the functionality has diverged, or you'll create bugs, which costs money.

Broken mental model

Developers build up a mental model of the code they work with. If certain types are difficult to reason about, that mental model breaks. Developers will misuse your types, causing subtle bugs. Perhaps they don't call methods in the order that you require. Perhaps they miss calling a method that they should have. Perhaps they just misunderstand what the code is doing and pass the wrong information to it. Any of these will introduce fragility into your codebase.

Reduced testing

Code that is hard to use is hard to test. It doesn't matter if it's a complicated interface, a large chain of dependencies, or involved interactions; if you can't easily test the code, fewer tests will be written. The fewer tests that are written, the fewer bugs you'll catch when things change. It is very frustrating to deal with tests breaking in subtle ways every time a seemingly unrelated change is made.

Hard-to-use code will make your codebase unhealthy. You must take special care when designing your interfaces. Try to adhere to this rule of thumb from Scott Meyers:

Make interfaces easy to use correctly and hard to use incorrectly.[1]

You want developers to find your type easy to use, as if everything behaved as expected (this is a subtle restatement of the Law of Least Surprise, as mentioned in Chapter 1). Furthermore, you also want to prevent users from using your types the wrong way. It is your job to think about all the behaviors that you should support and forbid in your interface. To do this, you need to get into the heads of your collaborators.

Thinking Like a User

It's tricky to think like a user, for you have been bestowed with the Curse of Knowledge. No arcane hex or mystical spell causes this; it is a by-product of your time with the codebase. As you build out ideas, you become so intimately familiar with them that it can blind you to how new users perceive your code. The first step to dealing with cognitive biases is to acknowledge them. From that point, you can take biases into account as you try to get into your users' mindspace. Here are some useful strategies you can employ.

Test-driven development

Test-driven development (TDD), formulated by Kent Beck in the early 2000s, is a popular framework for testing your code.[2] TDD revolves around a simple loop:

- Add a failing test.
- Write just enough code to pass that test.
- Refactor.

---

1 Kevlin Henney and Scott Meyers. "Make Interfaces Easy to Use Correctly and Hard to Use Incorrectly." Chap. 55 in *97 Things Every Programmer Should Know: Collective Wisdom from the Experts*. Sebastopol: O'Reilly Media, 2010.

2 Kent Beck. *Test Driven Development: By Example*. Upper Saddle River, NJ: Addison-Wesley Professional, 2002.

There are entire books written about TDD, so I won't go into too much detail about the mechanics.[3] However, the intent of TDD is *fabulous* for understanding how to use a type.

Many developers think that test-*driven* development (writing tests first) has similar benefits to test-*after* development (writing tests second). In both cases, you have tested code, right? When simplified to this degree, TDD doesn't seem worth the effort.

However, this is an unfortunate oversimplification. The confusion stems from thinking of TDD as a testing methodology, when in fact, it is a *design methodology*. The tests are important, but they are merely a by-product of the methodology. The true value lies in how tests help design your interface.

With TDD, you are able to see how calling code looks before you write the implementation. Since you write the test first, you are given a chance to pause and ask yourself if how you interact with your types feels frictionless. If you find yourself making confusing function calls, building up long chains of dependencies, or having to write tests in a fixed order, you are experiencing red flags that should alert you that the type you're building is too complicated. In these cases, reevaluate or refactor your interface. How great is it that you can simplify this code before you even write it?

As an additional benefit, your tests serve as a form of documentation. Other developers will want to know how to use your code, especially the parts that are not described in top-level documentation. A good set of comprehensive unit tests provides working documentation of exactly how to use your type; you want them to leave a good first impression. Just as your code is a single source of truth for the behavior in your system, your tests are the single source of truth for interacting with your code.

README-driven development

Similar to TDD, README-driven development (RDD), coined by Tom Preston-Werner (*https://oreil.ly/qd16A*), is another design methodology aimed at catching hard-to-use code before it's written. The goal with RDD is to distill your top-level ideas and most important interactions with your code into a single document that lives in your project: a README file. This is a great way to formulate how different parts of your code interact, and might provide higher level patterns for users to follow.

RDD boasts some of the following benefits:

---

3 I recommend *Test-Driven Development with Python* (*https://oreil.ly/PJARR*) by Harry Percival (O'Reilly, 2017) if you'd like more information.

- No need to create every level of documentation up front, like you would in a Waterfall methodology.

- A README is often the first thing a developer sees; RDD gives you a chance to craft the best first impression you can.

- It is easier to change the documentation based on team discussion than it is to change written code.

- You don't need to use the README to explain poor code decisions; instead, the code needs to morph to support the ideal use cases.

Remember, you are only successful in building maintainable software if future developers can actually maintain it. Give them every chance you can to succeed and craft them an experience starting at your documentation.

Usability testing

Ultimately, you are trying to think about how your users think. There is a whole discipline dedicated to this very task: user experience (UX). UX is another area where there are countless books available, so I'll just focus on one strategy that has done me wonders in simplifying code: usability testing.

Usability testing is the process of actively asking your users what they think of your product. It sounds so simple, doesn't it? In order to think about how your users will behave, just ask them. The simplest thing you can do is talk to potential users (in this case, other developers), but it's easy to overlook.

It's incredibly easy to get started with usability testing through hallway testing. As you design your interface, just grab the first person to walk down your hallway and ask them to give feedback on your design. This is a great low-cost way of learning pain points. Don't take this advice too literally though. Feel free to expand beyond whoever you see in a hallway and ask teammates, peers, or testers to evaluate your interface.

However, for interfaces that will be used by a much broader audience (such as the interface of a popular open source library), you may want something a tad more formal. In these cases, usability testing involves placing your prospective users in front of the interface that you're writing. You give them a set of tasks to complete, and then observe. Your role is not to teach them or lead them through the exercises, but to see where they struggle and where they excel. Learn from their struggles; they are showing areas that are definitively hard to use.

Usability testing is a great task for the more junior members on your team. Their curse of knowledge won't be as strong as with the senior members, and they will be more likely to evaluate the design with a fresh set of eyes.

Natural Interactions

Donald Norman describes a mapping as a relationship between "controls and their movements with results in the real world." That mapping is natural if it "takes advantage of physical analogies and cultural standards, [leading] to immediate understanding."[4] This is what you strive for when you write an interface. You want that immediate understanding to eliminate confusion.

The "controls and their movements" in this case are the functions and types that make up your interface. The "results in the real world" represent the behavior of the code. For this to feel natural, the operations have to agree with the mental model of the user. This is what Donald Norman means when talking about "physical analogies and cultural standards." You must connect with the readers of your code in a way that they understand, drawing on their experiences and knowledge. The best way to do this is mapping your domain and other common knowledge into your code.

When designing an interface, you need to think through the entire life cycle of a user's interactions and ask yourself if the entirety of it maps to what a user unfamiliar with your code would understand. Model your interface such that it is easy to comprehend for someone who knows the domain well, even if they aren't familiar with code. As you do this, your interface becomes intuitive, which lessens the chances of developers making mistakes.

Natural Interfaces in Action

For this chapter, you're going to design an interface for part of an automated grocery pick-up service. A user scans their recipes using their smartphone, and the app will automatically figure out what ingredients are required. After the user confirms the order, the app queries local grocery stores for ingredient availability and schedules delivery. Figure 11-1 provides a representation of this workflow.

I'm going to focus on the specific interface for building up an order given a set of recipes.

---

4 This is from *Design of Everyday Things* by Donald Norman (Basic Books). This classic book is essential to anyone wanting to get into a UX mindset.

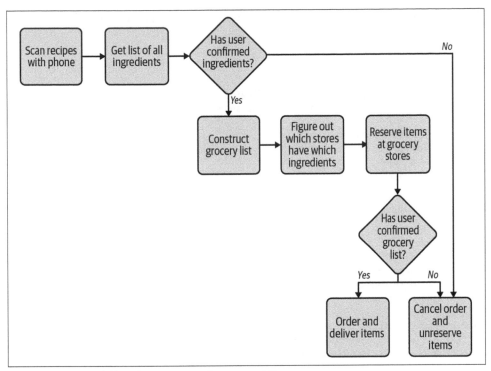

Figure 11-1. Workflow for automated grocery delivery app

To represent a recipe, I'll modify parts of the `Recipe` `dataclass` from Chapter 9:

```python
from dataclasses import dataclass
from enum import auto, Enum

from grocery.measure import ImperialMeasure

@dataclass(frozen=True)
class Ingredient:
    name: str
    brand: str
    amount: float = 1
    units: ImperialMeasure = ImperialMeasure.CUP

@dataclass
class Recipe:
    name: str
    ingredients: list[Ingredient]
    servings: int
```

The codebase also has functions and types to retrieve local grocery store inventory:

```python
import decimal
from dataclasses import dataclass
from typing import Iterable

from grocery.geospatial import Coordinates
from grocery.measure import ImperialMeasure

@dataclass(frozen=True)
class Store:
    coordinates: Coordinates
    name: str


@dataclass(frozen=True)
class Item:
    name: str
    brand: str
    measure: ImperialMeasure
    price_in_cents: decimal.Decimal
    amount: float

Inventory = dict[Store, List[Item]]
def get_grocery_inventory() -> Inventory:
    # reach out to APIs and populate the dictionary
    # ... snip ...

def reserve_items(store: Store, items: Iterable[Item]) -> bool:
    # ... snip ...

def unreserve_items(store: Store, items: Iterable[Item]) -> bool:
    # ... snip ...

def order_items(store: Store, items: Iterable[Item]) -> bool:
    # ... snip ...
```

The other developers in the codebase have already set up the code to figure out the recipes from smartphone scans, but now they need to generate the ingredient list to order from each grocery store. That's where you come in. Here's what they have so far:

```python
recipes: List[Recipe] = get_recipes_from_scans()

# We need to do something here to get the order
order = ????
# the user can make changes if needed
display_order(order) # TODO once we know what an order is
wait_for_user_order_confirmation()
if order.is_confirmed():
    grocery_inventory = get_grocery_inventory()
    # HELP, what do we do with ingredients now that we have grocery inventory
```

```
grocery_list =  ????
# HELP we need to do some reservation of ingredients so others
# don't take them
wait_for_user_grocery_confirmation(grocery_list)
# HELP - actually order the ingredients ????
deliver_ingredients(grocery_list)
```

Your goal is to fill in the blanks marked HELP or ????. I want you to get in the habit of deliberately designing your interface before you start coding. How would you describe the purpose of the code to a nontechnical product manager or marketing agent? Take a few minutes before looking at the following code: how do you want a user to interact with your interface?

Here's what I came up with (there are plenty of ways to solve this; it's OK if you have something vastly different):

1. For each recipe received, grab all the ingredients and aggregate them together. This becomes an Order.

2. An Order is a list of ingredients, and the user can add/remove ingredients as needed. However, once confirmed, the Order should not be changeable.

3. Once the order is confirmed, take all the ingredients and figure out what stores have the items available. This is a Grocery List.

4. A Grocery List contains a list of stores and the items to pick up from each store. Each item is reserved at the store until the app places the order. Items may come from different stores; the app tries to find the cheapest item that matches.

5. Once the user confirms the GroceryList, place the order. Grocery items are unreserved and set for delivery.

6. The order is delivered to the user's home.

 Isn't it amazing that you can come up with an implementation without having to know exactly how get_recipe_from_scans or get_grocery_inventory is implemented? This is the beauty of having types to describe domain concepts: if these were represented by tuples or dictionaries (or with no type annotations, which makes me shudder), you'd have to go digging through the codebase finding out what data you were dealing with.

That description of the interface contained no code concepts; it was all described in a way that is familiar to workers in the grocery domain. When designing an interface, you want to map as naturally to the domain as you can.

Let's start with the order handling by creating a class:

```
from typing import Iterable, Optional
from copy import deepcopy
class Order:
    ''' An Order class that represents a list of ingredients '''
    def __init__(self, recipes: Iterable[Recipe]):
        self.__ingredients: set[Ingredient] = set()
        for recipe in recipes:
            for ingredient in recipe.ingredients:
                self.add_ingredient(ingredient)

    def get_ingredients(self) -> list[Ingredient]:
        ''' Return a alphabetically sorted list of ingredients '''
        # return a copy so that users won't inadvertently mess with
        # our internal data
        return sorted(deepcopy(self.__ingredients),
                      key=lambda ing: ing.name)

    def _get_matching_ingredient(self,
                                 ingredient: Ingredient) -> Optional[Ingredient]:
        try:
            return next(ing for ing in self.__ingredients if
                        ((ing.name, ing.brand) ==
                         (ingredient.name, ingredient.brand)))
        except StopIteration:
            return None

    def add_ingredient(self, ingredient: Ingredient):
        ''' adds the ingredient if it's not already added,
            or increases the amount if it has
        '''
        target_ingredient = self._get_matching_ingredient(ingredient)
        if target_ingredient is None:
            # ingredient for the first time - add it
            self.__ingredients.add(ingredient)
        else:
            # add ingredient to existing set
            ????
```

Not too bad of a start. If I look at the first step of my description above, it matches pretty closely to the code. I am getting the ingredients from each recipe and aggregating them together in a set. I'm having some trouble with how I want to represent adding ingredients to the set I'm already tracking, but I'll come back to this in a bit, I promise.

For now, I want to make sure that I am properly representing the invariant of an Order. If the order is confirmed, a user should not be able to modify anything inside it. I'll change the Order class to do the following:

```
# create a new exception type so that users can explicitly catch this error
class OrderAlreadyFinalizedError(RuntimeError):
    # inheriting from RuntimeError to allow users to provide a message
    # when raising this exception
```

```
        pass

    class Order:
        ''' An Order class that represents a list of ingredients
            Once confirmed, it cannot be modified
        '''
        def __init__(self, recipes: Iterable[Recipe]):
            self.__confirmed = False
            # ... snip ...

        # ... snip ...

        def add_ingredient(self, ingredient: Ingredient):
            self.__disallow_modification_if_confirmed()
            # ... snip ...


        def __disallow_modification_if_confirmed():
            if self.__confirmed:
                raise OrderAlreadyFinalizedError('Order is confirmed -'
                                                 ' changing it is not allowed')

        def confirm(self):
            self.__confirmed = True

        def unconfirm(self):
            self.__confirmed = False

        def is_confirmed(self):
            return self.__confirmed
```

Now I have the first two items on my list represented in code, and the code mirrors the description pretty closely. By using a type to represent the Order, I have created an interface for the calling code to operate with. You can construct an order with order = Order(recipes) and then use that order to add ingredients, change the amount of existing ingredients, and handle confirmation logic.

The only thing that is missing is that ???? when adding an ingredient that I'm already tracking (such as adding an extra 3 cups of flour). My first instinct was to just add the amounts together, but that won't work if the units of measure are different, such as adding 1 cup of olive oil to 1 tablespoon. Neither 2 tablespoons nor 2 cups is the right answer.

I could do type conversions right here in the code, but that doesn't feel natural. What I really want to do is do something like already_tracked_ingredient += new_ingredient. But doing that gives me an exception:

```
TypeError: unsupported operand type(s) for +=: 'Ingredient' and 'Ingredient'
```

However, this is achievable; I just have to use a little Python magic to make it so.

Magic Methods

Magic methods allow you to define custom behavior when built-in operations are invoked in Python. A magic method is prefixed and suffixed by two underscores. Because of this, they are sometimes called *dunder* methods (or *double underscore* methods). You've already seen them in earlier chapters:

- In Chapter 10, I used the __init__ method to initialize a class. __init__ gets called whenever a class is instantiated.

- In Chapter 9, I used __lt__, __gt__, and others to define what happens when two objects were compared with < or >, respectively.

- In Chapter 5, I introduced __getitem__ for intercepting calls to indexing with brackets such as recipes['Stromboli'].

I can use the magic method __add__ to control behavior for addition:

```python
@dataclass(frozen=True)
class Ingredient:
    name: str
    brand: str
    amount: float = 1
    units: ImperialMeasure = ImperialMeasure.CUP

    def __add__(self, rhs: Ingredient):
        # make sure we are adding the same ingredient
        assert (self.name, self.brand) == (rhs.name, rhs.brand)
        # build up conversion chart (lhs, rhs): multiplication factor
        conversion: dict[tuple[ImperialMeasure, ImperialMeasure], float] = {
            (ImperialMeasure.CUP, ImperialMeasure.CUP): 1,
            (ImperialMeasure.CUP, ImperialMeasure.TABLESPOON): 16,
            (ImperialMeasure.CUP, ImperialMeasure.TEASPOON): 48,
            (ImperialMeasure.TABLESPOON, ImperialMeasure.CUP): 1/16,
            (ImperialMeasure.TABLESPOON, ImperialMeasure.TABLESPOON): 1,
            (ImperialMeasure.TABLESPOON, ImperialMeasure.TEASPOON): 3,
            (ImperialMeasure.TEASPOON, ImperialMeasure.CUP): 1/48,
            (ImperialMeasure.TEASPOON, ImperialMeasure.TABLESPOON): 1/3,
            (ImperialMeasure.TEASPOON, ImperialMeasure.TEASPOON): 1
        }

        return Ingredient(rhs.name,
                          rhs.brand,
                          rhs.amount + self.amount * conversion[(rhs.units,
                                                                 self.units)],
                          rhs.units)
```

Now with the __add__ method defined, I can add ingredients together with the + operator. The add_ingredient method can look like the following:

```
def add_ingredient(self, ingredient: Ingredient):
    '''Adds the ingredient if it's not already added,
       or increases the amount if it has '''

    target_ingredient = self._get_matching_ingredient(ingredient)
    if target_ingredient is None:
        # ingredient for the first time - add it
        self.__ingredients.add(ingredient)
    else:
        # add ingredient to existing set
        target_ingredient += ingredient
```

I can now express the idea of adding ingredients naturally. It doesn't stop here, either. I can define subtraction, or multiplication/division (for scaling serving numbers), or comparison. It is far easier for users to understand your codebase when such natural operations are available. Just about every operation in Python has a magic method backing it. There are so many that I can't even begin to enumerate them all. However, some common methods are listed in Table 11-1.

Table 11-1. Common magic methods in Python

Magic method	Used for
__add__, __sub__, __mul__, __div__	Arithmetic operations (add, subtract, multiply, divide)
__bool__	Implicitly converting to Boolean for if <expression> checks
__and__, __or__	Logical operations (and and or)
__getattr__, __setattr__, __delattr__	Attribute access (such as obj.name or del obj.name)
__le__, __lt__, __eq__, __ne__, __gt__, __ge__	Comparision (<=, <, ==, !=, >, >=)
__str__, __repr__	Converting to string (str()) or reproducible (repr()) forms

If you want to learn more, check out the Python documentation regarding the data model (*https://oreil.ly/jHBaZ*).

Discussion Topic

What are some types in your codebase that could benefit from a more natural mapping? Discuss where magic methods might make sense, and where they might not.

Context Managers

Your code can now handle orders, but it's time to fill in the other half: the grocery list handling. I want you to take a break from reading and think about filling in the blanks of the grocery list handling code. Take what you learned from the last section and create an interface that naturally maps to the written description of the problem.

Here's a reminder of the grocery list handling:

1. A Grocery List contains a list of stores and the items to pick up from each store. Each item is reserved at the store until the app places the order. Items may come from different stores; the app tries to find the cheapest item that matches.

2. Once the user confirms the GroceryList, place the order. Grocery items are unreserved and set for delivery.

From a calling code perspective, here's what I have:

```
order = Order(recipes)
# the user can make changes if needed
display_order(order)
wait_for_user_order_confirmation()
if order.is_confirmed():
    grocery_inventory = get_grocery_inventory()
    grocery_list = GroceryList(order, grocery_inventory)
    grocery_list.reserve_items_from_stores()
    wait_for_user_grocery_confirmation(grocery_list)
    if grocery_list.is_confirmed():
        grocery_list.order_and_unreserve_items()
        deliver_ingredients(grocery_list)
    else:
        grocery_list.unreserve_items()
```

Given this grocery list interface, this is certainly easy to use (if I do say so myself). It's clear what the code is doing, and if making the interface intuitive were the full story, I'd be golden. But I forgot the other half of Scott Meyers's quote. I forgot to make the code *hard to use incorrectly*.

Take a look again. What happens if the user doesn't confirm their order? What if some exception were thrown while waiting? If this were to happen, I would never unreserve the items, leaving them reserved in perpetuity. Sure, I could hope that calling code would always try to catch an exception, but that's easy to forget to do. In fact, it'd be quite easy to use incorrectly, wouldn't you agree?

 You can't only focus on the happy path, which is the execution of the code when everything goes as planned. Your interface must also handle all the possible ways problems can arise.

Wanting to automatically invoke some sort of function when you are done with an operation is a common case in Python. File open/close, session authenticate/logout, database command batching/submission; these are all examples where you want to always make sure to invoke the second operation, regardless of what the previous code did. If you don't, you often leak resources or otherwise tie up the system.

Chances are, you've actually run across how to handle this: using a with block.

```
with open(filename, "r") as handle:
    print(handle.read())
# at this point, the with block has ended, closing the file handle
```

This is something you learn early on in your Python journey as a best practice. As soon as the with block is finished (when the code returns to the original indent level of the with statement), Python closes the opened file. This is a convenient way of making sure that an operation occurs, even with no explicit user interaction. This is the key you need to making your grocery list interface hard to use incorrectly—what if you could make the grocery list unreserve items automatically, regardless of what path the code takes?

To do this, you need to employ a *context manager*, which is a Python construct that lets you take advantage of with blocks. Using a context manager, I can make our grocery list code much more fault-tolerant:

```
from contextlib import contextmanager

@contextmanager
def create_grocery_list(order: Order, inventory: Inventory):
    grocery_list = _GroceryList(order, inventory)
    try:
        yield grocery_list
    finally:
        if grocery_list.has_reserved_items():
            grocery_list.unreserve_items()
```

Any function decorated with @contextmanager will be usable alongside a with block. I construct a _GroceryList (notice how it's private, so nobody should be creating a grocery list in ways other than create_grocery_list), then *yield* it. Yielding a value interrupts this function, returning the value yielded to the calling code. The user can then use it like so:

```
# ... snip ...
if order.is_confirmed():
    grocery_inventory = get_grocery_inventory()
    with create_grocery_list(order, grocery_inventory) as grocery_list:
        grocery_list.reserve_items_from_stores()
        wait_for_user_grocery_confirmation(grocery_list)
        grocery_list.order_and_unreserve_items()
        deliver_ingredients(grocery_list)
```

The yielded value becomes grocery_list in the example above. When the with block exits, execution is returned to the context manager, right after the yield statement. It doesn't matter if an exception is thrown, or if the with block finishes normally; because I wrapped our yield in a try...finally block, the grocery list will always clear any reserved items.

This is how you can effectively force a user to clean up after themselves. You are eliminating an entire class of errors that can happen when you use context managers—the errors of omission. Errors of omission are so easy to make; you literally have to do nothing. Instead, a context manager lets users do the right thing, even when they do nothing. It's a sure sign of a robust codebase when a user can do the right thing without even knowing it.

 Context managers will not finish if the program is forcibly closed, such as a force kill from the operating system or a power loss. Context managers are just a tool to keep developers from forgetting to clean up after themselves; make sure your system can still handle things outside a developer's control.

Closing Thoughts

You can create all the types in the world, but if other developers can't use them without error, your codebase will suffer. Just like a house needs a strong foundation to stand upon, the types you create and vocabulary you surround them with need to be rock solid for your codebase to be healthy. When you have natural interfaces to your code, future developers will be able to reach for these types and build new features effortlessly. Have empathy for those future developers, and design your types with care.

You'll need to think through the domain concepts your types represent, and how users interact with those types. By building a natural mapping, you tie real-world operations to your codebase. The interfaces you build should feel intuitive; remember, they should be easy to use correctly and hard to use incorrectly. Use every trick and tip at your disposal, from proper naming to magic methods to context managers.

In the next chapter, I'm going to cover how types relate to one another when you create subtypes. Subtypes are a way of specializing a type's interface; they allow for extension without modifying the original types. Any modification to existing code is a potential regression, so being able to create new types without changing old ones can significantly reduce erratic behavior.

## CHAPTER 12

Subtyping

Most of Part II has focused on creating your own types and defining interfaces. These types do not exist in isolation; types are often related to one another. So far, you've seen *composition*, where types use other types as members. In this chapter, you'll learn about *subtyping*, or creating types based on other types.

When applied correctly, subtyping makes it incredibly easy to extend your codebase. You can introduce new behaviors without ever worrying about breaking the rest of your codebase. However, you must be dilligent when creating a subtyping relationship; if you do it poorly, you can decrease the robustness of your codebase in unexpected ways.

I'll start with one of the most common subtype relationships: inheritance. Inheritance is seen as a traditional pillar of object-oriented programming (OOP).[1] Inheritance can be tricky if not applied correctly. I'll then move on to other forms of subtyping present in the Python programming language. You'll also learn about one of the more fundamental SOLID design principles, the Liskov Substitution Principle. This chapter will help you make sense of when and where subtyping is appropriate and where it is not.

---

1 Object-oriented programming is a programming paradigm where you organize your code around encapsulated data and their behaviors. If you'd like an introduction to OOP, I suggest *Head First Object-Oriented Analysis and Design* (*https://oreil.ly/6djy9*) by Brett McLaughlin, Gary Pollice, and Dave West (O'Reilly).

Inheritance

Most developers immediately think of inheritance when they talk about subtyping. *Inheritance* is a way of creating a new type from another type, copying all the behaviors into the new type. This new type is known as a *child class, derived class,* or *subclass.* In contrast, the type being inherited from is known as a *parent class, base class,* or *superclass.* When talking about types in this way, we say that the relationship is an *is-a* relationship. Any object of a derived class is also an instance of a base class.

To illustrate this, you are going to design an app that helps owners of restaurants organize operations (tracking finances, customizing menus, etc.). For this scenario, a restaurant has the following behaviors:

- A restaurant has the following attributes: a name, a location, a list of employees and their schedules, inventory, a menu, and current finances. All of these attributes are mutable; even a restaurant can be renamed or change locations. When a restaurant changes locations, its location attribute reflects its final destination.

- An owner can own multiple restaurants.

- Employees can be moved from one restaurant to another, but they cannot work at two restaurants at the same time.

- When a dish is ordered, the ingredients used are removed from the inventory. When a specific item is depleted in the inventory, any dish requiring the ingredient is no longer available through the menu.

- Whenever a menu item is sold, the restaurant's funds increase. Whenever new inventory is purchased, the restaurant's funds decrease. For every hour that an employee works at that restaurant, the restaurant's funds decrease according to the employee's salary and/or wage.

Restaurant owners will use this app to view all their restaurants, manage their inventory, and track profits in real time.

Since there are specific invariants about the restaurant, I'll use a class to represent a restaurant:

```python
from restaurant import geo
from restaurant import operations as ops
class Restaurant:
    def __init__(self,
                 name: str,
                 location: geo.Coordinates,
                 employees: list[ops.Employee],
                 inventory: list[ops.Ingredient],
                 menu: ops.Menu,
                 finances: ops.Finances):
```

```
    # ... snip ...
    # note that location refers to where the restaurant is located when
    # serving food

    def transfer_employees(self,
                           employees: list[ops.Employee],
                           restaurant: 'Restaurant'):
        # ... snip ...

    def order_dish(self, dish: ops.Dish):
        # ... snip ..

    def add_inventory(self, ingredients: list[ops.Ingredient],
                      cost_in_cents: int):
        # ... snip ...

    def register_hours_employee_worked(self,
                                       employee: Employee,
                                       minutes_worked: int):
        # ... snip ...

    def get_restaurant_data(self) -> ops.RestaurantData:
        # ... snip ...

    def change_menu(self, menu: ops.Menu):
        self.__menu = menu

    def move_location(self, new_location: geo.Coordinates):
        # ... snip ...
```

In addition to a "standard" restaurant, as described above, there are a few "specialized" restaurants: a food truck and a pop-up stall.

Food trucks are mobile: they drive around to different spots and change their menu based on the occasion. Pop-up stalls are transient; they appear for a limited time with a limited menu (typically for some sort of event like a festival or fair). While slightly different in how they operate, both a food truck and pop-up stall are still restaurants. This is what I mean when I say an *is-a* relationship—a food truck *is a* restaurant and a pop-up stall *is a* restaurant. Because this is an *is-a* relationship, inheritance is an appropriate construct to use.

You denote inheritance by specifying the base class when you define your derived class:

```
class FoodTruck(Restaurant):
    #... snip ...

class PopUpStall(Restaurant):
    # ... snip ...
```

Figure 12-1 shows how this relationship is typically drawn.

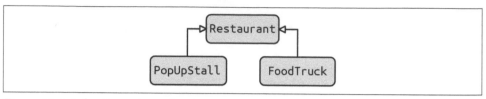

Figure 12-1. Inheritance tree of restaurants

By defining inheritance in this fashion, you ensure that the derived classes will inherit all the methods and attributes from the base class, without needing to redefine them.

This means that if you were to instantiate one of the derived classes, such as Food Truck, you would be able to use all the same methods as if you were interacting with a Restaurant.

```
food_truck = FoodTruck("Pat's Food Truck", location, employees,
                        inventory, menu, finances)
food_truck.order_dish(Dish('Pasta with Sausage'))
food_truck.move_location(geo.find_coordinates('Huntsville, Alabama'))
```

What's really nice about this is that a derived class can be passed to a function expecting a base class and the typechecker will not complain one bit:

```
def display_restaurant_data(restaurant: Restaurant):
    data = restaurant.get_restaurant_data()
    # ... snip drawing code here ...

restaurants: list[Restaurant] = [food_truck]
for restaurant in restaurants:
    display_restaurant_data(restaurant)
```

By default, the derived class operates exactly like the base class. If you'd like the derived class to do something different, you can override methods or redefine the methods in the derived class.

Suppose I want my food truck to automatically drive to the next location when the location changes. For this use case, however, when asking for restaurant data, I only want the final location, not the location while the food truck is en route. Developers can call a separate method to show the current location (for use in a separate food truck–only map). I'll set up a GPS locator in the FoodTruck's __init__ method, and override move_location to start the automatic driving:

```
from restaurant.logging import log_error
class FoodTruck(Restaurant):
    def __init__(self,
                    name: str,
                    location: geo.Coordinates,
                    employees: list[ops.Employee],
                    inventory: list[ops.Ingredient],
                    menu: ops: Menu,
```

```
                finances: ops.Finances):
            super().__init__(name, location, employees,inventory, menu, finances)
            self.__gps = initialize_gps()

        def move_location(self, new_location: geo.Coordinates):
            # schedule a task to drive us to our new location
            schedule_auto_driving_task(new_location)
            super().move_location(new_location)

        def get_current_location(self) -> geo.Coordinates:
            return self.__gps.get_coordinates()
```

I am using a special function, super(), to access the base class. When I call super().__init__(), I am actually calling Restaurant's __init__ method. When I call super().move_location, I am calling Restaurant's move_location, not Food Truck's move_location. This way, the code can behave exactly like the base class.

Take a moment and reflect on the implications of extending code through subclassing. You can insert new behaviors into existing code without ever modifying that existing code. If you avoid modifying existing code, you drastically reduce the chance of introducing new bugs; you won't inadvertently break consumers' assumptions if you aren't changing the code they depend on. A well-designed inheritance structure can greatly improve maintainability. Unfortunately, the inverse is true as well; design your inheritance poorly, and maintainability suffers. When working with inheritance, you always need to be thinking about how easy it is to substitute your code.

Multiple Inheritance

In Python, it is possible to inherit from multiple classes:

```
class FoodTruck(Restaurant, Vehicle):
    # ... snip ...
```

In this case, you inherit all the methods and attributes from both base classes. When you call super(), you now have to decide exactly which class is initialized. This can get very confusing for beginners, and there is a complex set of rules governing the resolution order of methods. You can learn more about Method Resolution Ordering (MRO) and how multiple base classes interact in the Python documentation (*https://oreil.ly/BZox9*).

Do not reach for multiple inheritance often. When a single class inherits two separate sets of invariants from its base classes, it creates extra cognitive burden for your readers. They not only have to keep two sets of invariants in their head but also the potential interactions between those invariants. Furthermore, the complex rules surrounding MRO make it incredibly easy to make mistakes if you don't fully understand Python's behavior. For the cases where you absolutely must use multiple inheritance, document it well with comments to explain why you need it and how you're using it.

However, there is one case that I am fond of for multiple inheritance: mixins. Mixins are classes that you can inherit generic functionality from. These base classes typically do not contain any invariants or data; they are just a set of methods that are not intended to be overridden.

For example, in the Python standard library, there are abstractions for creating a TCP socket server:

```
from socketserver import TCPServer
class Server(TCPServer):
    # ... snip ...
```

You can customize this server to use multiple threads by also inheriting socket server.ThreadingMixIn:

```
from socketserver import TCPServer, ThreadingMixIn
class Server(TCPServer, ThreadingMixIn):
    # ... snip ...
```

This mixin does not bring in any invariants, and none of its methods need to be called or overridden from the derived class. Just the mere act of inheriting the mixin provides everything you need. This simplification makes it much easier for maintainers to reason about your class.

Substitutability

As described earlier, inheritance is all about modeling an *is-a* relationship. Describing something with an *is-a* relationship may sound simple, but you'd be surprised just how wrong things can go. To model *is-a* relationships properly, you need to understand substitutability.

Substitutability states that when you derive from a base class, you should be able to use that derived class in every instance that you use a base class.

If I were to create a function that could display relevant restaurant data:

```
def display_restaurant(restaurant: Restaurant):
    # ... snip ...
```

I should be able to pass a `Restaurant`, a `FoodTruck`, or a `PopUpStall`, and this function should be none the wiser. Again, this sounds simple; what's the catch?

There is indeed a catch. To show you, I'd like to step away from the food concept for a second, and go back to a fundamental question that any first grader should be able to answer: is a square a rectangle?

From your early days of school, you probably know the answer as "yes, a square is a rectangle." A rectangle is a polygon that has four sides, and each intersection of two sides is a 90-degree angle. A square is the same, with the extra requirement that each side must be the exact same length.

If I were to model this with inheritance, I might do so as follows:

```python
class Rectangle:
    def __init__(self, height: int, width: int):
        self._height = height
        self._width = width

    def set_width(self, new_width):
        self._width = new_width

    def set_height(self, new_height):
        self._height = new_height

    def get_width(self) -> int:
        return self._width

    def get_height(self) -> int:
        return self._height

class Square(Rectangle):
    def __init__(self, length: int):
        super().__init__(length, length)

    def set_side_length(self, new_length):
        super().set_width(new_length)
        super().set_height(new_length)

    def set_width(self, new_width):
        self.set_side_length(new_width)

    def set_height(self, new_height):
        self.set_side_length(new_height)
```

So yes, from a geometry perspective a square is indeed a rectangle. But this assumption when mapped to *is-a* relationships is flawed. Take a few moments and see if you can catch where my assumptions break down.

Still don't see it? Here's a hint: what if I asked you if a Square is *substitutable* for a Rectangle for every use case? Can you construct a use case for a rectangle that a square would not be substitutable for?

Suppose the user of the app selects squares and rectangles on a map of restaurants to gauge market size. A user can draw a shape on the map, and then expand it as needed. One of the functions to handle this is as follows:

```python
def double_width(rectangle: Rectangle):
    old_height = rectangle.get_height()
    rectangle.set_width(rectangle.get_width() * 2)
```

```
# check that the height is unchanged
assert rectangle.get_height() == old_height
```

With this code, what would happen if I were to pass a Square as the argument? All of a sudden, a previously passing assertion would start to fail, since the height of a square changes when the length changes. This is catastrophic; the whole intention of inheritance is to extend functionality without breaking existing code. In this case, by passing in a Square (since it's also a Rectangle, the type checker won't complain), I have introduced a bug just waiting to happen.

This sort of mistake impacts the derived class as well. The error above stems from overriding set_width in Square so that the height is changed as well. What if set_width were not overridden and the Rectangle's set_width function were invoked? Well, if this were the case, and you passed a Square into the function, the assertion would not fail. Instead, something far less obvious but much more detrimental happens: the function succeeds. No longer do you receive an AssertionError with a stack trace that leads you to the bug. Now, you create a square that is no longer a square; the width is changed, but the height has not. You have committed a cardinal sin and have broken the invariants of that class.

What makes this so sinister is that the goal of inheritance is to decouple, or remove dependencies from, existing code and new code. Implementers and consumers of the base class have no view into different derived classes at runtime. It might be that the derived class definitions live in a completely different codebase, owned by a different organization. With this error case, you make it so that every time a derived class changes, you need to look at every invocation and use of the base class and assess whether or not your changes will break code.

In order to solve this, you have a few options available to you. First, you can not inherit Square from Rectangle in the first place and avoid the whole problem. Second, you can restrict the methods of Rectangle so that the Square does not contradict it (such as making the fields immutable). Last, you can abolish the class hierarchy altogether and provide an is_square method in the Rectangle.

These sorts of errors can break your codebase in subtle ways. Consider the use case where I want to franchise my restaurants; franchisees are allowed to create their own menu, but must always have a common set of dishes.

Here's a potential implementation:

```
class RestrictedMenuRestaurant(Restaurant):

    def __init__(self,
                 name: str,
                 location: geo.Coordinates,
                 employees: list[ops.Employee],
                 inventory: list[ops.Ingredient],
```

```
                    menu: ops.Menu,
                    finances: ops.Finances,
                    restricted_items: list[ops.Ingredient]):
            super().__init__(name,location,employees,inventory,menu,finances)
            self.__restricted_items = restricted_items

    def change_menu(self, menu: ops.Menu):
        if any(not menu.contains(ingredient)
               for ingredient in self.__restricted_items):
            # new menus MUST contain restricted ingredients
            return super().change_menu(menu)
```

In this case, the function returns early if any of the restricted items aren't in the new menu. What seems sensible in isolation completely falls apart when put in an inheritance hierarchy. Put yourself in another developer's shoes, one who wants to implement the UI for changing menus in the app. They see a Restaurant class, and code against that interface. When a RestrictedMenuRestaurant inevitably gets used in place of a Restaurant, the UI will try to change a menu and have no indication that the update didn't actually occur. The only way this bug could have been caught earlier would be for a developer to trawl through the codebase looking for derived classes that broke invariants. And if there's any theme to this book, it's that any time a developer has to go searching through a codebase to understand one piece of code, it's a sure sign of fragility.

What if I wrote the code to throw an exception instead of just returning? Unfortunately, this doesn't solve any problems either. Now, when users change the menu of a Restaurant, they are liable to receive an exception. If they look at the Restaurant class's code, there is no indication that they would ever need to think about an exception. Nor should they be paranoid and wrap every call in a try...except block, worried that a derived class somewhere might throw an exception.

In both of these cases, subtle errors are introduced when a class inherits from a base class but does not behave exactly as that base class does. These errors require a specific combination of conditions to occur: code must execute methods on the base class, it must depend on specific behavior of that base class, and a derived class breaking that behavior has to be substituted as a base class. The tricky thing is that any of these conditions can be introduced long after the original code was written. This is why substitutability is so important. As a matter of fact, the importance of substitutability is embodied in a very important principle: the Liskov Substitution Principle.

The Liskov Substitution Principle (LSP), named after Barbara Liskov, states the following:[2]

> *Subtype Requirement*: Let $\Phi(X)$ be a property provable about objects X of type T. Then $\Phi(Y)$ should be true for objects Y of type S where S is a subtype of T.

Don't let the formal notation scare you. The LSP is quite simple: in order for a subtype to exist, it must adhere to all the same properties (behaviors) as the supertype. It all comes back to substitutability. You should keep the LSP in mind whenever you think about properties of supertypes and what they mean for subtypes. When designing with inheritance, think through the following:

Invariants

Chapter 10 focused mostly on invariants (truths about your types that must not be violated). When you're subtyping from other types, the subtypes *must* preserve all invariants. When I subtyped `Square` from `Rectangle`, I disregarded the invariant that heights and widths can be set independent of one another.

Preconditions

A precondition is anything that must be true before interacting with a type's property (such as calling a function). If the supertype defines preconditions that happen, the subtype *must not* be more restrictive. This is what happened when I subtyped `RestrictedMenuRestaurant` from `Restaurant`. I added an extra precondition that certain ingredients were mandatory when changing the menu. By throwing an exception, I've made it so that previously good data would now fail.

Postcondition

A postcondition is anything that must be true after interacting with a type's property. If a supertype defines postconditions, the subtype must not *weaken* those postconditions. A postcondition is weakened if any of its guarantees are not met. When I subtyped `RestrictedMenuRestaurant` from `Restaurant` and returned early instead of changing the menu, I violated a postcondition. The base class guaranteed a postcondition that the menu would be updated, regardless of the menu contents. When subtyped like I did, I could no longer guarantee that postcondition.

If at any time you break an invariant, precondition, or postcondition in an overridden function, you are begging for an error to show up. Here are some red flags that I look for in the derived class's overridden functions when evaluating inheritance relationships:

---

2 Barbara H. Liskov and Jeannette M. Wing. "A Behavioral Notion of Subtyping." *ACM Trans. Program. Lang. Syst.* 16, 6 (Nov. 1994), 1811–41. *https://doi.org/10.1145/197320.197383*.

Conditionally checking arguments

A good way to know if a precondition is more restrictive is to see if there are any `if` statements at the beginning of the function checking the arguments being passed in. If there are, there's a good chance they are different from the base class's checks, typically meaning that the derived class is restricting the arguments further.

Early return statements

If a subtype's function returns early (in the middle of the function block), this indicates that the latter part of the function is not going to execute. Check that latter part for any postcondition guarantees; you don't want to omit those by returning early.

Throwing an exception

Subtypes should only throw exceptions that match what the supertype throws (either exactly or a derived exception type). If any exceptions are different, callers are not going to expect them, let alone write code to catch them. It's even worse if you throw an exception when the base class doesn't indicate any possibility of an exception at all. The most flagrant violation of this that I've seen is throwing `NotImplementedError` exceptions (or similar).

Not calling `super()`

By definition of substitutability, the subtype must offer the same behavior as the supertype. If you aren't calling `super()` as part of your subtype's overridden functions, your subtype has no defined relationship to that behavior in code. Even if you were to copy-paste the supertype's code into your subtype, there's no guarantee that these will stay synchronized; a developer could make an innocuous change to the supertype's function and not even realize that there is a subtype that needs to change as well.

You need to be extra careful when modeling types with inheritance. Any mistake can introduce subtle bugs that could have catastrophic effects. When designing with inheritance, tread with utmost caution.

Discussion Topic

Have you encountered any of the red flags in your codebase? Has it led to surprising behavior when inheriting from other classes? Discuss why these break assumptions and what errors can happen in those cases.

Design Considerations

Take precautions whenever you are writing classes intended to be derived from. Your goal is to make it as easy as possible for other developers to write derived classes. Here are a few guidelines for writing base classes (I'll cover guidelines for derived classes afterward):

Don't change invariants

Normally, changing invariants is a bad idea in the first place. Countless pieces of code can depend on your types, and changing an invariant will break assumptions made on your code. Unfortunately, derived classes can break if a base class changes invariants as well. If you have to change your base class, try to only add new functionality, not modify existing functionality.

Be cautious tying invariants to protected fields

Protected fields are inherently meant to be interacted with by derived classes. If you tie invariants to these fields, you are fundamentally restricting what operations should be invoked. This creates a tension that other developers may not be aware of. It's better to keep invariants to private data and force derived classes to interact with public or protected methods in order to interact with that private data.

Document your invariants

This is the number one most important thing you can do to help your other developers. While some invariants are representable in code (as you saw in Chapter 10), there are simply some invariants that cannot be mathematically proven by a computer, such as guarantees around exceptions being thrown or not. You must document these invariants when you design your base class, and make it easy for derived classes to discover them, such as in a docstring.

Ultimately, it is the derived class's responsibility to adhere to the base class's invariants. If you are writing a derived class, heed the following guidelines:

Know the base class invariants

You can't write a derived class properly without knowing the invariants. It is your job to understand all the base class's invariants in order to preserve them. Look through code, documentation, and anything else related to the class to understand what you should and should not be doing.

Extend functionality in the base class

If you need to write code that doesn't jive with your current invariants, you may want to put that functionality in the base class instead. Take the example of not supporting an overridable method. Rather than throw a `NotImplementedError`, you could create a Boolean flag indicating functionality support in the base class instead. If you do this, take note of all the guidelines earlier in this chapter for modifying the base class.

Every overridden method should contain super()

If you don't call super() in an overridden method, you have no guarantee that your subclass is behaving exactly like the base class, especially if the base class changes at all in the future. If you are going to override a method, make sure you call super(). The only time you can get away with this is when the base method is empty (such as an abstract base class) and you are sure it will remain empty for the remainder of the codebase's life cycle.

Composition

It's also important to know when not to use inheritance. One of the biggest mistakes I've seen is using inheritance solely for the purpose of code reuse. Don't get me wrong, inheritance is a great way to reuse code, but the primary reason for inheritance is modeling a relationship where subtypes are used in place of the supertype. If you never interact with the subtype in the code that assumes the supertype, you aren't modeling an *is-a* relationship.

In such cases, you want to use composition, also known as a *has-a* relationship. *Composition* is when you put member variables inside a type. I have primarily used composition to group types together. For instance, the restaurant from earlier:

```
class Restaurant:
    def __init__(self,
                 name: str,
                 location: geo.Coordinates,
                 employees: list[ops.Employee],
                 inventory: list[ops.Ingredient],
                 menu: ops: Menu,
                 finances: ops.Finances):
        self.name = name
        self.location = location
        self.employees = employees
        # ... etc etc snip snip ...
```

Discussion Topic

Where in your codebase have you overused inheritance? Are you using it anywhere as a conduit for reuse only? Discuss how to transform this to use composition instead.

Each of the member fields set in __init__ is an example of composition. It doesn't make sense for a Restaurant to be substitutable for a Menu (*is-a* relationship), but it does make sense for a restaurant to be composed of a menu (*has-a* relationship), among other things. You should prefer composition to inheritance anytime you need to reuse code but aren't going to substitute types for one another.

Composition is preferable to inheritance as a reuse mechanism because it is a weaker form of *coupling*, which is another term for dependencies between entities. All other things being equal, you want weaker forms of coupling, as it makes it easier to reorganize classes and refactor functionality. If classes have high coupling between them, changes in one more directly affect the behavior of the other.

 Mixins are the exception to preferring composition over inheritance, as they are classes explicitly meant to be inherited to provide additions to a type's interface.

With inheritance, a derived class is beholden to the base class's changes. A developer must be cognizant of not only the public interface changing, but also changes to invariants and protected members. By contrast, when another class has an instance of your class, that class is only affected by a subset of changes: those impacting the public methods and invariants it depends on. By limiting the impact of changes, you lessen the chance of broken assumptions, decreasing fragility. To write robust code, use inheritance judiciously.

Subtyping Outside Inheritance

Most of this chapter has focused exclusively on class-based subtyping, or inheritance. However, the notion of subtyping is much broader, mathematically speaking. Back in Chapter 2, I described how types are really just a communication method around behaviors. You can apply this notion to subtypes as well: a subtype is a set of behaviors that can be completely used in place of some other supertype's behaviors.

In fact, duck typing is a subtype/supertype relationship as well:

```
def double_value(x):
    return x + x

>>> double_value(3)
6
>>> double_value("abc")
abcabc
```

In this case, the supertype is the parameter. It supports the addition method, which must return the same type as its addends. Note that a supertype does not necessarily have to be a named type in Python; it is all about the expected behaviors.

The guidelines earlier in this chapter around designing your supertypes and subtypes are not exclusive to inheritance. Duck typing is a form of subtyping; all the same guidelines apply. Also, as a consumer, make sure that you are not passing in arguments that are not substitutable for the supertype. Otherwise, you are making it much harder for your other developers; duck typing obscures the supertype/subtype relationship just like inheritance does. Stick to the guidelines in this chapter to avoid headaches.

Closing Thoughts

Subtyped relationships are a very powerful concept in programming. You can use them to extend existing functionality without modifying it. However, inheritance is often overused, or used improperly. Subtypes should only be used if they are directly substitutable for their supertype. If this isn't the case, reach for composition instead.

Special care should be taken when introducing supertypes or subtypes. It may not be easy for developers to know of all the subtypes associated with a single supertype; some subtypes may even live in other codebases. Supertypes and subtypes are very closely coupled, so be cautious whenever you make changes. With the proper diligence, you can reap all the benefits of subtyping without introducing a slew of headaches.

In the next chapter, I'm going to focus on a specific application of subtyping known as protocols. These are the missing link between the typechecker and duck typing. Protocols bridge the gap in an important way: they help your typechecker catch some of the errors introduced in a supertype/subtype relationship. Any time you catch more errors, especially through a typechecker, you are contributing to the robustness of your codebase.

## CHAPTER 13

Protocols

I have a confession to make. I've been skirting around something in the Python type system that, upon first glance, is contradictory. It has to do with a key difference in philosophy between the Python runtime type system and the static type hints.

Back in Chapter 2, I described how Python supports duck typing. Recall that this means you can use objects in a context as long as that object supports a specific set of behaviors. You don't need any sort of parent class or predefined inheritance structure to use duck typing.

However, the typechecker has no clue how to handle duck typing without any assistance. The typechecker knows how to handle types known at static analysis time, but how does it handle duck-typed decisions made at runtime?

To remedy this, I'm going to introduce protocols, a feature introduced in Python 3.8. Protocols solve the contradiction listed above; they annotate duck-typed variables during typechecking. I'll cover why you need protocols, how to define your own, and how to use them in advanced scenarios. But before you start, you need to understand the disconnect between Python's duck typing and static typecheckers.

Tension Between Typing Systems

In this chapter, you are going to build an automated lunch shop's digital menu system. This restaurant has a variety of entries that are "splittable," meaning you can get a half order. Deli sandwiches, wraps, and soups can be split, but entries like drinks and hamburgers cannot be split. In the interest of deduplication, I want one method that does all the splitting. Here are some entries as an example:

```
class BLTSandwich:
    def __init__(self):
        self.cost = 6.95
        self.name = 'BLT'
        # This class handles a fully constructed BLT sandwich
        # ...

    def split_in_half(self) -> tuple['BLTSandwich', 'BLTSandwich']:
        # Instructions for how to split a sandwich in half
        # Cut along diagonal, wrap separately, etc.
        # Return two sandwiches in return

class Chili:
    def __init__(self):
        self.cost = 4.95
        self.name = 'Chili'
        # This class handles a fully loaded chili
        # ...

    def split_in_half(self) -> tuple['Chili', 'Chili']:
        # Instructions for how to split chili in half
        # Ladle into new container, add toppings
        # Return two cups of chili in return
        # ...

class BaconCheeseburger:
    def __init__(self):
        self.cost = 11.95
        self.name = 'Bacon Cheeseburger'
        # This class handles a delicious Bacon Cheeseburger
        # ...

    # NOTE! no split_in_half method
```

Now, the split method might look something like this:

```
import math
def split_dish(dish: ???) -> ????:
    dishes = dish.split_in_half()
    assert len(dishes) == 2
    for half_dish in dishes:
        half_dish.cost = math.ceil(half_dish.cost) / 2
        half_dish.name = "½ " + half_dish.name
    return dishes
```

What should the parameter dish be typed as? Remember, a type is a set of behaviors, not necessarily a concrete Python type. I may not have a name for this set of behaviors, but I do want to make sure that I uphold them. In this example, the type must have these behaviors:

- The type must have a function called split_in_half. This must return an iterable collection of two objects.

- Each object returned from `split_in_half` must have an attribute called `cost`. This `cost` must be able to have the ceiling applied to it and to be integer-divided by two. This `cost` must be mutable.

- Each object returned from `split_in_half` must have an attribute called `name`. This `name` must be allowed to set the text "½ " prefixed before it. This `name` must be mutable.

A `Chili` or a `BLTSandwich` object will work just fine as a subtype, but `BaconCheese burger` will not. `BaconCheeseburger` does not have the structure that the code is looking for. If you did try to pass in `BaconCheeseburger`, you'd get an `Attribute Error` specifying that `BaconCheeseburger` has no method called `split_in_half()`. In other words, `BaconCheeseburger` does not match the structure of the expected type. In fact, this is where duck typing earns its other name: *structural subtyping*, or subtyping based on structure.

In contrast, most of the type hinting that you've been exploring throughout this part of the book is known as *nominal subtyping*. This means that types that have different names are separate from one another. Do you see the problem? These two types of subtyping are opposed to each other. One is based on names of types and the other is based on structure. In order to catch errors during typechecking, you will need to come up with a named type:

```
def split_dish(dish: ???) -> ???:
```

So, to ask again, what should the parameter be typed as? I've listed some options below.

Leave the Type Blank or Use Any

```
def split_dish(dish: Any)
```

I cannot condone this, certainly not in a book all about robustness. This conveys no intent to future developers, and typecheckers will not detect common errors. Moving on.

Use a Union

```
def split_dish(dish: Union[BLTSandwich, Chili])
```

Ah, this is a bit better than leaving it blank. An order can be either a `BLTSandwich` or `Chili`. And for this limited example, it does work. However, this should feel slightly off to you. I need to figure out how to reconcile structural subtyping and nominal subtyping, and all I've done is hardcode a few classes into the type signature.

What's worse about this is that it's fragile. Every time somebody needs to add a class that can be splittable, they have to remember to update this function. You can only hope that this function is somewhat near where classes are defined so that future maintainers might stumble upon it.

There's another hidden danger here. What if this automated lunch maker is a library, meant to be used in automated kiosks by different vendors? Presumably, they would pull in this lunch-making library, make their own classes, and call split_dish on those classes. With the definition of split_dish in library code, there are very few reasonable ways that a consumer can get their code to typecheck.

Use Inheritance

Some of you who are experienced in an object-oriented language such as C++ or Java may be yelling that an interface class is appropriate here. It'd be simple to have both of these classes inherit from some base class that defined the methods you want.

```
class Splittable:
    def __init__(self, cost, name):
        self.cost = cost
        self.name = name

    def split_in_half(self) -> tuple['Splittable', 'Splittable']:
        raise NotImplementedError("Must implement split in half")

class BLTSandwich(Splittable):
    # ...

class Chili(Splittable):
    # ...
```

This type hierarchy is modeled in Figure 13-1.

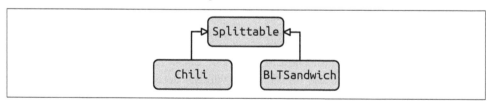

Figure 13-1. Type hierarchy for splittable

And this does work:

```
def split_dish(dish: Splittable):
```

In fact, you can even annotate the return type:

```
def split_dish(dish: Splittable) ->
    tuple[Splittable, Splittable]:
```

But what if there is a more complicated class hierarchy at play? What if your class hierarchy looks like Figure 13-2?

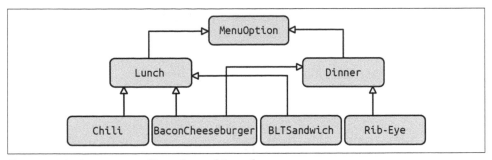

Figure 13-2. A more complicated type hierarchy

Now, you have a tough decision in front of you. Where do you put the `Splittable` class in the type hierarchy? You can't put it in the parent of the tree; not every dish should be splittable. You could make the `Splittable` class into a `SplittableLunch` class and jam it right between `Lunch` and whichever class that can be splittable, like in Figure 13-3.

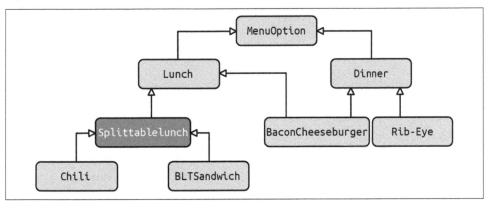

Figure 13-3. A more complicated type hierarchy with `Splittable` injected in

This will fall apart as your codebase grows. For one, if you want to use `Splittable` anywhere else (say for dinner, or checks, or anything else), you'll have to duplicate that code; nobody wants a billing system that inherits from `SplittableLunch`. Also, `Splittable` might not be the only parent class you want to introduce. You may have other attributes, such as being able to share an entree, having it available for curbside pickup, specifying that it allows substitutions, and so on. The number of classes you have to write explodes with each option you introduce.

Use Mixins

Now, some languages solve this through the mixins, which I introduced in Chapter 11. Mixins shift the burden to each class at the bottom of the class hierarchy

without polluting any classes above. If I want my BLTSandwich to be Shareable, Pick
Uppable, Substitutable, and Splittable, then I don't have to modify anything else
besides BLTSandwich.

```
class BLTSandwich(Shareable,
                  PickUppable,
                  Substitutable,
                  Splittable):
    # ...
```

Only the classes that need the functionality need to change. You reduce the need to
coordinate across large codebases. Still, this is not perfect; users still need to add multiple inheritance to their classes to address this problem, and it would be great if you
could minimize the changes needed to typecheck. It also introduces a physical
dependency when you import the parent class, which may not be ideal.

In fact, none of the options above feels right. You're changing existing classes just for
the sake of typechecking, which feels very *unpythonic* to me. Many developers fell in
love with Python because it doesn't require such verbosity. Fortunately, there is a better solution in the form of *protocols*.

Protocols

Protocols provide a way of closing the gap between type hinting and the runtime type
system. They allow you to provide structural subtyping during typechecking. As a
matter of fact, you probably are familiar with a protocol without even knowing it: the
iterator protocol.

The iterator protocol is a defined set of behaviors that objects may implement. If an
object implements these behaviors, you can loop over the object. Consider:

```
from random import shuffle
from typing import Iterator, MutableSequence
class ShuffleIterator:
    def __init__(self, sequence: MutableSequence):
        self.sequence = list(sequence)
        shuffle(self.sequence)

    def __iter__(self):
        return self

    def __next__(self):
        if not self.sequence:
            raise StopIteration
        return self.sequence.pop(0)

my_list = [1, 2, 3, 4]
iterator: Iterator = ShuffleIterator(my_list)
```

```
for num in iterator:
    print(num)
```

Notice how I didn't have to subclass `Iterator` in order for the typing to work. This is because the `ShuffleIterator` has the two methods needed for iterators to work: an `__iter__` method for looping over iterators, and a `__next__` method for getting the next item in the sequence.

This is exactly the sort of pattern I want to achieve with the `Splittable` examples. I want to be able to have typing work based on the structure of the code. To do this, you can define your own protocol.

Defining a Protocol

Defining a protocol is extremely simple. If you want something to be splittable, you define `Splittable` in terms of a protocol:

```
from typing import Protocol
class Splittable(Protocol):
    cost: int
    name: str

    def split_in_half(self) -> tuple['Splittable', 'Splittable']:
        """ No implementation needed """
        ...
```

This looks pretty close to the example for subclassing earlier in this chapter, but you use it a tad differently.

To have the `BLTSandwich` be splittable, you don't have to indicate anything different in the class. There is no subclassing needed:

```
class BLTSandwich:
    def __init__(self):
        self.cost = 6.95
        self.name = 'BLT'
        # This class handles a fully constructed BLT sandwich
        # ...

    def split_in_half(self) -> ('BLTSandwich', 'BLTSandwich'):
        # Instructions for how to split a sandwich in half
        # Cut along diagonal, wrap separately, etc.
        # Return two sandwiches in return
```

There is no explicit parent class for `BLTSandwich`. If you'd like to be explicit, you can still subclass from `Splittable`, but it's not a requirement.

The `split_dish` function can now expect to use anything that supports the new `Splittable` protocol:

```
def split_dish(order: Splittable) -> tuple[Splittable, Splittable]:
```

The typechecker will detect that a BLTSandwich is Splittable just by virtue of the fields and method it has defined. This simplifies class hierarchies immensely. You don't need a complicated tree structure, even as you add more protocols. You can simply define a different protocol for each set of required behaviors, including Sharea ble, Substitutable, or PickUppable. Functions that depend on those behaviors can then rely on those protocols instead of any sort of base class. The original classes don't need to change in any form, as long as they implement the needed functionality.

Do Protocols Eliminate the Need for Inheritance?

Once you get used to protocols, inheritance appears redundant. While inheritance makes a lot of sense for nominal subtyping, it is too heavyweight for anything regarding structural subtyping. You are introducing linkages that don't need to be there, increasing the maintenance cost of your system.

To decide whether to use a protocol or subclass, I want you to remember the lessons learned in Chapter 12. Anything subclassing another class or adhering to a protocol is a subtype. Therefore, it needs to uphold the contract of the parent type. If the contract just defines the structure of the type (such as being Splittable, which just needed certain attributes to be defined), use a protocol. However, if the parent type's contract defines behaviors that need to be upheld, such as how to operate in certain conditions, use inheritance to better reflect the *is-a* relationship.

Advanced Usage

I've covered the primary use case for protocols so far, but there's a little more I'd like to show you. You won't be reaching for these features as often, but they fill out a critical niche for protocols.

Composite Protocols

I talked in the last section about how a class might satisfy multiple protocols. For instance, a single lunch item may be Splittable, Shareable, Substitutable, and PickUppable. While you can mix in these protocols quite easily, what if you found out that over half the lunch entries fall into this category? You could designate these

---

lunch entries as a `StandardLunchEntry`, allowing you to refer to all four protocols as a single type.

Your first attempt might just be to write a type alias to cover your bases:

```
StandardLunchEntry = Union[Splittable, Shareable,
                           Substitutable, PickUppable]
```

However, this will match anything that satisfies at least one protocol, not all four. To match all four protocols, you need to use a composite protocol:

```
class StandardLunchEntry(Splittable, Shareable, Substitutable,
                         PickUppable, Protocol):
    pass

# Remember, you don't need to explicitly subclass from the protocol
# I do so here for clarity's sake
class BLTSandwich(StandardLunchEntry):
    # ... snip ...
```

Then, you can use `StandardLunchEntry` anywhere an item should support all four protocols. This allows you to group protocols together, without having to duplicate the same combinations again and again throughout your codebase.

 `StandardLunchEntry` also subclasses from `Protocol`. This is required; if it is left out, `StandardLunchEntry` would not be a protocol, even though it subclasses from other protocols. Put more generally: classes subclassed from a protocol do not automatically become a protocol.

Runtime Checkable Protocols

Throughout all of this protocol discussion, I've stayed in the realm of static type-checking. Sometimes, you just need to check a type at runtime, though. Unfortunately, protocols out of the box do not support any sort of `isinstance()` or `issubclass()` check. It's easy to add, though:

```
from typing import runtime_checkable, Protocol

@runtime_checkable
class Splittable(Protocol):
    cost: int
    name: str

    def split_in_half(self) -> tuple['Splittable', 'Splittable']:
        ...

class BLTSandwich():
    # ... snip ..
```

```
assert isinstance(BLTSandwich(), Splittable)
```

As long as you throw the `runtime_checkable` decorator in there, you can do an `isinstance()` check to see if an object satisfies a protocol. When you do, `isinstance()` is essentially calling a `__hasattr__` method on each of the expected variables and functions of the protocol.

 `issubclass()` will only work if your protocol is a nondata protocol, which is one that does not have any protocol variables. This has to deal with edge cases concerning setting variables in `__init__` methods.

You will typically mark protocols as `runtime_checkable` when you are using a `Union` of protocols. Functions may expect either one protocol or a different protocol, and those functions might need some way to differentiate the two inside the body of a function at runtime.

Modules Satisfying Protocols

While I've so far only talked about objects satisfying protocols, there's a narrower use case that is worth mentioning. It turns out that modules can satisfy protocols, too. After all, a module is still an object.

Suppose I want to define a protocol around a restaurant and each restaurant is defined in a separate file. Here's one such file:

```
name = "Chameleon Café"
address = "123 Fake St."

standard_lunch_entries = [BLTSandwich, TurkeyAvocadoWrap, Chili]
other_entries = [BaconCheeseburger, FrenchOnionSoup]

def render_menu() -> Menu:
    # Code to render a menu
```

Then, I need some code that will define the `Restaurant` protocol and be able to load a restaurant:

```
from typing import Protocol
from lunch import LunchEntry, Menu, StandardLunchEntry

class Restaurant(Protocol):
    name: str
    address: str
    standard_lunch_entries: list[StandardLunchEntry]
    other_entries: List[LunchEntry]
```

```
    def render_menu(self) -> Menu:
        """ No implementation needed """
        ...

def load_restaurant(restaurant: Restaurant):
    # code to load restaurant
    # ...
```

Now, I can pass imported modules to my `load_restaurant` function:

```
import restaurant
from load_restaurant import load_restaurant

# Loads our restaurant model
load_restaurant(restaurant)
```

In `main.py`, the call to `load_restaurant` will typecheck just fine. The restaurant module satisfies the `Restaurant` protocol I've defined. Protocols are even smart enough to ignore the `self` argument in `render_menu` when a module is passed in. Using a protocol to define a module isn't an everyday Python sort of thing, but you'll see it crop up if you have Python configuration files or plug-in architectures that need to enforce a contract.

 Not every typechecker may support using a module as a protocol just yet; double-check the bugs and documentation of your favorite typechecker for support.

Closing Thoughts

Protocols were just introduced in Python 3.8, so they are still relatively new. However, they patch a huge hole in what you can do with Python's static typechecking. Remember, while the runtime is structurally subtyped, most of the static typechecking is nominally subtyped. Protocols fill that gap and let you do structural subtyping during typechecking. You'll most commonly use them whenever you're writing library code and want to provide a solid API that users can depend on, without relying on a specific type. Using protocols reduces physical dependencies of code, which helps with maintainability, but you still can catch errors early.

In the next chapter, you'll learn about one more way to enhance your types: modeled types. Modeling a type allows you to create a rich set of constraints that are checked at typecheck and runtime, and can eliminate a whole class of errors without having to manually write validation for every field. Even better, by modeling your types, you provide built-in documentation for what is and what is not allowed in your codebase. Throughout the next chapter, you'll see how to do all of this using the popular library pydantic.

CHAPTER 14

Runtime Checking With pydantic

The central theme of robust code is making it easier to detect errors. Errors are an inevitable part of developing complex systems; you can't avoid them. By writing your own types, you create a vocabulary that makes it harder to introduce inconsistencies. Using type annotations provides you a safety net, letting you catch mistakes as you are developing. Both of these are examples of *shifting errors left*; instead of finding errors during testing (or worse, in production), you find them earlier, ideally as you develop code.

However, not every error is easily found through code inspection and static analysis. There is a whole class of errors that will only be detectable at runtime. Any time you interact with data supplied from outside your program (such as databases, config files, network requests), you run the risk of inputting invalid data. Your code can be rock-solid in how you retrieve and parse data, but there's not much you can do to prevent users from passing in invalid data.

Your first inclination might be to write a lot of *validation logic*: if statements and checks to see if all of the data passed in is correct. The problem is that validation logic is often complex, sprawling, and tough to understand at a glance. The more comprehensive your validation, the worse it gets. If your goal is to find errors, reading all the code (and tests) will be your best shot. In that case, you need to minimize the amount of code you look at. Herein lies the rub: you will understand more of the code the more you read, but the more you read, the higher the cognitive burden you will have, decreasing your chances of finding an error.

In this chapter, you'll learn how using the pydantic library will fix this problem. pydantic lets you define modeled classes, reducing the amount of validation logic you need to write, without sacrificing readability. pydantic will easily parse user-supplied data, providing guarantees about output data structures. I'll go through a few basic examples of what you can do with it, and then end the chapter with some advanced pydantic usage.

Dynamic Configuration

In this chapter, I'm going to build out types describing restaurants. I'll start by providing a way for a user to specify restaurants through configuration files. Here is a list of configurable fields (and their constraints) per restaurant:

- Name of the restaurant
  - For legacy reasons, the name must be less than 32 characters long, and only contain letters, numbers, quotation marks, and spaces (no Unicode, sorry).
- Owner's full name
- Address
- List of employees
  - There must be at least one chef and one server.
  - Each employee has a name and position (chef, server, host, sous chef, or delivery driver).
  - Each employee either has a mailing address for a check or direct deposit details.
- List of dishes
  - Each dish has a name, price, and description. The name is limited to 16 characters, and the description is limited to 80 characters. Optionally, there is a picture (in the form of a filename) with each dish.
  - Each dish must have a unique name.
  - There must be at least three dishes on the menu.
- Number of seats
- Offers to-go orders (Boolean)
- Offers delivery (Boolean)

This information is stored in a YAML file (https://yaml.org) that looks like this:

```
name: Viafore's
owner: Pat Viafore
address: 123 Fake St. Fakington, FA 01234
employees:
  - name: Pat Viafore
    position: Chef
    payment_details:
      bank_details:
        routing_number: "123456789"
```

```
              account_number: "123456789012"
    - name: Made-up McGee
      position: Server
      payment_details:
        bank_details:
          routing_number: "123456789"
          account_number: "123456789012"
    - name: Fabricated Frank
      position: Sous Chef
      payment_details:
        bank_details:
          routing_number: "123456789"
          account_number: "123456789012"
    - name: Illusory Ilsa
      position: Host
      payment_details:
        bank_details:
          routing_number: "123456789"
          account_number: "123456789012"
  dishes:
    - name: Pasta and Sausage
      price_in_cents: 1295
      description: Rigatoni and sausage with a tomato-garlic-basil sauce
    - name: Pasta Bolognese
      price_in_cents: 1495
      description: Spaghetti with a rich tomato and beef Sauce
    - name: Caprese Salad
      price_in_cents: 795
      description: Tomato, buffalo mozzarella, and basil
      picture: caprese.png
  number_of_seats: 12
  to_go: true
  delivery: false
```

The pip-installable library `yaml` makes it easy to read this file, providing a dictionary:

```python
with open('code_examples/chapter14/restaurant.yaml') as yaml_file:
    restaurant = yaml.safe_load(yaml_file)

print(restaurant)
>>> {
    "name": "Viafore's",
    "owner": "Pat Viafore",
    "address": "123 Fake St. Fakington, FA 01234",
    "employees": [{
        "name": "Pat Viafore",
        "position": "Chef",
        "payment_details": {
            "bank_details": {
                "routing_number": '123456789',
                "account_number": '123456789012'
            }
        }
    }
```

```
    },
    {
        "name": "Made-up McGee",
        "position": "Server",
        "payment_details": {
            "bank_details": {
                "routing_number": '123456789',
                "account_number": '123456789012'
            }
        }
    },
    {
        "name": "Fabricated Frank",
        "position": "Sous Chef",
        "payment_details": {
            "bank_details": {
                "routing_number": '123456789',
                "account_number": '123456789012'
            }
        }
    },
    {
        "name": "Illusory Ilsa",
        "position": "Host",
        "payment_details": {
            "bank_details": {
                "routing_number": '123456789',
                "account_number": '123456789012'
            }
        }
    }],
    "dishes": [{
        "name": "Pasta and Sausage",
        "price_in_cents": 1295,
        "description": "Rigatoni and sausage with a tomato-garlic-basil sauce"
    },
    {
        "name": "Pasta Bolognese",
        "price_in_cents": 1495,
        "description": "Spaghetti with a rich tomato and beef Sauce"
    },
    {
        "name": "Caprese Salad",
        "price_in_cents": 795,
        "description": "Tomato, buffalo mozzarella, and basil",
        "picture": "caprese.png"
    }],
    'number_of_seats': 12,
    "to_go": True,
    "delivery": False
}
```

I want you to put on your tester hat for a second. The requirements I've just given are certainly not exhaustive; how would you refine them? I want you to take a few minutes and list out all the different constraints you can think of with just the dictionary given. Assuming the YAML file parses and returns a dictionary, how many invalid test cases can you think of?

You may notice that the routing number and account numbers are strings in the example above. This is intentional. Despite being a string of numerals, I do not want this to be a numeric type. Numeric operations (such as addition or multiplication) do not make sense, and I do not want an account number of 000000001234 to be truncated to 1234.

Here are some ideas to think about when enumerating test cases:

- Python is a dynamic language. Are you sure that everything is the right type?
- Dictionaries don't require any sort of required fields—are you sure every field is present?
- Are all the constraints from the problem statement tested for?
- What about additional constraints (correct routing numbers, account numbers, and addresses?)
- What about negative numbers where there shouldn't be?

I came up with 67 different test cases with invalid data in about five minutes. Some of my test cases included (the full list is included in the GitHub repo for this book (*https://github.com/pviafore/RobustPython*)):

- Name is zero characters.
- Name is not a string.
- There are no chefs.
- Employee has no bank details or address.
- Employee's routing number is truncated (0000123 becomes 123).
- Number of seats is negative.

This, admittedly, is not a very complex class. Could you imagine the number of test cases for a much more involved class? Even with 67 test cases, could you imagine opening up an __init__ method of a type and checking 67 different conditions? In most of the codebases I've worked on, the validation logic is nowhere near as comprehensive. However, this is user-configurable data and I want errors to be caught as early as possible in runtime. You should prefer catching the errors at data injection over first use. After all, the first use of these values might not happen until you are in a separate system, decoupled from your parse logic.

Discussion Topic

Think about some user data represented as data types in your system. How complex is that data? How many ways can you construct it incorrectly? Discuss the impact of creating this data incorrectly and how confident you are that your code will catch all the errors.

Throughout this chapter, I'll show you how to create a type that is easy to read and models all the constraints listed. Since I've focused on type annotations so much, it'd be nice if I can catch missing fields or wrong types at typecheck time. A first idea is to use a TypedDict (see Chapter 5 for more information on TypedDict):

```python
from typing import Literal, TypedDict, Union
class AccountAndRoutingNumber(TypedDict):
    account_number: str
    routing_number: str

class BankDetails(TypedDict):
    bank_details: AccountAndRoutingNumber

AddressOrBankDetails = Union[str, BankDetails]

Position = Literal['Chef', 'Sous Chef', 'Host',
                   'Server', 'Delivery Driver']

class Dish(TypedDict):
    name: str
    price_in_cents: int
    description: str

class DishWithOptionalPicture(Dish, TypedDict, total=False):
    picture: str

class Employee(TypedDict):
    name: str
    position: Position
    payment_information: AddressOrBankDetails

class Restaurant(TypedDict):
    name: str
    owner: str
    address: str
    employees: list[Employee]
    dishes: list[Dish]
    number_of_seats: int
    to_go: bool
    delivery: bool
```

This is a huge step in readability; you can tell exactly what types are needed to construct your type. You could write the following function:

```
def load_restaurant(filename: str) -> Restaurant:
    with open(filename) as yaml_file:
        return yaml.safe_load(yaml_file)
```

Downstream consumers would automatically benefit from the types I've just laid out. However, there are a few problems with this approach:

- I can't control construction of a TypedDict, so I can't validate any fields as part of type construction. I must force consumers to do the validation.
- TypedDict cannot have additional methods on it.
- TypedDict does no validation implicitly. If you create the wrong dictionary from YAML, the typechecker will not complain.

That last point is important. In fact, I could have the following contents as the entirety of my YAML file, and the code will still typecheck:

```
invalid_name: "This is the wrong file format"
```

Typechecking will not catch errors at runtime. You need something stronger. Enter pydantic.

pydantic

pydantic (https://pydantic-docs.helpmanual.io) is a library that provides runtime checking of your types without sacrificing readability. You can use pydantic to model your classes like so:

```
from pydantic.dataclasses import dataclass
from typing import Literal, Optional, TypedDict, Union

@dataclass
class AccountAndRoutingNumber:
    account_number: str
    routing_number: str

@dataclass
class BankDetails:
    bank_details: AccountAndRoutingNumber

AddressOrBankDetails = Union[str, BankDetails]

Position = Literal['Chef', 'Sous Chef', 'Host',
                   'Server', 'Delivery Driver']

@dataclass
class Dish:
```

```
    name: str
    price_in_cents: int
    description: str
    picture: Optional[str] = None

@dataclass
class Employee:
    name: str
    position: Position
    payment_information: AddressOrBankDetails

@dataclass
class Restaurant:
    name: str
    owner: str
    address: str
    employees: list[Employee]
    dishes: list[Dish]
    number_of_seats: int
    to_go: bool
    delivery: bool
```

You decorate each class with a `pydantic.dataclasses.dataclass` instead of inheriting from `TypedDict`. Once you have this, pydantic does validation upon type construction.

To construct the pydantic type, I'll change my load function as follows:

```
def load_restaurant(filename: str) -> Restaurant:
    with open(filename) as yaml_file:
        data = yaml.safe_load(yaml_file)
        return Restaurant(**data)
```

If a future developer violates any constraint, pydantic will throw an exception. Here are some example exceptions:

If a field is missing, such as a missing description:

```
pydantic.error_wrappers.ValidationError: 1 validation error for Restaurant
dishes -> 2
  __init__() missing 1 required positional argument:
    'description' (type=type_error)
```

When an invalid type is provided, such as putting the number 3 as an employee's position:

```
pydantic.error_wrappers.ValidationError: 1 validation error for Restaurant
employees -> 0 -> position
  unexpected value; permitted: 'Chef', 'Sous Chef', 'Host',
                                'Server', 'Delivery Driver'
                               (type=value_error.const; given=3;
                                permitted=('Chef', 'Sous Chef', 'Host',
                                           'Server', 'Delivery Driver'))
```

Pydantic can work with mypy, but you may need to enable the pydantic plug-in for typechecking in your *mypy.ini* to take advantage of all the features. Your *mypy.ini* will need the following in it:

```
[mypy]
plugins = pydantic.mypy
```

For more information, check out the pydantic documentation (*https://oreil.ly/FBQXX*).

By modeling types with pydantic, I can catch entire classes of errors without writing my own validation logic. The pydantic data classes above catch 38 of the 67 test cases that I came up with earlier. But I can do better. This code still is missing functionality for those other 29 test cases, but I can use pydantic's built-in validators to catch even more errors on type construction.

Validators

Pydantic offers a ton of built-in *validators*. Validators are custom types that will check for specific constraints upon a field. For instance, if I wanted to make sure that strings were a certain size or that all integers were positive, I could use pydantic's constrained types:

```
from typing import Optional

from pydantic.dataclasses import dataclass
from pydantic import constr, PositiveInt

@dataclass
class AccountAndRoutingNumber:
    account_number: constr(min_length=9,max_length=9) ❶
    routing_number: constr(min_length=8,max_length=12)

@dataclass
class Address:
    address: constr(min_length=1)

# ... snip ...

@dataclass
class Dish:
    name: constr(min_length=1, max_length=16)
    price_in_cents: PositiveInt
    description: constr(min_length=1, max_length=80)
    picture: Optional[str] = None

@dataclass
class Restaurant:
    name: constr(regex=r'^[a-zA-Z0-9 ]*$', ❷
                 min_length=1, max_length=16)
```

```
    owner: constr(min_length=1)
    address: constr(min_length=1)
    employees: List[Employee]
    dishes: List[Dish]
    number_of_seats: PositiveInt
    to_go: bool
    delivery: bool
```

❶ I'm constraining a string to be a certain length.

❷ I'm constraining a string to match a regular expression (in this case, only alpha-
numeric characters and spaces).

If I pass in an invalid type (such as a restaurant name with special characters or a negative number of seats), I get the following error:

```
pydantic.error_wrappers.ValidationError: 2 validation errors for Restaurant
name
  string does not match regex "^[a-zA-Z0-9 ]$" (type=value_error.str.regex;
                                                pattern=^[a-zA-Z0-9 ]$)
number_of_seats
  ensure this value is greater than 0
    (type=value_error.number.not_gt; limit_value=0)
```

I can even constrain lists to enforce further restrictions.

```
from pydantic import conlist,constr
@dataclass
class Restaurant:
    name: constr(regex=r'^[a-zA-Z0-9 ]*$',
                 min_length=1, max_length=16)
    owner: constr(min_length=1)
    address: constr(min_length=1)
    employees: conlist(Employee, min_items=2) ❶
    dishes: conlist(Dish, min_items=3) ❷
    number_of_seats: PositiveInt
    to_go: bool
    delivery: bool
```

❶ This list is constrained to Employee types and must have at least two employees.

❷ This list is constrained to Dish types and must have at least three dishes.

If I pass in something that doesn't follow these constraints (such as forgetting a dish):

```
pydantic.error_wrappers.ValidationError: 1 validation error for Restaurant
dishes
  ensure this value has at least 3 items
    (type=value_error.list.min_items; limit_value=3)
```

With constrained types, I catch an additional 17 of my previously thought-up test
cases, bringing my total up to 55 out of 67 test cases covered. Pretty nice, isn't it?

To catch the remaining set of errors, I can use custom validators to embed those last pieces of validation logic:

```
from pydantic import validator
@dataclass
class Restaurant:
    name: constr(regex=r'^[a-zA-Z0-9 ]*$',
                 min_length=1, max_length=16)
    owner: constr(min_length=1)
    address: constr(min_length=1)
    employees: conlist(Employee, min_items=2)
    dishes: conlist(Dish, min_items=3)
    number_of_seats: PositiveInt
    to_go: bool
    delivery: bool

    @validator('employees')
    def check_chef_and_server(cls, employees):
        if (any(e for e in employees if e.position == 'Chef') and
              any(e for e in employees if e.position == 'Server')):
                return employees
        raise ValueError('Must have at least one chef and one server')
```

If I then fail to provide at least one chef and server:

```
pydantic.error_wrappers.ValidationError: 1 validation error for Restaurant
employees
  Must have at least one chef and one server (type=value_error)
```

I will leave it up to you to write custom validators for other error cases (such as valid addresses, valid routing numbers, or a valid image that exists on a filesystem).

Validation Versus Parsing

Admittedly, pydantic is not strictly a validation library, but also a *parsing* library. The difference is slight, but needs to be called out. In all my examples, I have been using pydantic to check arguments and types, but it is not a strict validator. Pydantic advertises itself as a *parsing library*, which means it is providing a guarantee of what comes *out* of the data model, not what goes in. That is, when you are defining pydantic models, pydantic will do whatever it can to coerce data into the types you defined.

If you were to have a model:

```
from pydantic import dataclass
@dataclass
class Model:
    value: int
```

There is no problem passing in a string or a float into this model; pydantic will do its best to coerce the value to an integer (or throw an exception if the value is not coercible). This code throws no exceptions:

```
Model(value="123") # value is set to the integer 123
Model(value=5.5) # this truncates the value to 5
```

Pydantic is parsing these values, not validating them. You are not guaranteed to pass an integer into the model, but you are always guaranteed an int comes out on the other side (or an exception is thrown).

If you'd like to restrict this sort of behavior, you can use pydantic's strict fields:

```
from pydantic.dataclasses import dataclass
from pydantic import StrictInt
@dataclass
class Model:
    value: StrictInt
```

Now, when constructing from another type,

```
x = Model(value="0023").value
```

you will get an error:

```
pydantic.error_wrappers.ValidationError: 1 validation error for Model
value
   value is not a valid integer (type=type_error.integer)
```

So, while pydantic advertises itself as a parsing library, it is possible to enforce more strict behavior in your data models.

Closing Thoughts

I've been harping on the importance of typecheckers throughout this book, but that doesn't mean catching errors at runtime is meaningless. While typecheckers catch their fair share of errors and reduce runtime checks, they can't catch everything. You still need validation logic to fill in the gaps.

For these sorts of checks, the pydantic library is a great tool in your toolbox. By embedding your validation logic directly into your types (without writing tons of tedious if statements), you improve robustness twofold. First, you dramatically increase readability; developers reading your type definition will know exactly what constraints are imposed upon it. Second, it gives you that much-needed layer of protection with runtime checking.

I find that pydantic also helps fill in the middle ground between a data class and a class. Each constraint is technically fulfilling invariants about that class. I normally advise not to give your data classes an invariant because you can't protect it; you don't control construction and property access is public. However, pydantic protects the invariant even when you initialize a type or set a field. But, if you have fields that are interdependent (such as needing to set both at the same time or needing to set only one field based on the value of another), stick with a class.

That's it for Part II. You've learned how to create your own types with Enums, data classes, and classes. Each of these fits a specific use case, so be mindful about your intentions when writing types. You learned how types can model *is-a* relationships with subtyping. You also learned why your API is so important to each class; it's the first chance other developers get to understand what you're doing. You finished up with this chapter, learning about the need to do runtime validation in addition to static typechecking.

In the next part, I'm going to take a step back and look at robustness from a much broader viewpoint. Pretty much all of the guidance in the first two parts of this book has focused on type annotations and typecheckers. Readability and error checking are important benefits of robustness, but they are not all there is. Other maintainers need to be able to make big changes to your codebase to introduce new functionality, not just small changes interacting with your types. They need to extend your codebase. Part III will focus on extensibility.

PART III

Extensible Python

Robust code is maintainable code. In order to be maintainable, code must be easy to read, easy to check for errors, and easy to change. Parts I and II of this book focused on readability and error detection, but not necessarily how to extend or modify existing code. Type annotations and typecheckers provide confidence to maintainers when interacting with individual types, but what about larger changes in a codebase, such as introducing new workflows or switching out a key component?

Part III examines larger changes and shows you how to enable future developers to make them. You'll learn about extensibility and composability, both core principles that improve robustness. You'll learn how to manage dependencies, to make sure that simple changes don't create a ripple effect of bugs and errors. You'll then apply these concepts to architectural models, such as plug-in-based systems, reactive programming, and task-oriented programs.

CHAPTER 15

Extensibility

This chapter focuses on extensibility. Extensibility underpins this part of the book; it's important to understand this key concept. Once you know how extensibility affects robustness, you'll start seeing opportunities to apply it throughout your codebase. Extensible systems allow other developers to enhance your codebase with confidence, reducing the chance of errors. Let's examine how.

What Is Extensibility?

Extensibility is the property of systems that allows new functionality to be added without modifying existing parts of your system. Software is not static; it will change. Throughout your codebase's lifetime, developers will change your software. The *soft* part of *software* indicates as much. These changes can be quite large. Think about the times you need to swap out a key piece of your architecture as you scale, or add in new workflows. These changes touch multiple parts of your codebase; simple type-checking won't catch all errors at this level. After all, you may be redesigning your types completely. The goal of extensible software is to be designed in such a way that you have provided easy extension points for future developers, especially in areas of code that are changed often.

To illustrate this idea, let's consider a restaurant chain that wants to implement some sort of notification system to help suppliers respond to demand. A restaurant may have a special, or be out of a certain ingredient, or indicate that some ingredient has gone bad. In each case, the restaurant wants the supplier to automatically be notified that a restock is needed. The supplier has provided a Python library to do the actual notifications.

The implementation looks like the following:

```
def declare_special(dish: Dish, start_date: datetime.datetime,
                     end_time: datetime.datetime):
    # ... snip setup in local system ...
    # ... snip send notification to the supplier ...

def order_dish(dish: Dish):
    # ... snip automated preparation
    out_of_stock_ingredients = {ingred for ingred in dish
                                if out_of_stock(ingred)}
    if out_of_stock_ingredients:
        # ... snip taking dishes off menu ...
        # ... snip send notification to the supplier ...


# called every 24 hours
def check_for_expired_ingredients():
    expired_ingredients = {ing for ing in ingredient in get_items_in_stock()}:
    if expired_ingredients:
        # ... snip taking dishes off menu ...
        # ... snip send notifications to the supplier ...
```

This code is pretty straightforward at first glance. Whenever an event of note occurs, the appropriate notification can be sent to the supplier (imagine some dictionary being sent as part of a JSON request).

Fast forward a few months, and a new work item comes in. Your boss at the restaurant is so pleased with the notification system that they want to expand it. They want notifications to come to their email address. Sounds simple enough, right? You make the declare_special function take an email address as well:

```
def declare_special(notification: NotificationType,
                     start_date: datetime.datetime,
                     end_time: datetime.datetime,
                     email: Email):
    # ... snip ...
```

This has far-reaching implications, though. A function calling declare_special will also need knowledge of what email to pass down. Thankfully, typecheckers will catch any omission. But what if other use cases start rolling in? You take a look at your backlog and the following tasks are present:

- Notify sales team about specials and items out of stock.
- Notify the restaurant's customers of new specials.
- Support different APIs for different suppliers.
- Support text message notifications so your boss can get notifications, too.
- Create a new notification type: New Menu Item. Marketers and the boss want to know about this, but not the supplier.

As developers implement these features, `declare_special` gets bigger and bigger. It handles more and more cases, and as the logic gets more complex, the potential for making a mistake grows. What's worse, any changes to the API (such as adding a list of email addresses or phone numbers for texting) will have repercussions for all the callers. At some point, doing simple things like adding a new email address to the list of marketers touches multiple files in your codebase. This is colloquially known as "shotgun surgery":[1] where a single change spreads out in a blast pattern, impacting a variety of files. Furthermore, developers are modifying existing code, increasing the chances of a mistake. To top it off, we've only covered `declare_special`, but `order_dish` and `check_for_expired_ingredients` need their own custom logic as well. Handling the notification code duplicated everywhere would be quite tedious. Ask yourself if you would enjoy having to look for every notification snippet in the codebase just because a new user wants text notifications.

This all stems from the code not being very extensible. You start requiring developers to know about all the intricacies of multiple files in order to make their changes. It will take significantly more work for a maintainer to implement their features. Recall from Chapter 1 the discussion between accidental complexity and necessary complexity. Necessary complexity is intrinsic to your problem domain; accidental complexity is the complexity you introduce. In this case, the combination of notifications, recipients, and filters is necessary; it is a required functionality of the system.

However, how you implement the system dictates how much accidental complexity you incur. The way I've described is chock full of accidental complexity. Adding any one simple thing is quite a monumental undertaking. Requiring developers to hunt through the codebase to find all the places that need to change is just asking for trouble. Easy changes should be easy to make. Otherwise, extending the system becomes a chore every single time.

The Redesign

Let's look at the `declare_special` function again:

```
def declare_special(notification: NotificationType,
                    start_date: datetime.datetime,
                    end_time: datetime.datetime,
                    email: Email):
    # ... snip ...
```

The problem all started with adding email as a parameter to the function. This is what caused a ripple effect that affected other parts of the codebase. It's not the future developer's fault; they are often constrained by time, trying to jam their feature into a

---

1 Martin Fowler. *Refactoring: Improving the Design of Existing Code.* 2nd ed. Upper Saddle River, NJ: Addison-Wesley Professional, 2018.

part of the codebase they are unfamiliar with. They will typically follow the patterns already laid out for them. If you can lay groundwork to lead them in the right direction, you increase the maintainability of your code. If you let the maintainability fester, you start seeing methods like the following:

```
def declare_special(notification: NotificationType,
                    start_date: datetime.datetime,
                    end_time: datetime.datetime,
                    emails: list[Email],
                    texts: list[PhoneNumber],
                    send_to_customer: bool):
    # ... snip ...
```

The function will grow and grow out of control until it's a tangled mess of dependencies. If I need to add a customer to a mailing list, why do I need to look at how specials are declared?

I need to redesign the notification system so that changes are easy to make. First, I'll look at use cases and think about what needs to be made easy for future developers. (If you'd like additional advice around designing interfaces, revisit Part II, specifically Chapter 11.) In this specific use case, I want future developers to be able to add three things easily:

- New notification types
- New notification methods (such as email, text message, or APIs)
- New users to notify

Notification code is littered around the codebase, so I want to make sure that as developers make these changes, they don't need to engage in any shotgun surgery. Remember, I want the easy things to be easy.

Now, think about my *necessary* complexities. In this case, there will be multiple notification methods, multiple notification types, and multiple users needing to be notified. These are three separate complexities; I want to limit the interactions between these. Part of the problem of declare_special is that the combination of concerns it has to account for are daunting. Multiply that complexity by every function needing slightly different notification needs and you have a real nightmare of maintenance on your hand.

The first thing to do is decouple the intents as best as you can. I'll start by creating classes for each notification type:

```
@dataclass
class NewSpecial:
    dish: Dish
    start_date: datetime.datetime
    end_date: datetime.datetime
```

```
@dataclass
class IngredientsOutOfStock:
    ingredients: Set[Ingredient]

@dataclass
class IngredientsExpired:
    ingredients: Set[Ingredient]

@dataclass
class NewMenuItem:
    dish: Dish

Notification = Union[NewSpecial, IngredientsOutOfStock,
                     IngredientsExpired, NewMenuItem]
```

If I think about how I want `declare_special` to interact with the codebase, I really only want it to know about this `NotificationType`. Declaring a special should not require knowing who is signed up for that special and how they will be notified. Ideally, the `declare_special` (and any other function needing to send notifications) should look something like this:

```
def declare_special(dish: Dish, start_date: datetime.datetime,
                    end_time: datetime.datetime):
    # ... snip setup in local system ...
    send_notification(NewSpecial(dish, start_date, end_date))
```

`send_notification` can just be declared like such:

```
def send_notification(notification: Notification):
    # ... snip ...
```

This means that if any part of the codebase wants to send a notification, it merely needs to invoke this function. All you need to pass in is a notification type. Adding new notification types is simple; you add a new class, add that class to the `Union`, and call the `send_notification` with the new notification type.

Next, you have to make it easy to add new notification methods. Again, I'll add new types to represent each notification method:

```
@dataclass
class Text:
    phone_number: str

@dataclass
class Email:
    email_address: str

@dataclass
class SupplierAPI:
    pass

NotificationMethod = Union[Text, Email, SupplierAPI]
```

Somewhere in the codebase, I need to actually send a different notification type per method. I can create a few helper functions to handle that functionality:

```python
def notify(notification_method: NotificationMethod, notification: Notification):
    if isinstance(notification_method, Text):
        send_text(notification_method, notification)
    elif isinstance(notification_method, Email):
        send_email(notification_method, notification)
    elif isinstance(notification_method, SupplierAPI):
        send_to_supplier(notification)
    else:
        raise ValueError("Unsupported Notification Method")

def send_text(text: Text, notification: Notification):
    if isinstance(notification, NewSpecial):
        # ... snip send text ...
        pass
    elif isinstance(notification, IngredientsOutOfStock):
        # ... snip send text ...
        pass
    elif isinstance(notification, IngredientsExpired):
        # ... snip send text ...
        pass
    elif isinstance(notification, NewMenuItem):
        # .. snip send text ...
        pass
    raise NotImplementedError("Unsupported Notification Method")

def send_email(email: Email, notification: Notification):
    # .. similar to send_text ...


def send_to_supplier(notification: Notification):
    # .. similar to send_text
```

Now, adding a new notification method is straightforward as well. I add a new type, add it to the union, add an `if` statement in `notify`, and write a corresponding method to handle all different notification types.

It may seem unwieldy to handle all the notification types in each `send_*` method, but this is necessary complexity; there is different functionality per method/type combo due to different messages, different information, and different formats. If the sheer amount of code did grow, you could make a dynamic lookup dictionary (so that adding a new key-value would be all that's needed for adding a notification method), but in these cases you will trade off early error detection with typechecking for more readability.

Now I have easy ways to add a new notification method or type. I just have to tie it all together so that it's easy to add new users. To do that, I will write a function to get the list of users needing to be notified:

```
users_to_notify: Dict[type, List[NotificationMethod]] = {
    NewSpecial: [SupplierAPI(), Email("boss@company.org"),
                 Email("marketing@company.org"), Text("555-2345")],
    IngredientsOutOfStock: [SupplierAPI(), Email("boss@company.org")],
    IngredientsExpired: [SupplierAPI(), Email("boss@company.org")],
    NewMenuItem: [Email("boss@company.org"), Email("marketing@company.org")]
}
```

In practice, this data could be coming from a config file or some other declarative source, but for the brevity needed for a book example, it will do. To add new users, I just add a new entry to this dictionary. Adding new notification methods or notification types for a user is just as easy. The code for users to notify is much easier to handle.

To put it all together, I'll implement send_notification using all of these concepts:

```
def send_notification(notification: Notification):
    try:
        users = users_to_notify[type(notification)]
    except KeyError:
        raise ValueError("Unsupported Notification Method")
    for notification_method in users:
        notify(notification_method, notification)
```

That's it! All of this code for notifications can live in one file, and the rest of the codebase only needs to know one function—send_notification—to interact with the notification system. This becomes much easier to test once there's no need to interact with any other part of the codebase. Furthermore, this code is extensible; developers can easily add new notification types, methods, or users without trawling through the codebase for all the myriad invocations. You want to make it easy to add new functionality to your codebase while minimizing modifications to existing code. This is known as the Open-Closed Principle.

Open-Closed Principle

The *Open-Closed Principle* (OCP) states that code should be open for extension and closed for modification.[2] This is the heart of extensibility. Our redesign in the previous section tried to uphold this principle. Rather than requiring new functionality to touch multiple parts of the codebase, it instead required adding new types or functions. Even when existing functions changed, all I did was add a new conditional check instead of modifying an existing check.

It may seem like all I've done is aim for code reuse, but the OCP goes a step further. Yes, I've deduplicated the notification code, but more importantly, I've made it easier for developers to manage the complexity. Ask yourself which you prefer: implement-

---

2 The OCP was first described in *Object-Oriented Software Construction* by Bertrand Meyer (Pearson).

ing a feature by examining call stacks and not being sure if you found every place that needs to be changed, or one file that is easy to modify and doesn't require extensive changes. I know what I'd pick.

You've already been exposed to the OCP in this book. Duck typing (in Chapter 2), subtyping (in Chapter 12), and protocols (in Chapter 13) are all mechanisms that can help with the OCP. The common thread among all these mechanisms is that they allow you to program in a generic fashion. You no longer need to handle every special case directly where the functionality is used. Instead, you provide extension points for other developers to utilize, allowing them to inject their own functionality without modifying your code.

The OCP is the heart of extensibility. Keeping your code extensible will improve robustness. Developers can implement functionality with confidence; there is one place to make the change, and the rest of the codebase is all geared up to support the change. Less cognitive overhead and less code to change will lead to fewer errors.

Detecting OCP Violations

How can you tell if you should be writing code to be more extensible, adhering to the OCP? Here are some indicators that should raise an eyebrow as you think about your codebase:

Are the easy things hard to do?
> Some things should be conceptually easy in your codebase. The effort needed to implement the concept should match the domain complexity. I once worked in a codebase that required 13 different files to be modified in order to add a user-configurable option. For a product that had hundreds of configurable options, this should have been an easy task. Suffice to say, it was not.

Do you encounter pushback against similar features?
> If feature requesters are constantly pushing back on timelines for a feature, especially if it, in their words, "is almost identical to previous feature *X*", ask yourself if the disconnect is due to complexity. It might be that the complexity is inherent in the domain, in which case you should make sure the feature requester is on the same page as you. If the complexity is accidental, though, your code probably needs to be reworked to make it easier to work in.

Do you have consistently high estimates?
> Some teams use estimates to predict the amount of work they will do in a given timeline. If features consistently have high estimates, ask yourself the source of the estimate. Is complexity driving the high estimate, and is that complexity necessary? Is it risk and fear of the unknown? If it's the latter, ask why your codebase feels risky to work in. Some teams split features into separate estimates by

splitting the work. If you're doing this consistently, ask if restructuring the codebase could have mitigated the split.

Do commits contain large changesets?

Look for commits in your version control system that have a large number of files. This is a great indication that shotgun surgery is happening, especially if the same files keep showing up in multiple commits. Keep in mind this is a guideline; big commits don't always indicate a problem, but if they happen frequently, it's worth checking into.

Discussion Topic

Which OCP violations have you encountered in your codebase? How could you restructure code to avoid them?

Drawbacks

Extensibility is not a panacea to all of your coding woes. In fact, you can actually *degrade* your codebase with too much flexibility. If you overdo the OCP and try to make everything configurable and extensible, you will quickly find yourself in a mess. The problem is that while making your code extensible reduces accidental complexity in making changes, it can *increase* accidental complexity in other areas.

First, readability suffers. You are creating a whole new layer of abstraction that separates your business logic from other parts of your codebase. Anyone who wants to understand the entire picture has to jump through a few extra hoops. This will affect new developers getting up to speed, as well as hinder debugging efforts. You can mitigate this with good documentation and explaining your code structure.

Secondly, you introduce a coupling that may not have been present before. Before, separate parts of the codebase were independent of each other. Now, they share a common subsystem; any change in that subsystem will affect all the consumers. I'll go more in depth in Chapter 16. Mitigate this with a strong set of tests.

Use the OCP in moderation and take care when applying these principles. Use them too much, and your codebase will be overabstracted with a confusing tangle of dependencies. Use it too little, and developers will take longer to make changes as well as introduce more bugs. Define extension points in areas that you are reasonably sure that someone will have to modify again, and you will drastically improve your future maintainer's experience with your codebase.

Closing Thoughts

Extensibility is one of the most important aspects of codebase maintenance. It allows your collaborators a way of adding functionality without modifying existing code. Any time you get away without modifying existing code is a time that you aren't introducing any regressions. Adding extensible code now prevents bugs in the future. Remember the OCP: keep code open to extension but closed for modification. Apply this principle judiciously and you will see your codebase become more maintainable.

Extensibility is an important theme that will weave throughout the next few chapters. In the next chapter, I'm going to focus on dependencies and how relationships in your codebase can constrain its extensibility. You'll learn about the different types of dependencies and how to manage them. You'll learn how to visualize and understand your dependencies, and why some parts of your codebases can have more dependencies than others. Once you start managing your dependencies, you will find it much easier to extend and modify code.

## CHAPTER 16

Dependencies

It is difficult to write a program with no dependencies. Functions depend on other functions, modules depend on other modules, and programs depend on other programs. Architecture is fractal; no matter what level you're looking at, your code can be represented as some sort of box-and-arrows diagram, like in Figure 16-1. It doesn't matter if it's functions, classes, modules, programs, or systems, you can draw a similar diagram to Figure 16-1 to represent the dependencies in your code.

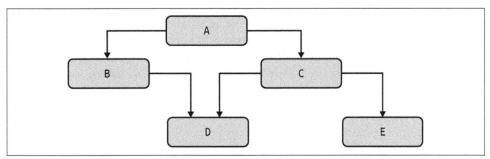

Figure 16-1. Box-and-arrows diagram

However, if you don't actively manage your dependencies, you soon get to what's known as "spaghetti code," making your box-and-arrows diagram look like Figure 16-2.

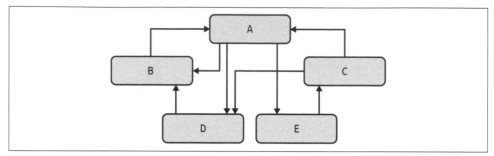

Figure 16-2. A tangled mess of dependencies

In this chapter, you are going to learn all about dependencies and how to keep them under control. You'll learn about different types of dependencies, all of which should be managed with different techniques. You'll learn how to graph your dependencies, and how to interpret whether you have a healthy system. You'll learn how to truly simplify your code architecture, which will help you manage complexity and increase the robustness of your codebase.

Relationships

Dependencies are, in essence, relationships. When a piece of code requires another piece of code to behave in some specific way, we call that a *dependency*. You typically use a dependency to benefit from code reuse in some fashion. Functions call other functions to reuse behaviors. Modules import other modules to reuse the types and functions defined in that module. It doesn't make sense in most codebases to write literally everything from scratch. Reusing other parts of the codebase, or even code from other organizations, can be immensely beneficial.

When you reuse code, you save time. You don't need to waste effort writing code; you can just call or import the functionality that you need. Furthermore, any code you are depending on is presumably used in other places. This means that some layer of testing has already been done, which should reduce the number of bugs. Bonus points if the code is readily available to read. As *Linus's Law* (as in Linus Torvalds, creator of Linux) states:[1]

> "Given enough eyeballs, all bugs are shallow."

Put another way, the likeliness of finding bugs is higher because so many people are looking at the code. This is another point in favor of readability leading to maintainability. If your code is readable, other developers will find and fix errors in it more easily, helping your robustness grow.

---

1 Eric S. Raymond. *The Cathedral & the Bazaar*. Sebastopol, CA: O'Reilly Media, 2001.

There's a catch, though. There is no such thing as a free lunch when talking about dependencies. Every dependency you create contributes to *coupling*, or tying two entities together. If a dependency changes in an incompatible way, your code needs to change as well. If this happens often, your robustness will suffer; you are constantly struggling to stay afloat as your dependencies change.

There's also a human factor with dependencies. Every piece of code you depend on is maintained by a living, breathing human (maybe even a group of them). These maintainers have their own schedules, their own deadlines, and their own vision for the code they develop. Chances are those will not align with your schedules, deadlines, and vision. The more a piece of code is reused, the less likely it is that it meets all of the needs of every consumer. As your dependencies diverge from your implementation, you either live with the difficulties, choose an alternative dependency (possibly one you control), or fork it (and maintain it yourself). The choice you make depends on your specific scenario, but in each case, robustness takes a hit.

Any JavaScript developer who was working in 2016 can tell you how dependencies went wrong in "the left-pad debacle." Due to a policy dispute, a developer removed a library named left-pad from the package repository and the next morning, thousands of projects were suddenly broken and unable to build. Many large projects (including React, a very popular library) depended on left-pad not directly, but transitively, through their own dependencies. That's right, dependencies have their own dependencies and you get them too when you depend on other code. The moral of the story: don't forget the human factor and the associated costs related to their workflows. Be prepared for any of your dependencies to change in the worst way, including being removed. Dependencies are liabilities. Necessary, but still liabilities.

Dependencies also broaden the attack surface from a security perspective. Every dependency (and their own dependencies) has potential to compromise your system. There are entire websites dedicated to tracking security vulnerabilities, such as *https://cve.mitre.org*. A keyword search of "Python" shows you how many vulnerabilities exist today, and naturally, those websites can't even count the not-yet-known vulnerabilities. This is even more perilous with dependencies maintained by your organization; unless you have security-minded individuals constantly looking at all of your code, unknown vulnerabilities may be ever-present in your codebase.

To Pin or Not to Pin

Some developers tend to pin their dependencies, which means those dependencies are frozen at a specific point in time. That way, you don't run the risk of breaking code because of an updated dependency; projects keep chugging along using an old version. For a very mature project that isn't updated often, this isn't too bad of a setup to minimize risk, but you need to be wary of a few things.

For this to work, you need to be diligent about what you pin. If any dependencies are unpinned, they shouldn't depend on any other pinned dependency. Otherwise, when the unpinned dependencies change, they are liable to have a conflict with the pinned dependencies.

Secondly, in order to pin dependencies, those dependencies actually need to be pinnable. The dependencies need to be represented as a specific commit or version number to reference. You cannot pin dependencies that are solely inside your codebase, such as an individual function or class.

Lastly, you need to evaluate the likelihood of actually needing to update the pin at any time. Think about new features, security updates, or bug fixes that might happen. Any one of these will inevitably cause a pin to get updated. The longer you wait on updating a pin, the more changes that may have been introduced, incompatible with your codebase's assumptions. This can make for a painful integration.

If you foresee the need to change the pinning of a dependency, you need a strategy for updating those dependencies. I recommend keeping the dependencies pinned, but lean on a continuous integration workflow and dependency managers such as `poetry` to update those dependencies. With continuous integration, you are constantly scanning for new dependencies. When dependencies change, the tools will update the dependencies, run tests, and if tests pass, check in the new pins for the updated dependencies. This way, dependencies stay up to date, but you always maintain a checked-in set of pins for reproducibility. The downside here is that you need to have the discipline and supporting culture to fix the failed integrations as they appear. Tackling failures piecemeal is much less effort in the long run than delaying the integration.

Carefully balance your use of dependencies. Your code will inherently have dependencies, and that is a good thing. The trick is to be smart with how you manage them. Being careless will lead to a sloppy, tangled mess. To learn how to handle dependencies, you first need to know how to identify the different types.

Types of Dependencies

I group dependencies into three classifications: physical, logical, and temporal. Each impacts your code's robustness in different ways. You have to be able to spot them and know when they go awry. When wielded correctly, dependencies can keep your code extensible without bogging it down.

Physical Dependencies

When most developers think about dependencies, it's the physical dependencies they think about. *Physical dependencies* are a relationship observed directly in code. Functions calling functions, types composed of other types, modules importing modules, classes inheriting from other classes...these are all examples of physical dependencies. They are static, meaning they aren't changing at runtime.

Physical dependencies are the easiest to reason about; even tools can look at the codebase and map out physical dependencies (you'll see this in just a few pages). They are easy to read and understand at first glance, which is a win for robustness. When future maintainers are reading or debugging the code, it becomes quite apparent how the dependency chain resolves; they can follow a trail of imports or function calls to get to the end of the chain.

Figure 16-3 focuses on a completely automated pizza café named *PizzaMat*. Franchisees can purchase a PizzaMat as an entire module, and deploy it anywhere to get instant (and delicious) pizza. PizzaMat has a few different systems: the pizza-making system, a system to control payment and ordering, and a system to handle table management (seating, refills, and order delivery).

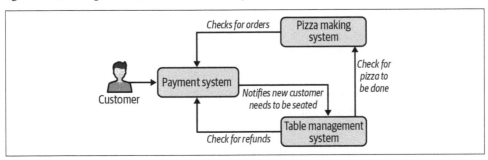

Figure 16-3. An automated pizza café

Each of these three systems interacts with the others (that's what the arrows represent). The customer interacts with the payment/ordering system to order their pizza. Once they're done, the pizza maker checks for any new orders and starts making the pizzas, and the table management system starts seating the customer. Once the table management service learns the pizza is done, it preps it for the table and serves it to the customer. If for any reason the customer is unhappy with the pizza, the table management system returns the pizza and the payment system issues a refund.

Each of these dependencies is a relationship, and only with these systems working together do we have a working pizza shop. Physical dependencies are absolutely necessary to make sense of large systems; they allow you to break the problem down into smaller entities and define the interactions between each entity. I could take any one of these systems and break that down into modules, or take any module and break it down into functions. What I want to focus on is how those relationships impact maintainability.

Suppose these three systems are maintained by three separate entities. You and your team maintain the pizza-making system. Another team in your company (but in a different building) owns the table management system, and an independent contractor has been providing the payment system. You've been part of a huge rollout to provide a new item in your pizza maker: stromboli. You've been working for weeks, carefully coordinating changes. Every system requires changes to handle the new menu item. After countless late nights (all pizza-fueled, of course), you are ready for the big update for your customers. However, as soon as the update rolls out, error reports start rolling in. An unfortunate set of events has introduced a bug, leading to pizza shops around the world breaking. As more and more systems come online, the problem becomes more dire. Management decides that you need to fix it as soon as possible.

Take a minute to ask how you would like your night to go. Do you want to spend it frantically trying to reach all of the other teams, attempting to hack in a fix across the three systems? You happen to know that the contractor has already turned off notifications for the night and the other team got a little too carried away with their launch celebration after work today. Or do you want to take a look at the code and realize that it's incredibly easy to remove stromboli from all three systems by just messing with a few lines of code, with no input from the other teams?

Dependencies are a one-way relationship. You are beholden to your dependencies. If they don't do exactly what you want when you need it, you have little recourse. Remember, living, breathing humans are on the other side of your dependencies and they won't necessarily jump when you ask them to jump. How you construct your dependencies will directly impact how you maintain a system.

In our stromboli example, the dependencies are a circle; any one change can potentially affect the other two systems. You need to think about every direction of your dependencies and how changes ripple through your system. With PizzaMat, the support of the pizza-making equipment is our single source of truth; there's no use in setting up billing and table management for pizza products that don't exist. However, in the example above, all three systems were written with their own copy of what menu items are available. Based on the direction of the dependencies, the pizza maker could take out the stromboli code, but stromboli would still show up in the payment system. How could you make this more extensible to avoid these dependency problems?

 The tricky thing about large architectural changes is that the right answer always depends on the context of your specific problem. If *you* were to build an automated pizza maker, you might draw your dependency tree differently, based on a variety of different factors and constraints. It's important to focus on *why* you are drawing your dependencies the way you are, not making sure that they are always drawn the same way as someone else's system.

To start, you can construct your system such that all the menu definitions live in the pizza-making system; after all, it is the system that knows what it can and cannot make. From there, the pricing system can query the pizza maker as to what items are actually available. That way, if you need to remove stromboli in an emergency, you can do it in the pizza-making system; the pricing system doesn't control what is and is not available. By inverting, or reversing the direction of, the dependency, you restore control to the pizza-making system. If I were to invert this one dependency, the dependency graph looks like Figure 16-4.

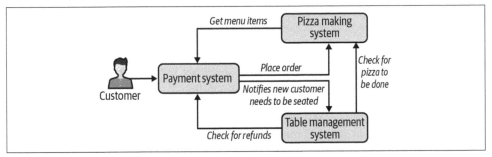

Figure 16-4. More sensible dependencies

Now the pizza maker calls the shots for what can and cannot be ordered. This can go a long way toward limiting the amount of changes needed. If the pizza maker needs to stop supporting a type of ingredient in a dish, the payment system will pick up the changes automatically. Not only will this save your hide during an emergency, but it gives your business more flexibility in the future. You've added the ability to optionally display different dishes in the payment system depending on what the pizza maker can automatically make, all without needing to coordinate with an external payment team.

Discussion Topic

Think through how you would add a feature that prevents the payment system from showing certain options if the pizza maker was out of ingredients. Consider the systems in Figures 16-3 and 16-4.

As an additional discussion topic, discuss the cycle between the table management system and payment system. How can you break that cycle? What are the pros and cons of each direction of dependencies?

When Code Gets Too DRY

The DRY principle (Don't Repeat Yourself—see Chapter 10 for more detail) is ingrained in most developers' heads. Anytime you see very similar code in your codebase, you are required to shout "DUPLICATION!" to warn other developers, and dutifully refactor that code so that it lives in one place. After all, you don't want to fix the same bug in multiple places.

It's possible for the DRY principle to go too far, though. Every time you refactor code, you are introducing a physical dependency to the refactored code. If other parts of your codebase depend on this piece of code, you are coupling them together. If that refactored central piece of code needs to change, it can affect a large amount of code.

When applying the DRY principle, don't deduplicate code just because it looks the same; deduplicate it only if that code has the same *reasons* to change. Otherwise, you'll start getting into cases where the refactored code needs to change for one reason, but that reason is incompatible with other parts of code that depend on the refactored code. You need to start putting special logic into the deduplicated code to handle special cases. Any time you increase complexity like this, you start to reduce maintainability and make code harder to reuse for general purposes.

Logical Dependencies

A *logical dependency* is when two entities have a relationship but no direct linkage in code. The dependency is abstracted; it contains a layer of indirection. It's a dependency that is only present at runtime. In our pizza maker example, we have three subsystems interacting with one another. We represented the dependency with arrows in Figure 16-3. If those arrows are imports or function calls, then they are physical dependencies. However, it's possible to link these subsystems at runtime without function calls or imports.

Suppose subsystems live on different computers and communicate over HTTP. If the pizza maker were to notify the table management service on when the pizza is made over HTTP using the requests library, it would look something like this:

```
def on_pizza_made(order: int, pizza: Pizza):

    requests.post("table-management/pizza-made", {
        "id": order,
        "pizza": pizza.to_json()
    })
```

The physical dependency is no longer from the pizza maker to our table management system, but from the pizza maker to the requests library. As far as the pizza maker is concerned, it just needs an HTTP endpoint that it can post to an endpoint called

"/pizza-done" from some web server named "table-management." That endpoint needs to accept an ID and pizza data formatted as JSON.

Now, in reality, your pizza maker still needs a table management service to work. This is the logical dependency at play. Even though there is no direct dependency, there is still a relationship between the pizza maker and table management systems. This relationship doesn't just disappear; it transforms from physical to logical.

The key benefit for introducing a logical dependency is substitutability. It is much easier to replace a component when nothing is physically depending on it. Take the example with the `on_pizza_done` over HTTP request. You could completely replace the table management service, as long as it upholds the same contract as the original service. If that sounds familiar, it should, as it's the exact same idea you learned about in Chapter 12. Subtyping, whether through duck typing, inheritance, or something similar, introduces logical dependencies. Calling code physically depends on the base class, but the logical dependency of which child class is used isn't determined until runtime.

Improving substitutability improves maintainability. Remember, maintainable code is easy to change. If you can substitute entire swaths of functionality with minimal impact, you give your future maintainers immense flexibility in making decisions. If a specific function or class or subsystem isn't growing to your needs, you can just replace it. Code that is easy to delete is inherently easy to change.

As with anything though, logical dependencies come with a cost. Every logical dependency is an indirect reference to some relationship. Because there is no physical linkage, tooling has a very hard time identifying logical dependencies. You won't be able to create a nice box-and-arrows diagram of logical dependencies. Furthermore, as developers read your code, the logical dependencies won't be immediately apparent. Often, a reader of code will see the physical dependency to some layer of abstraction, while the logical dependency isn't noticed or resolved until runtime.

This is the trade-off of introducing a logical dependency. You increase maintainability by increasing substitutability and reducing coupling, but you also decrease maintainability by making your code harder to read and understand. Too many layers of abstraction create a tangled mess just as easily as too few layers of abstraction. There is no hard and fast rule for what the right number of layers of abstraction are; you need to use your best judgment for whether you need flexibility or readability for your specific scenario.

Some logical dependencies create relationships that aren't detectable through tooling, such as depending on the specific ordering of a collection or relying on specific fields to be present in a class. When found, these often surprise developers because there was little indication they existed without close inspection.

I once worked on a codebase that stored network interfaces. Two pieces of code depended on these interfaces: one system for performance statistics and one for setting up communication paths with other systems. The problem was they had different assumptions about the ordering of those interfaces. It worked for years, until new network interfaces were added. Due to how communication paths worked, new interfaces needed to be put in the front of the list. But the performance statistics would have only worked with those interfaces in the back. Due to a hidden logical dependency, these two parts of code were inextricably linked (I never would have thought that adding communication paths would break performance statistics).

In hindsight, the fix was easy. I created a function that mapped the ordering from the communication path expectations to a reordered list. The performance statistics system then depended on this new function. However, that didn't retroactively fix the bug (or give me back the hours of my time spent trying to figure out why performance statistics were broken). Whenever you create a dependency on something that is not directly apparent in code, find a way to make it apparent. Leave a trail of breadcrumbs, preferably with a separate codepath (like the intermediary function above) or types. If you can't do that, leave a comment. Had one comment in the network interface list indicated a dependency upon a specific ordering, I never would have had such a headache with that code.

Temporal Dependencies

The last type of dependency is the temporal dependency. This is actually a type of logical dependency, but how you handle it is slightly different. A *temporal dependency* is a dependency that is linked by time. Anytime there is a concrete order of operations, such as "dough must be laid down before sauce and cheese" or "an order must be paid for before the pizza begins being made," you have a temporal dependency. Most temporal dependencies are straightforward; they are a natural part of your business domain. (Where would you put pizza sauce and cheese without the dough, anyway?) These are not the temporal dependencies that will cause you problems. Instead, it's the ones that aren't always so apparent.

Temporal dependencies bite you the most in situations where you must do certain operations in a specific order, but you have no indication that you need to do so. Imagine if your automated pizza maker could be configured in two modes: single-pizza (for high-quality pizzas) or mass-produce (for cheap and fast pizzas). Whenever a pizza maker goes from single-pizza to mass-produce, it needs an explicit reconfiguration. If that reconfiguration doesn't happen, the machine's failsafe kicks in and refuses to make pizzas until a manual operator override occurs.

When this option is first introduced, developers take the utmost care in making sure that before any call to mass_produce, such as:

```
pizza_maker.mass_produce(number_of_pizzas=50, type=PizzaType.CHEESE)
```

There has to be a check:

```
if not pizza_maker.is_configured(ProductionType.MASS_PRODUCE):
    pizza_maker.configure_for_mass_production()
    pizza_maker.wait_for_reconfiguration()
```

Developers diligently look for this code in code reviews and make sure that the proper checks are always made. However, as the years go by, and developers cycle in and out of the project, the team's knowledge of mandatory checks starts to dwindle. Imagine a newer automated pizza maker model comes to market, which doesn't need reconfiguration (calls to configure_for_mass_production result in no change to the system). Developers who are only familiar with this new model may never think to call configure_for_mass_production in these cases.

Now, put yourself in a developer's shoes a few years in the future. Let's say you are writing new functionality for the pizza maker, and the mass_produce function fits the exact use case you need. How would you know that you need to do explicit checking for mass production, especially for older models? Unit tests won't help you, as they don't exist yet for the new functionality. Do you really want to wait until integration tests fail (or a customer complains) to find out that you missed that check?

Here are some strategies to mitigate missing such a check:

Lean on your type system
> By restricting certain operations to specific types, you can prevent confusion. Imagine if mass_produce was only callable from a MassProductionPizzaMaker object. You could write function calls to make sure that a MassProductionPizza Maker was only created after reconfiguration. You are using the type system to make it impossible to a mistake (NewType does something very similar, as described in Chapter 4).

Embed preconditions deeper
> The fact that the pizza maker has to be configured before use is a *precondition*. Consider making this precondition of the mass_produce function by moving the checks inside mass_produce. Think about how you will handle error conditions (such as throwing an exception). You'll be able to prevent violating the temporal dependency, but you've introduced a different error at runtime. Your specific use case will dictate what you consider to be the lesser of two evils: violating the temporal dependency or dealing with a new error case.

Leave breadcrumbs

This isn't necessarily a strategy to catch a violated temporal dependency. Instead it is more of a last-ditch effort to alert developers about temporal dependencies if all other efforts fail. Try to organize temporal dependencies in the same file (ideally within a few lines of each other). Leave comments and documentation to notify future developers of this linkage. With any luck, those future developers will see the clues and know that there is a temporal dependency.

In any linear program, most lines have a temporal dependency on the lines that precede them. This is normal, and you don't need to apply mitigations for each of these cases. Instead, look for temporal dependencies that might only be applied in certain cases (such as machine reconfiguration on older models), or temporal dependencies that are catastrophic if missed (such as not sanitizing a user input string before passing it to a database). Weigh the cost of violating a temporal dependency against the effort to detect it and mitigate it. It will depend on your use case, but when you do mitigate a temporal dependency, it can save you immense headaches later on.

Visualizing Your Dependencies

It can be challenging to find these sorts of dependencies and understand where to look for potential problem points. Sometimes you need a more visual representation. Fortunately, tools exist to help you make sense of your dependencies visually.

 For many of the following examples, I will be using the GraphViz library to display pictures. To install it, follow the instructions on the GraphViz website (*https://graphviz.org*).

Visualizing Packages

Chances are, your code uses other packages, installed by pip. It can be helpful to know all the packages that you depend on, their dependencies, the dependencies of those dependencies, and so on.

To do so, I'm going to install two packages, `pipdeptree` and GraphViz. `pipdeptree` is a useful tool to tell you how packages interact with one another, and GraphViz does the actual visualization part. For this example, I'll be using the mypy codebase. I've downloaded the mypy source code, created a virtual environment, and installed mypy from source.[2]

---

2 Creating a virtual environment is a great way to isolate your dependencies from your system's Python installation.

From within that virtual environment, I've installed `pipdeptree` and GraphViz:

```
pip install pipdeptree graphviz
```

Now I run the following command:

```
pipdeptree --graph-output png --exclude pipdeptree,graphviz > deps.png
```

You can see the results in Figure 16-5.

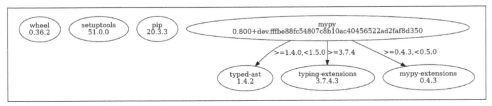

Figure 16-5. Visualizing packages

I'm going to ignore wheel, setuptools, and pip packages, and focus on mypy. In this case, I see the exact version of mypy that is installed, as well as the direct dependencies (in this case typed_ast 1.4.2, typing-extensions 3.7.4.3, and mypy-extensions 0.4.3. `pipdeptree` is also nice enough to specify what version constraints exist (such as only allowing mypy-extensions to be a version greater or equal to 0.4.3, but less than 0.5.0). With these tools, you can get a handy pictorial representation of your packaged dependencies. This is extremely useful for projects with a large number of dependencies, especially if you actively maintain a lot of the packages.

Visualizing Imports

Visualizing packages is quite a high-level view, so it helps to go one step deeper. How can you find out what's being imported at the module level? Another tool, called `pydeps`, is great for this.

To install it, you can:

```
pip install pydeps
```

Once installed, you can run:

```
pydeps --show-deps <source code location> -T png -o deps.png
```

I ran this for mypy and received a very complex and dense graph. Reproducing it in print would be a waste of paper, so I've decided to zoom into a specific section in Figure 16-6.

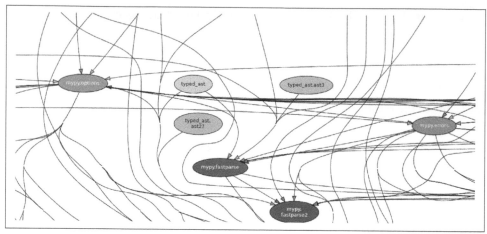

Figure 16-6. Visualizing imports

There's a mess of arrows going on even in this small section of the dependency graph. However, you can see that quite a few different areas of the codebase depend on `mypy.options`, as well as the `fastparse` and `errors` modules. Because of the size of these graphs, I recommend digging into smaller subsystems of your codebase one at a time.

Visualizing Function Calls

If you want even *more* information than an import graph, you can see which functions call each other. This is known as a *call graph*. First, I'll look at a *static* call graph generator. These generators look at your source code and see which functions call which; no code is executed. For this example, I'll use the library pyan3, which can be installed with:

```
pip install pyan3
```

To run pyan3, you execute the following on the command line:

```
pyan3 <Python files> --grouped --annotated --html > deps.html
```

When I run this on the *dmypy* folder inside of mypy (I picked a subfolder to limit the amount of information drawn), I receive an interactive HTML page that lets me explore the dependencies. Figure 16-7 shows a snippet from the tool.

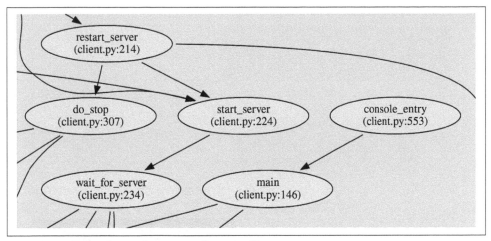

Figure 16-7. Visualizing function calls statically

Note that this only tracks physical dependencies, as logical dependencies aren't known until runtime. If you'd like to see a call graph at runtime, you will need to execute your code in concert with a *dynamic* call graph generator. For this purpose, I like using the built-in Python profiler. A *profiler* audits all function calls you are making during the execution of a program and records performance data. As a side benefit, the entire function call history is preserved in the profile. Let's try this out.

I'll first build the profile (I'm profiling a test file in mypy for size reasons):

```
python -m cProfile -o deps.profile mypy/test/testutil.py
```

Then I'll convert the profile into a file that GraphViz can understand: a dot file.

```
pip install gprof2dot
gprof2dot --format=pstats deps.profile -o deps.dot
```

Finally, I'll use GraphViz to convert the *.dot* file to a *.png*.

```
dot deps.dot -Tpng > deps.png
```

Again, this produces oodles of boxes and arrows, so Figure 16-8 is just a small screen-shot illustrating part of the call graph.

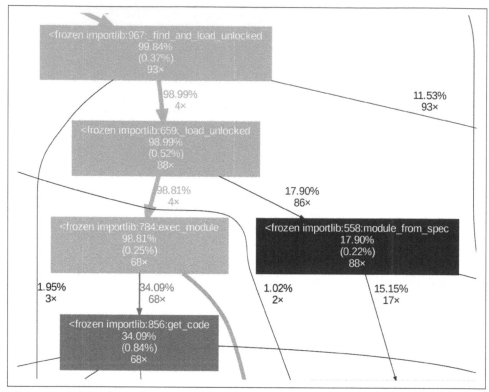

Figure 16-8. Visualizing function calls dynamically

You can find out how many times the function gets called, as well as how much of the execution time was spent in the function. This can be a great way to find performance bottlenecks in addition to understanding your call graph.

Interpreting Your Dependency Graph

Alright, you've drawn all these pretty graphs; what can you do with them? When you see your dependencies graphed out in this fashion, you get a pretty good idea where your maintainability hotspots are. Remember, every dependency is a reason for code to change. Whenever anything changes in your codebase, it can ripple up through physical and logical dependencies, potentially impacting large swaths of code.

With this in mind, you need to think about the relationships between what you're changing and the things that depend upon them. Consider the amount of code depending on you, as well as the code that you yourself depend upon. If you have a lot of dependencies coming in, but not going out, you have what's known as high *fan-in*. Conversely, if you don't have a lot of dependencies coming in, but you depend on a large number of other entities, this is known as high *fan-out*. Figure 16-9 illustrates the difference between fan-in and fan-out.

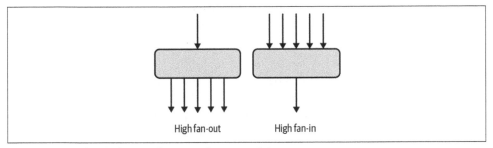

High fan-out   High fan-in

Figure 16-9. The difference between fan-in and fan-out

You want the entities in your system that have a high amount of fan-in to be leaves of your dependency graph, or at the bottom. Large parts of your codebase depend on these entities; every dependency you have is a dependency the rest of your codebase will have as well. You also want these entities to be stable, which means that they should be changing infrequently. Every time you introduce change, you potentially impact most of your codebase due to the large fan-in.

On the other hand, fan-out entities should be toward the top of your dependency graph. This is where most of your business logic will likely live; it will change as the business evolves. These parts of your codebase can withstand a much higher rate of change; due to their relatively few upstream dependencies, their code won't break as often when behaviors change.

Changing fan-out entities won't impact as much of your codebase's assumptions, but I can't say whether or not it will break customer's assumptions. How much you want external behavior to remain backward compatible is a UX concern and outside the scope of this book.

Closing Thoughts

The presence of dependencies does not dictate how robust your code is. It's about how you utilize and manage those dependencies. Dependencies are absolutely crucial to sane reuse in your system. You can break code into smaller chunks and reorganize your codebase appropriately. By giving your dependencies the right directionality, you can actually increase the robustness of your code. You can make your code more maintainable by increasing substitutability and extensibility.

But, as with anything in engineering, there is always a cost. Dependencies are a coupling; linking different parts of your codebase together and making changes can have a wider impact than you might be looking for. There are different types of dependencies that must be handled in different ways. Physical dependencies are easy to visualize through tooling, but are also rigid in the structure they impose. Logical dependencies provide an extensibility to your codebase, but their nature is hidden until runtime. Temporal dependencies are a necessary part of executing Python in a linear fashion, but when those dependencies become unintuitive, they incur a ton of future pain.

All of these lessons assume that you have pieces of code that you can depend upon. In the next chapter, you'll explore *composable code*, or breaking code into smaller pieces for reuse. You'll learn how to compose objects, looping patterns, and functions to reorganize your code into new use cases. When you think in terms of composable code, you'll start building in new functionality with ease. Your future maintainers will thank you.

## CHAPTER 17

Composability

One of the biggest challenges you face as a developer is predicting how future developers will change your system. Businesses evolve, and the assertions of today become the legacy systems of the future. How would you support such a system? How do you reduce the friction that future developers will face when adapting your system? You will need to develop your code so that it can perform in all sorts of circumstances.

In this chapter, you are going to learn how to develop that code by thinking in terms of composability. When you write with composability in mind, you create your code to be small, discrete, and reusable. I'll show you an architecture that is not composable and how that can hinder development. You'll then learn how to fix it with composability in mind. You'll learn how to compose objects, functions, and algorithms to make your codebase more extensible. But first, let's examine how composability increases maintainability.

Composability

Composability focuses on building small components with minimal interdependencies and little business logic embedded inside. The goal is that future developers can use any one of these components to build their own solutions. By making them small, you make them easier to read and understand. By reducing dependencies, you save future developers from worrying about all the costs involved in pulling new code (such as the costs you learned about in Chapter 16). By keeping the components mostly free of business logic, you allow your code to solve new problems, even if those new problems look nothing like the problems you encounter today. As the number of composable components increases, developers can mix'n'match your code to create brand-new applications with the utmost ease. By focusing on composability, you make it easier to reuse and extend your code.

Consider the lowly spice rack in a kitchen. What sort of meals would you create if you were to stock your spice rack exclusively with blends of spices, such as pumpkin pie spice (cinnamon, nutmeg, ginger, and cloves) or Chinese five-spice (cinnamon, fennel, star anise, Sichuan peppercorns, and cloves)? You'd end up predominantly making recipes that centered on these spice mixes, such as pumpkin pie or five-spice chicken. While these blends make specialized meals incredibly easy to prepare, what happens if you need to make something that just uses individual ingredients, such as a cinnamon-clove syrup? You could try to substitute pumpkin pie spice or five-spice powder and hope that the extra ingredients don't clash, or you could buy cinnamon and cloves individually.

The individual spices are analogous to small, composable bits of software. You don't know what dishes you might want to make in the future, nor do you know what business needs you will have in the future. By focusing on discrete components, you give your collaborators flexibility in using what they need, without trying to make suboptimal substitutions or pulling other components along for the ride. And if you need a specialized blend of components (such as a pumpkin pie spice), you are free to build your application from those components. Software doesn't expire like spice mixes; you can have your cake (or pumpkin pie) and eat it too. Build the specialized applications from small, discrete, composable software, and you'll find that you can reuse those components in brand new ways next week or next year.

You've actually seen composability before when you learned about building your own types in Part II. I built up an array of small, discrete types that could be reused in multiple scenarios. Each type contributed to a vocabulary of concepts in the codebase. Developers could use these types to represent domain ideas, but also to build upon to define new concepts. Take a look at a definition of a soup from Chapter 9:

```python
class ImperialMeasure(Enum):
    TEASPOON = auto()
    TABLESPOON = auto()
    CUP = auto()

class Broth(Enum):
    VEGETABLE = auto()
    CHICKEN = auto()
    BEEF = auto()
    FISH = auto()

@dataclass(frozen=True)
# Ingredients added into the broth
class Ingredient:
    name: str
    amount: float = 1
    units: ImperialMeasure = ImperialMeasure.CUP

@dataclass
class Recipe:
```

```
aromatics: set[Ingredient]
broth: Broth
vegetables: set[Ingredient]
meats: set[Ingredient]
starches: set[Ingredient]
garnishes: set[Ingredient]
time_to_cook: datetime.timedelta
```

I was able to create a `Recipe` out of `Ingredient`, `Broth`, and `ImperialMeasure` objects. All of these concepts could have been embedded in `Recipe` itself, but this would have make reuse tougher (if somebody wanted to use an `ImperialMeasure`, it'd be confusing to depend on `Recipe` to do so.) By keeping each of these types disparate, I allow future maintainers to build new types, such as non–soup-related concepts, without needing to find ways to tease apart dependencies.

This was an example of *type composition*, where I created discrete types that could be mixed and matched in new ways. In this chapter, I'm going to focus on other common composition types in Python, such as composing functionality, functions, and algorithms. Take, for instance, the simple menu at a sandwich shop, like the one in Figure 17-1.

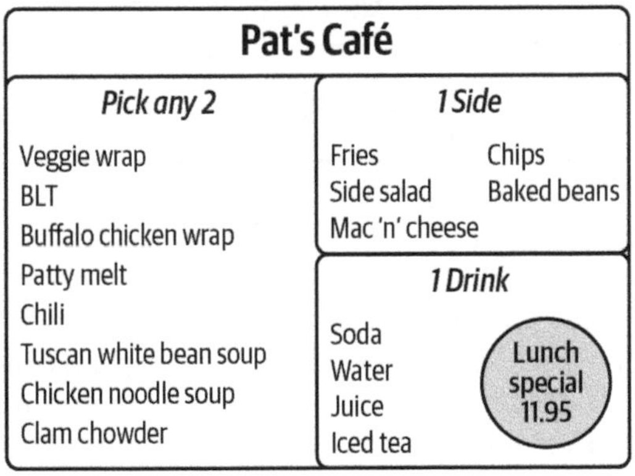

Pat's Café

Pick any 2	1 Side
Veggie wrap	Fries Chips
BLT	Side salad Baked beans
Buffalo chicken wrap	Mac 'n' cheese

	1 Drink
Patty melt	
Chili	Soda
Tuscan white bean soup	Water
Chicken noodle soup	Juice
Clam chowder	Iced tea

Lunch special 11.95

Figure 17-1. A fictional menu

This menu is another example of composability. Diners pick two entries off the first part of the menu, plus a side and a drink. They *compose* different parts of the menu to get the exact lunch they want. If this menu were not composable, you would have to list every single option to represent all the combinations possible (and with 1,120 options, that's a menu that puts most restaurants to shame). This is not tractable for any restaurant to handle; it's easier to break the menu into parts that can be pieced together.

I want you to think about your code in the same way. Code doesn't become composable just by existing; you have to actively design with composability in mind. You want to look at the classes, functions, and data types that you create and ask how you can write them so that future developers can reuse them.

Consider an automated kitchen, creatively named AutoKitchen, that serves as the backbone of Pat's Café. It is a fully automated system that is able to make any dish on the menu. I want it to be easy to add new dishes to this system; Pat's Café boasts an ever-changing menu, and the developers are tired of having to spend a lot of time modifying large chunks of the system each time. The design of AutoKitchen is shown in Figure 17-2.

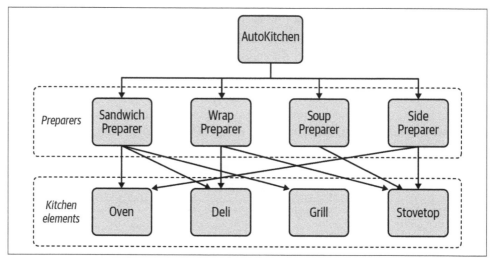

Figure 17-2. AutoKitchen design

This design is fairly straightforward. The AutoKitchen depends on various preparation mechanisms, known as *preparers*. Each preparer depends on kitchen elements to turn ingredients into a dish component (such as turning ground beef into a cooked hamburger). Kitchen elements, such as the oven or grill, are issued commands to cook various ingredients; they have no knowledge of the specific ingredients being used or the resulting dish component. Figure 17-3 illustrates what a specific preparer might look like.

This design is extensible, which is a good thing. Adding a new sandwich type is simple, because I don't have to modify any of the existing sandwich code. However, this is not very composable. If I wanted to take dish components and reuse them for new dishes (such as cooking bacon for a BLT wrap, or cooking hamburgers for cheeseburger soup), I would have to bring the entire BLT Maker or Patty Melt Maker with me. If I do that, I'd have to take a Bread Maker and Database with me as well. This is what I want to avoid.

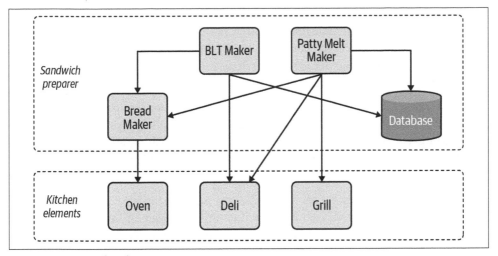

Figure 17-3. Sandwich Preparer

Now, I want to introduce a new soup: potato, leek, and bacon. The Soup Preparer already knows how to handle leeks and potatoes from other soups; I now want the Soup Preparer to know how to make bacon. While modifying Soup Preparer, I have a few options: introduce a dependency on a BLT Maker, write my own bacon-handling code, or find a way to reuse just the bacon-handling part separately from the BLT Maker.

The first option has issues: if I depend on a BLT Maker, I need to depend on all of its physical dependencies, such as a Bread Maker. A Soup Preparer might not want all that baggage. The second option is not great either, because now I have duplication of bacon handling in my codebase (and once you have two, don't be surprised if a third pops up eventually). The only good option is to find a way to split the bacon making from the BLT Maker.

However, code doesn't become reusable just because you wish it to be (it would be nice, though). You have to consciously design your code to be reusable. You need to make it small, discrete, and mostly independent from business logic to make it composable. And to do that, you need to separate policies from mechanisms.

Policy Versus Mechanisms

Policies are your business logic, or the code directly responsible for solving your business needs. The *mechanisms* are the pieces of code that provide *how* you will enact the policies. In the previous example, the policies of the system are the specific recipes. In contrast, *how* it makes those recipes are the mechanisms.

When you focus on making code composable, you need to separate the policies from the mechanisms. The mechanisms are often the thing you want to reuse; it doesn't help when they are linked together with a policy. It's this reason why a `Soup Preparer` depending on a `BLT Maker` doesn't make sense. You end up with policy depending on a completely separate and unrelated policy.

When you link two unrelated policies, you start creating a dependency that becomes tough to break later on. As you link more and more policies, you create spaghetti code. You get a tangled mess of dependencies, and extricating any one dependency becomes problematic. This is why you need to be cognizant of which parts of your codebase are policies and which are mechanisms.

A great example of policy versus mechanisms is the `logging` module (*https://oreil.ly/ xNhjh*) in Python. The policy outlines what you need logged and where to log it; the mechanisms are what let you set log levels, filter log messages, and format logs.

Mechanically, any module can call logging methods:

```
logging.basicConfig(format='%(levelname)s:%(message)s', level=logging.DEBUG)
logger.warning("Family did not match any restaurants: Lookup code A1503")
```

The `logging` module does not care what it is logging or about the format of the log message. The `logging` module simply provides the *how* of logging. It's up to any consuming application to define the policies, or the *what*, which outline what needs to get logged. Separating the policy from the mechanism makes the `logging` module reusable. You can easily extend your codebase's functionality without pulling along heaps of baggage. This is the model you should strive for in the mechanisms present in your codebase.

Composability in the Wild

Once you start thinking about separating policies and mechanisms, you will start to see composability patterns show up in your everyday development life.

Consider a Unix-style command line. Rather than defining new applications, the command line gives you small discrete programs that you can compose together through piping.

Instead of writing a hyper-specialized program, such as parsing a log to get the error code, sorted by `datetime`, I could write the following on the command line:

```
grep -i "ERROR" log.txt | cut 3,5 | sort -r
```

Another example is continuous integration pipelines with third-party integrations (such as GitHub Actions or Travis CI). Developers want to run a series of checks and actions as part of their check-in process; many of these checks are provided by third-party entities (such as security scanners or pushing to a container registry). Developers don't have to know the internals of how this is done. Instead, they define policies

---

that tell these third-party integrations what to do—policies such as which folder should be scanned or which tags to apply in the container registry. Developers aren't bogged down in the *how*; they reuse these integrations by composing them into their pipeline and move on with their work.

In the previous café example, I can change the code's architecture to split out the mechanisms. My goal is to design a system such that making any dish component is standalone and I can compose these components together to create a recipe. This will allow me to reuse code across systems and have flexibility in creating new recipes. Figure 17-4 demonstrates a more composable architecture (note that I have elided some systems in the interest of space).

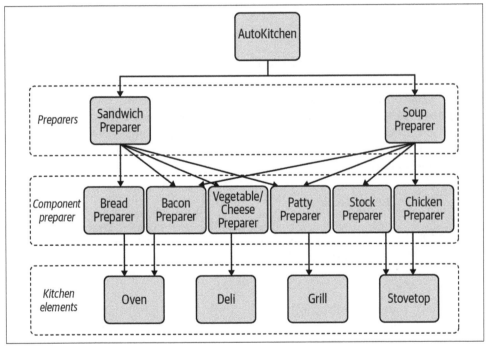

Figure 17-4. Composable architecture

By breaking out specific preparers into their own systems, I have both extensibility and composability. Not only is it easy to extend new dishes such as a new sandwich, but it becomes easy for new connections to be defined, such as letting the Soup Pre parer reuse the bacon preparation code.

When your mechanisms are split out like this, you find that writing your policies becomes much simpler. With none of the mechanisms tied to the policy, you can start to write *declaratively*, or in a style where you simply make declarations about what to do. Take a look at the following potato, leek, and bacon soup definition:

```
import bacon_preparer
import veg_cheese_preparer

def make_potato_leek_and_bacon_soup():
    bacon = bacon_preparer.make_bacon(slices=2)
    potatoes = veg_cheese_preparer.cube_potatoes(grams=300)
    leeks = veg_cheese_preparer.slice(ingredient=Vegetable.LEEKS, grams=250)

    chopped_bacon = chop(bacon)

    # the following methods are provided by soup preparer
    add_chicken_stock()
    add(potatoes)
    add(leeks)
    cook_for(minutes=30)
    blend()
    garnish(chopped_bacon)
    garnish(Garnish.BLACK_PEPPER)
```

By focusing solely on what a recipe is in code, I don't have to get bogged down with extraneous details such as how to make bacon or cube potatoes. I composed the Bacon Preparer and Vegetable/Cheese Preparer together with the Soup Preparer to define the new recipe. If a new soup (or any other dish) comes in tomorrow, it will be just as easy to define it as a linear set of instructions. Policies will change much more often than your mechanisms; make them easy to add, modify, or delete to meet your business needs.

Discussion Topic

What parts of your codebase have been easy to reuse? Which have been difficult? Have you wanted to reuse the policies or the mechanisms of the code? Discuss strategies for making your code more composable and reusable.

Try to make your mechanisms composable if you foresee a reason for reuse. You will accelerate development in the future because developers will be able to truly reuse your code with very few strings attached. You are increasing flexibility and reusability, which will make the code more maintainable.

There is a cost attached to composability, though. You reduce readability by spreading out functionality across more files, and you introduce more moving parts, which means a greater chance of a change having a negative impact. Look for opportunities to introduce composability, but beware making your code *too* flexible, requiring developers to explore entire codebases just to find out how to code simple workflows.

Composing on a Smaller Scale

The AutoKitchen example showed you how to compose different modules and sub-systems, but you can also apply composability principles at a smaller scale. You can write functions and algorithms to be composable, allowing you to build new code with ease.

Composing Functions

A lot of this book focuses on OOP principles (such as SOLID and class-based designs), but it's important to learn from other software paradigms as well. An increasingly popular paradigm is *functional programming* (FP). Where OOP's first-class citizens are objects, FP focuses on *pure functions*. A pure function is a function whose output is solely derived from the inputs. Given a pure function and a set of input arguments, it will always return the same output, regardless of any global state or environment change.

What makes functional programming so attractive is that pure functions are much easier to compose than functions laden with side effects. A *side effect* is anything a function does that is outside of its returned values, such as logging a message, making a network call, or mutating variables. By removing side effects from your functions, you make them easier to reuse. There are no hidden dependencies or surprising outcomes; the entire function is dependent on the input data, and the only observable effect is the data that is returned.

However, when you attempt to reuse code, you must pull in all of that code's physical dependencies as well (and provide logical dependencies at runtime if needed). With pure functions, you don't have any physical dependencies outside of a function call graph. You don't need to pull in extra objects with complicated setup or global variables. FP encourages developers to write short, single-purpose functions that are inherently composable.

Developers get used to treating functions just like any other variable. They create *higher-order* functions, which are functions that take other functions as arguments, or functions that return other functions as a return value. The simplest example is something that takes a function and calls it twice:

```
from typing import Callable
def do_twice(func: Callable, *args, **kwargs):
    func(*args, **kwargs)
    func(*args, **kwargs)
```

This isn't a very exciting example, but it opens the door for some very interesting ways of composing functions. In fact, there is an entire Python module dedicated to higher-order functions: functools. Most of functools, as well as any function composition you write, will be in the form of decorators.

Decorators

Decorators are functions that take another function and *wrap* it, or specify behavior that must execute before the function executes. It provides a way for you to compose functions together without requiring the function bodies to know about each other.

Decorators are one of the main ways of wrapping functions in Python. I can rewrite the do_twice function into a more generic repeat function like such:

```python
def repeat(times: int = 1) -> Callable:
    ''' this is a function that calls the wrapped function
        a specified number of times
    '''
    def _repeat(func: Callable):
        @functools.wraps(func)
        def _wrapper(*args, **kwargs):
            for _ in range(times):
                func(*args, **kwargs)
        return _wrapper
    return _repeat

@repeat(times=3)
def say_hello():
    print("Hello")

say_hello()
>>> "Hello"
"Hello"
"Hello"
```

Once again, I've separated the policy (saying hello repeatedly) from the mechanisms (actually repeating the function calls). That mechanism is something I can use throughout other codebases without any repercussions. I can apply this decorator to all sorts of functions in my codebase, such as making two hamburger patties at once for a double cheeseburger or mass-producing specific orders for a catering event.

Of course, decorators can do so much more than simply repeating a function invocation. One of my favorite decorators comes from the backoff library (*https://oreil.ly/ 4V6Ro*). backoff helps you define *retry logic*, or the actions you take to retry nondeterministic parts of your code. Consider the AutoKitchen from earlier needing to save data in a database. It will save orders taken, current inventory levels, and time spent making each dish.

At its simplest, the code would look like this:

```python
# setting properties of self.*_db objects will
# update data in the database
def on_dish_ordered(dish: Dish):
    dish_db[dish].count += 1

def save_inventory_counts(inventory):
```

```
    for ingredient in inventory:
        inventory_db[ingredient.name] = ingredient.count

def log_time_per_dish(dish: Dish, number_of_seconds: int):
    dish_db[dish].time_spent.append(number_of_seconds)
```

Whenever you work with a database (or any other I/O request), you always need to be prepared for errors. The database may be down, the network might be out, there might be a conflict with the data you are entering, or any other error might pop up. You can't always rely on this code executing without errors. The business doesn't want the code to give up on the first error; these operations should retry a set number of times or for a certain time period before giving up.

I can use the `backoff.on_exception` to specify that these functions should be retried if they throw an exception:

```
import backoff
import requests
from autokitchen.database import OperationException
# setting properties of self.*_db objects will
# update data in the database
@backoff.on_exception(backoff.expo,
                      OperationException,
                      max_tries=5)
def on_dish_ordered(dish: Dish):
    self.dish_db[dish].count += 1

@backoff.on_exception(backoff.expo,
                      OperationException,
                      max_tries=5)
@backoff.on_exception(backoff.expo,
                      requests.exceptions.HTTPError,
                      max_time=60)
def save_inventory_counts(inventory):
    for ingredient in inventory:
        self.inventory_db[ingredient.name] = ingredient.count

@backoff.on_exception(backoff.expo,
                      OperationException,
                      max_time=60)
def log_time_per_dish(dish: Dish, number_of_seconds: int):
    self.dish_db[dish].time_spent.append(number_of_seconds)
```

Through the use of decorators, I am able to modify behavior without messing with the function body. Each function will now back off exponentially (take longer between each retry) when specific exceptions are raised. Each function also has its own conditions for how much time to take or how many times to retry before giving up completely. I've defined the policy in this code, but left the actual *how* to do it, the mechanisms, abstracted away in the `backoff` library.

Take special note of the `save_inventory_counts` function:

```
@backoff.on_exception(backoff.expo,
                       OperationException,
                       max_tries=5)
@backoff.on_exception(backoff.expo,
                       requests.exceptions.HTTPError,
                       max_time=60)
def save_inventory_counts(inventory):
    # ...
```

I have two decorators defined here. In this case, I'll retry up to five times on an `Opera tionException` or up to 60 seconds for a `requests.exceptions.HTTPError`. This is composability at work; I can mix'n'match completely separate `backoff` decorators to define the policies however I want.

Contrast this with writing the mechanisms directly into the function:

```
def save_inventory_counts(inventory):
    retry = True
    retry_counter = 0
    time_to_sleep = 1
    while retry:
        try:
            for ingredient in inventory:
                self.inventory_db[ingredient.name] = ingredient.count
        except OperationException:
            retry_counter += 1
            if retry_counter == 5:
                retry = False
        except requests.exception.HTTPError:
            time.sleep(time_to_sleep)
            time_to_sleep *= 2
            if time_to_sleep > 60:
                retry = False
```

The amount of code needed to handle retry mechanisms ends up obscuring the actual intent of the function. It is difficult to ascertain what this function is doing at a quick glance. Furthermore, you would need to write similar retry logic into every function that needs to handle nondeterministic operations. It is far easier to compose decorators to define your business needs, and avoid tedious repetition throughout your code.

`backoff` is not the only useful decorator out there. There is a bevy of composable decorators that you can use to simplify your code, such as `functools.lru_cache` for saving function results, `click.command` from the `click` library (*https://oreil.ly/FlBcj*) for command-line applications, or `timeout_decorator.timeout` from the `timeout_deco rator` library (*https://oreil.ly/H5FcA*) for limiting execution time of functions. Don't be afraid to write your own decorators either. Find areas of your code that have similar program structure, and look for ways to abstract the mechanisms away from the policies.

Composing Algorithms

Functions are not the only small-scale composition you can make; you also can compose *algorithms*. Algorithms are a description of defined steps needed to solve a problem, like sorting a collection or diffing snippets of text. To make an algorithm composable, you again need to divorce the policies from the mechanisms.

Consider the meal recommendation for a café meal in the last section. Suppose the algorithm is as follows:

```
Recommendation Algorithm #1

Look at all daily specials
Sort based on number of matching surplus ingredients
Select the meals with the highest number of surplus ingredients
Sort by proximity to last meal ordered
    (proximity is defined by number of ingredients that match)
Take only results that are above 75% proximity
Return up to top 3 results
```

If I wrote this all out with `for` loops, it might look like this:

```python
def recommend_meal(last_meal: Meal,
                   specials: list[Meal],
                   surplus: list[Ingredient]) -> list[Meal]:
    highest_proximity = 0
    for special in specials:
        if (proximity := get_proximity(special, surplus)) > highest_proximity:
            highest_proximity = proximity

    grouped_by_surplus_matching = []
    for special in specials:
        if get_proximity(special, surplus) == highest_proximity:
            grouped_by_surplus_matching.append(special)

    filtered_meals = []
    for meal in grouped_by_surplus_matching:
        if get_proximity(meal, last_meal) > .75:
            filtered_meals.append(meal)

    sorted_meals = sorted(filtered_meals,
                          key=lambda meal: get_proximity(meal, last_meal),
                          reverse=True)

    return sorted_meals[:3]
```

It's not the prettiest code. If I didn't list out the steps in text beforehand, it would take a little longer to understand the code and make sure it is bug free. Now, suppose a developer comes to you and tells you that not enough customers are picking recommendations and they want to try out a different algorithm. The new algorithm goes like this:

```
Recommendation Algorithm #2

Look at all meals available
Sort based on proximity to last meal
Select the meals with the highest proximity
Sort the meals by number of surplus ingredients
Take only results that are a special or have more than 3 surplus ingredients
Return up to top 5 results
```

The catch is that this developer wants to A/B test these algorithms (and any other algorithm they come up with). With A/B testing, they want 75% of customers to be presented recommendations from the first algorithm and 25% of customers from the second. That way, they can measure how well the new algorithm works in relation to the old. This means your codebase has to support both algorithms (and be flexible to support new algorithms in the future). You don't want to see your codebase littered with ugly recommendation algorithm methods.

You need to apply composability principles to the algorithm itself. Copy-pasting the for loop code snippet and tweaking it is not a viable answer. To solve this, you once again need to separate your policies and mechanisms. This will help you break down the problem and improve the codebase.

Your policy this time is the actual details of the algorithm: what you're sorting, how you're filtering, and what you're ultimately selecting. The mechanisms are the iteration patterns that describe how we're shaping the data. In fact, I've already used an iteration mechanism in my code above: sorting. Instead of manually sorting (and forcing readers to understand what I'm doing), I used the `sorted` method. I indicated what I want sorted and in the key to sort by, but I really don't care (nor do I expect my readers to care) about the actual sorting algorithm.

If I were to compare the two algorithms, I can break down the mechanisms into the following (I'll mark policies with <angle brackets>):

```
Look at <a list of meals>
Sort based on <initial sorting criteria>
Select the meals with the <grouping criteria>
Sort the meals by <secondary sorting criteria>
Take top results that match <selection criteria>
Return up to top <number> results
```

The `itertools` module (*https://oreil.ly/NZCCG*) is a fantastic source of composable algorithms, all centered on iteration. It serves as a great example of what you can do when you create abstract mechanisms.

With that in mind, and the help of the `itertools` module, I'll take another crack at writing the recommendation algorithm:

```python
import itertools
def recommend_meal(policy: RecommendationPolicy) -> list[Meal]:
    meals = policy.meals
    sorted_meals = sorted(meals, key=policy.initial_sorting_criteria,
                          reverse=True)
    grouped_meals = itertools.groupby(sorted_meals, key=policy.grouping_criteria)
    _, top_grouped = next(grouped_meals)
    secondary_sorted = sorted(top_grouped, key=policy.secondary_sorting_criteria,
                              reverse=True)
    candidates = itertools.takewhile(policy.selection_criteria, secondary_sorted)
    return list(candidates)[:policy.desired_number_of_recommendations]
```

Then, to use this with an algorithm, I do the following:

```python
# I've used named functions to increase readability in the following example
# instead of lambda functions
recommend_meal(RecommendationPolicy(
    meals=get_specials(),
    initial_sorting_criteria=get_proximity_to_surplus_ingredients,
    grouping_criteria=get_proximity_to_surplus_ingredients,
    secondary_sorting_criteria=get_proximity_to_last_meal,
    selection_criteria=proximity_greater_than_75_percent,
    desired_number_of_recommendations=3)
)
```

Think of how nice it would be to be able to tweak the algorithm on the fly here. I created a different `RecommendationPolicy` and passed it into `recommend_meal`. By separating the algorithm's policy from the mechanism, I've provided a number of benefits. I've made the code easier to read, easier to extend, and more flexible.

Closing Thoughts

Composable code is reusable code. When you build small, discrete units of work, you'll find that they are easy to introduce into new contexts or programs. To make your code composable, focus on separating your policies and your mechanisms. It doesn't matter if you're working with subsystems, algorithms, or even functions. You will find that your mechanisms benefit from greater reuse, and policies become easier to modify. Your system's robustness will greatly improve as you identify composable code.

In the next chapter, you're going to learn how to apply extensibility and composability at an architectural level with event-based architectures. Event-based architectures help you decouple your code into publishers and consumers of information. They provide a way for you to minimize dependencies while still retaining extensibility.

## CHAPTER 18

Event-Driven Architecture

Extensibility is important at every level of your codebase. At the code level, you employ extensibility to make your functions and classes flexible. At the abstract level, you utilize the same principles in your codebase's architecture. *Architecture* is the set of high-level guidelines and constraints that shape how you design software. It is the vision that influences all developers, past, present, and future. This chapter, as well as the next one, are going to show two examples of how architectural examples improve maintability. Everything you've learned so far in this part of the book applies: good architecture promotes extensibility, manages dependencies well, and fosters composability.

In this chapter, you will learn about event-driven architecture. *Event-driven architecture* revolves around events, or notifications in your system. It is a fantastic way to decouple different parts of your codebase, as well as extend your system for new functionality or performance. Event-driven architectures allow you to introduce new changes easily with minimal impact. First, I want to talk about the flexibility that event-driven architectures provide. Then, I'll cover two separate variations of event-driven architectures: simple events and streaming events. While they are similar, you will use them in slightly different scenarios.

How It Works

When you focus on event-driven architectures, you are revolving around reactions to stimuli. You deal with reactions to simuli all the time, whether it's pulling a casserole out of the oven or picking up a delivery from your front door after a phone notification. In an event-driven architecture, you architect your code to represent this model. Your stimulus is some *producer* of events. A *consumer* of these events is the reaction to that stimulus. An event is just a transmission of information from a producer to a consumer. Table 18-1 shows some common producer–consumer pairs.

Table 18-1. Everyday events and their consumers

Producer	Consumer
Kitchen timer going off	Chef retrieves a casserole from the oven
Cook ringing a bell when a dish is done	Server picks it up and serves it
Alarm clock going off	Late sleeper wakes up
A last call for boarding at an airport	Rushing family rushes, trying to make their connection

You actually deal with producers and consumers every time you program. Any function that returns a value is a producer, and any piece of code that uses that returned value is a consumer. Observe:

```
def complete_order(order: Order):
    package_order(order)
    notify_customer_that_order_is_done(order)
    notify_restaurant_that_order_is_done(order)
```

In this case, `complete_order` is *producing* information in the form of a completed order. Based on the function names, the customer and the restaurant are *consuming* the fact that an order is done. There is a direct linkage where the producer notifies the consumer. Event-driven architectures aim to sever this physical dependency. The goal is to decouple producers and consumers. Producers do not know about the consumers, and consumers do not know about the producers. This is what drives the flexibility of an event-driven architecture.

With this decoupling, it becomes incredibly easy to add onto your system. If you need new consumers, you can add them without ever touching the producer. If you need different producers, you can add them without ever touching the consumers. This bidirectional extensibility allows you to substantially change multiple parts of your codebase in isolation.

What's happening behind the scenes is quite ingenious. Instead of any dependencies between producer and consumer, they both depend on a transport mechanism, as shown in Figure 18-1. A *transport mechanism* is simply the way that two pieces of code pass data back and forth.

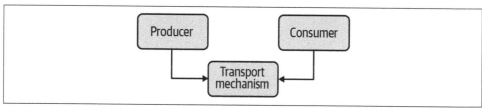

Figure 18-1. Producer–consumer relationship

Drawbacks

Because the producer and consumer depend on a transport mechanism, they have to agree on the message format. In most event-driven architectures, both the producer and consumer agree on a common identifier and message format. This does create a *logical* dependency between the two but not a physical one. If either party changes the identifier or message format in an incompatible way, the scheme breaks down. And like most logical dependencies, it is difficult to link the dependencies together through inspection. Consult Chapter 16 to learn more about how to mitigate these problems.

Because of this separation of code, your typechecker will not be much help when things go wrong. If a consumer starts depending on the wrong event type, the typechecker will not flag it. Be extra careful when changing the type of a producer or consumer, because you will have to update all the other producers–consumers to match.

Event-driven architectures can make debugging harder. When stepping through code in a debugger, you will get to the code that produces an event, but when you step into the transport mechanism, you often are stepping into third-party code. In the worst case, the code that actually transports your events may be running in a different process, or even on a different machine. You may need multiple debuggers active (one per process or system) to properly debug event-driven architectures.

Finally, error handling becomes a little more difficult when using event-driven architectures. Most producers are decoupled from their consumers; when a consumer throws an exception or returns an error, it's not always easy to handle it from the producer side.

As a thought experiment, consider what would happen if a producer produced an event and five consumers consumed it. If the third consumer that was notified threw an exception, what should happen? Should the other consumers get the exception, or should the execution stop in its tracks? Should the producer know about any error conditions, or should the errors get swallowed up? If the producer receives an exception, what happens if different consumers produce different exceptions? There is no one right answer to all of these questions; consult the tools you're using for event-driven architectures to better understand what happens in these cases.

Despite these drawbacks, event-driven architectures are worthwhile in situations where you need to give your system much-needed flexibility. Future maintainers can replace your producers or consumers with minimal impact. They can bring in new producers and consumers to create new functionality. They can quickly integrate with external systems, opening the door for new partnerships. And best of all, they are working with small, modular systems that are easy to test in isolation and easy to understand.

Simple Events

The simplest case for event-oriented architectures is dealing with *simple events* such as acting or alerting you when certain conditions change. Your producer of information is the one sending the event, and your consumer receives and acts upon the event. There are two typical ways of implementing this: with or without a message broker.

Using a Message Broker

A message broker is a specific piece of code that acts as a transport of data. Producers will publish data, known as a message, to a specific *topic* on the message broker. The topic is simply a unique identifier, such as a string. It could be something simple, like "orders," or complex, like "sandwich order is finished." It's just a namespace that distinguishes one message channel from another. Consumers use the same identifier to *subscribe* to a topic. The message broker then sends the message to all consumers subscribed to the topic. This type of system is also known as *publisher/subscriber*, or pub/sub for short. Figure 18-2 shows a hypothetical pub/sub architecture.

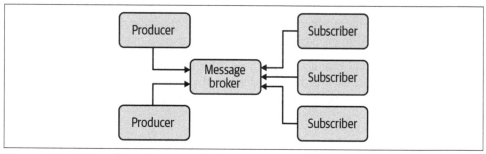

Figure 18-2. A hypothetical message broker–based architecture

For this chapter, I will design the notification system for an automated drone delivery service for restaurants. When a customer order is cooked, the drone system kicks into action, picks up the order, and delivers the meal to the correct address. There are five notifications that happen in this system, and I've broken them down into producer–consumer in Table 18-2.

Table 18-2. Producers and consumers in the automated drone delivery system

Producer	Consumer
Meal has finished cooking	Drone is notified for pickup
Meal has finished cooking	Customer is notified that the meal is cooked
Drone is en route	Customer is notified about an ETA
Drone has delivered meal	Customer is notified about delivery
Drone has delivered meal	Restaurant is notified about delivery

I don't want any of these systems to directly know about one another, as the code handling customers, drones, and restaurants should remain independent (they are maintained by separate teams and I want to keep physical dependencies low).

First, I will define the topics that exist in the system: a meal has finished cooking, the drone is en route, and the order is delivered.

For this example, I will use the Python library PyPubSub (*https://oreil.ly/8xLj7*), which is a publish-subscribe API used in single-process applications. To use it, you need to set up code to subscribe to a topic and other code to publish to the topic. First, you need to install pypubsub:

```
pip install pypubsub
```

Then, to subscribe to the topic, you specify the topic and the function you want to be called:

```
from pubsub import pub

def notify_customer_that_meal_is_done(order: Order):
    # ... snip ...

pub.subscribe(notify_customer_that_meal_is_done, "meal-done")
```

Then to publish to this topic, you do the following:

```
from pubsub import pub

def complete_order(order: Order):
    packge_order(order)
    pub.publish("meal-done", order)
```

 Subscribers operate in the same thread as the publisher, which means that any blocking I/O, such as waiting on a socket to be read, will block the publisher. This will affect all other subscribers and should be avoided.

These two pieces of code have no knowledge of each other; all they depend upon is the PyPubSub library as well as agreeing on the topic/message data. This makes it incredibly easy to add new subscribers:

```
from pubsub import pub

def schedule_pick_up_for_meal(order: Order):
    '''Schedule a drone pick-up'''
    # ... snip ...

pub.subscribe(schedule_pick_up_for_meal, "meal-done")
```

You can't get much more extensible. By defining topics that exist within the system, you can create new producers or consumers with the utmost ease. As your system needs to grow, you extend it by interacting with the existing messaging system.

PyPubSub also comes with a few options to help with debugging. You can add audit operations by adding your own functionality for things like new topics being created or a message being sent. You can add error handlers for any subscriber exception being thrown. You can also set up subscribers for *all* topics at once. If you would like to learn more about any of these features, or any other piece of functionality in PyPubSub, check out the PyPubSub documentation (*https://pypubsub.readthedocs.io*).

 PyPubSub is meant for single-process applications; you cannot publish to code running in other processes or systems. Other applications can be used to provide this functionality, such as Kafka (*https://kafka.apache.org*), Redis (*https://redis.io*), or RabbitMQ (*https://www.rabbitmq.com*). Check out each of these tool's documentation to learn how to use them in Python.

The Observer Pattern

If you don't want to use a message broker, you can choose to implement the Observer Pattern.[1] With the Observer Pattern, your producer contains of a list of *observers*: the consumers in this scenario. The Observer Pattern does not need a separate library to act as a message broker.

To avoid directly linking producers and consumers, you need to keep the knowledge of observers *generic*. In other words, keep any specific knowledge about the observers abstracted away. I will do this by just using functions (type annotated as a `Callable`). Here is how I would rewrite the previous example to use an Observer Pattern:

```
def complete_order(order: Order, observers: list[Callable[Order]]):
    package_order(order)
    for observer_func in observers:
        observer(order)
```

In this case, the producer only knows about a list of functions to call to notify. To add new observers, you just need to add them to the list passed in as an argument. Furthermore, since this is just function calls, your typechecker will be able to detect when a producer or its observers change in an incompatible way, which is a huge benefit over the message broker paradigm. It is also easier to debug, as you don't need to step through third-party message broker code in your debugger.

---

1 The Observer Pattern is first described in *Design Patterns: Elements of Reusable Object-Oriented Software* by Erich Gamma, Richard Helm, Ralph Johnson, and John Vlissides (Addison-Wesley Professional). This book is colloquially known as the "Gang of Four (GoF)" book.

Patterns Without Classes

The example in this chapter is not the typical representation of the Observer Pattern. The traditional implementation of this design pattern (as well as with many others) is represented in a very object-oriented fashion with classes, subclasses, inheritance, and interfaces. For example, the original Observer Pattern might be expressed in this way in Python:

```python
from typing import Any
class Subscriber:
    def notify(data: Any):
        raise NotImplementedError()

class Publisher:
    def __init__(self):
        self.subscribers = []

    def add_subscriber(self, sub: Subscriber):
        self.subscribers.append(sub)

    def notify_subscribers(self, data: Any):
        for subscriber in subscribers:
            subscriber.notify(data)
```

Classes that needed to publish or subscribe would then inherit from the appropriate base class. This is useful from a reuse standpoint, but it can be cumbersome to introduce classes when the example with functions is much simpler.

As such, design patterns have earned some criticism around the number of boilerplate classes and interfaces needed to implement them. As the development community has evolved, public opinion has soured toward many patterns because of their association with class-/interface-heavy code that was described as "object-oriented" in the mid 1990s and 2000s.

However, do not throw away the concept of many design patterns because of how the example was originally presented. There have been many iterations on these patterns that simplify implementation. Most patterns don't focus on the state management aspect of object-oriented code but on decoupling dependencies, and are still beneficial to larger system design.

The Observer Pattern above does have some drawbacks. First, you are a bit more sensitive to errors that crop up. If the observer throws an exception, the producer needs to be able to handle that directly (or use a helper function or class to handle the notification wrapped in a try...except). Second, the linking of producer to observer is more direct than in the message broker paradigm. In a message broker paradigm, the publisher and subscriber can become connected regardless of where they live in the codebase.

In contrast, the Observer Pattern requires the caller of the notification (in the previous case, this was `complete_order`) to know about the observers. If the caller doesn't know directly about the observers, then its caller needs to pass in the observers. This can continue all the way up the call stack until you are in a piece of code that directly knows about the observers. This can pollute a lot your function calls with extra parameters if there is a large gap between what knows about the observers and the actual code issuing the notification. If you find yourself passing observers through multiple functions to get to a producer deep in the call stack, consider using a message broker instead.

If you would like to go more in-depth into event-driven architectures with simple events, I recommend the book *Architecture Patterns with Python* (*https://oreil.ly/ JPpdr*) by Harry Percival and Bob Gregory (O'Reilly); its Part II is all about event-driven architecture.

Discussion Topic

How would event-driven architecture improve the decoupling within your codebase? Would the Observer Pattern or a message broker be more suitable for your needs?

Streaming Events

In the preceding section, simple events were each represented as a discrete event that happened when a certain condition was fulfilled. Message brokers and the Observer Pattern are great ways to handle simple events. However, some systems deal with a never-ending series of events. The events flow into the system as a continuous series of data known as a stream. Think about the drone systems described in the last section. Consider all the data that comes from each drone. There might be location data, battery levels, current speed, wind data, weather data, and current weight carried. This data will be coming in at regular intervals, and you need a way to handle it.

In these sorts of use cases, you don't want to build all the boilerplate of pub/sub or observers; you want an architecture that matches your use case. You need a programming model that centers on events and defines workflows for handling every single event. Enter reactive programming.

Reactive programming is an architectural style that revolves around streams of events. You define data sources as producers of these streams, and then link together multiple observers. Each observer is notified whenever there is a change in data and defines a series of operations for handling the data stream. The reactive programming style was popularized by ReactiveX (*http://reactivex.io*). In this section, I'll use the Python implementation of ReactiveX: RxPY.

I will install RxPy with `pip`:

```
pip install rx
```

From there, I need to define a stream of data. In RxPY parlance, this is known as an *observable*. For example purposes, I'll use a single hard-coded observable, but in practice, you will generate multiple observables from real data.

```
import rx
# Each one of these is simulating an independent real-world event streaming in
observable = rx.of(
    LocationData(x=3, y=12, z=40),
    BatteryLevel(percent=95),
    BatteryLevel(percent=94),
    WindData(speed=15, direction=Direction.NORTH),
    # ... snip 100s of events
    BatteryLevel(percent=72),
    CurrentWeight(grams=300)
)
```

This observable is generated from a list of events of different types for the drone data.

I next need to define what to do to process each event. Once I have an observable, observers can subscribe to it, in a similar manner to the pub/sub mechanism:

```
def handle_drone_data(value):
    # ... snip handle drone data ...

observable.subscribe(handle_drone_data)
```

This doesn't look too different from a normal pub/sub idiom.

The real magic comes with *pipable* operators. RxPY allows you to *pipe*, or chain, operations together to produce a pipeline of filters, transformations, and calculations. For instance, I can write an operator pipeline with `rx.pipe` to grab the average weight the drone has carried:

```
import rx.operators

get_average_weight = observable.pipe(
    rx.operators.filter(lambda data: isinstance(data, CurrentWeight)),
    rx.operators.map(lambda cw: cw.grams),
    rx.operators.average()
)

# save_average_weight does something with the final data
# (e.g. save to database, print to screen, etc.)
get_average_weight.subscribe(save_average_weight)
```

Similarly, I could write a pipeline chain that tracks the drone's maximum altitude once it's left the restaurant:

```
get_max_altitude = observable.pipe(
    rx.operators.skip_while(is_close_to_restaurant),
    rx.operators.filter(lambda data: isinstance(data, LocationData)),
    rx.operators.map(lambda loc: loc.z),
    rx.operators.max()
)

# save max altitude does something with the final data
# (e.g. save to database, print to screen, etc)
get_max_altitude.subscribe(save_max_altitude)
```

 A *lambda function* is just an inline function without a name. It is often used for functions that are only used once where you don't want to place the definition of the function too far away from its use.

This is our old friend *composability* (as seen in Chapter 17) coming to our aid. I can compose different operators however I want to produce a datastream that matches my use case. RxPY has support for over one hundred built-in operators, as well as a framework for defining your own operators. You can even compose the results from one pipe into a new stream of events that other parts of the program can observe. This composability, paired with the decoupled nature of event subscription, gives you a large amount of flexibility in writing code. Furthermore, reactive programming encourages immutability, which greatly decreases the chance of bugs. You can hook up new pipes, compose operators together, handle data asynchronously, and more with a reactive framework like RxPY.

It also becomes easy to debug in isolation. While you can't easily step through RxPY with a debugger (you'll end up in a lot of complicated code related to operations and observables), you can instead step into the functions that you pass to operators. Testing is a breeze too. Since all the functions are meant to be immutable, you can test any of them on their own. You end up with a lot of small, single-purpose functions that are easy to understand.

This type of model excels in systems that revolve around streams of data, such as data pipelines and extract, transform, load (ETL) systems. It is also incredibly useful in applications dominated by reactions to I/O events, such as server applications and GUI applications. If reactive programming fits your domain model, I encourage you to read the RxPY documentation (*https://rxpy.readthedocs.io/en/latest*). If you'd like more structured learning, I recommend the video course *Reactive Python for Data Science* (*https://oreil.ly/Kr9At*) or the book *Hands-On Reactive Programming with*

Python: Event-Driven Development Unraveled with RxPY (*https://oreil.ly/JCuf6*) by Romain Picard (O'Reilly).

Closing Thoughts

Event-driven architectures are incredibly powerful. An event-driven architecture allows you to separate producers and consumers of information. By decoupling the two, you introduce flexibility into your system. You can replace functionality, test your code in isolation, or extend new functionality by introducing new producers or consumers.

There are many ways to architect an event-driven system. You can choose to stay with simple events and the Observer Pattern for lightweight events in your system. As you scale up, you may need to introduce a message broker, such as with PyPubSub. You may even need to use another library as a message broker if you want to scale across processes or systems. Finally, as you approach streams of events, you can consider a reactive programming framework, such as RxPY.

In the next chapter, I will cover a different type of architectural paradigm: plug-in architectures. Plug-in architectures offer similar flexibility, composability, and extensibility to event-driven architectures, but in a completely different way. Whereas event-driven architectures focus on events, plug-in architecture focuses on pluggable units of implementation. You'll see how plug-in architectures can give you plenty of options to build a robust codebase that is easy to maintain.

## CHAPTER 19

Pluggable Python

The greatest challenge in building a robust codebase is predicting the future. You will never completely guess what a future developer will do. The best strategy is not being perfectly prescient, but instead creating flexibility so that future collaborators can hook into your system with minimal work. In this chapter, I will focus on creating *pluggable* code. Pluggable code allows you to define behaviors that are to be supplied later. You define a framework with *extension points*, or parts of your system that other developers will use to extend functionality.

Think about a stand mixer sitting on a kitchen counter. You can select a variety of attachments to use with your mixer: a hook for mixing bread, a whisk for beating eggs and cream, and a flat beater to do general-purpose mixing. Each attachment serves a specific purpose. What's great is that you can detach and attach hooks or blades as the situation calls for it. You don't need to buy an entire new mixer for each use case; you *plug in* whatever you need when you need it.

This is the goal for pluggable Python. You don't need to rebuild entire applications when new functionality is needed. You build extensions or attachments that snap onto a solid foundation. You pick the functionality you need for your specific use case and you plug that into your system.

In most of this book, I've been illustrating examples with automated food makers of some sort or another. In this chapter, I will perform the mother of mergers and design a system that can combine them all. I want to build a system that can take any of the recipes I've talked about and cook them. I call it the "Ultimate Kitchen Assistant" (if you think this is a terrible name, you now know why I don't work in marketing).

The Ultimate Kitchen Assistant contains all the instructions and gear you will need for working around the kitchen. It knows how to slice, dice, fry, sauté, bake, broil, and blend any ingredient. It comes with some premade recipes, but the real magic is that customers can buy off-the-shelf modules to extend its functionality (such as a "Pasta-Making Module" for sating Italian cuisine cravings).

The problem is, I don't want the code to become burdensome to maintain. There are a lot of different dishes to make, and I want to give the system some sort of flexibility without oodles of physical dependencies turning the system into spaghetti code (although your system making spaghetti itself in the kitchen is highly encouraged!). Just like plugging a new attachment onto the stand mixer, I want developers to affix different attachments to solve their use cases. I even want other organizations to build modules for the Ultimate Kitchen Assistant. I want this codebase to be extensible and composable.

I'll use this example to illustrate three separate ways of plugging into different Python constructs. First, I'll focus on how to plug in specific parts of an algorithm with the Template Method Pattern. Then, I'll talk through plugging in an entire class with the Strategy Pattern. Finally, I'll introduce you to an incredibly useful library, stevedore, to do plug-ins at a much larger architectural scale. All of these techniques will help you give future developers the extensibility they need.

The Template Method Pattern

The *Template Method Pattern* is a pattern for filling in the blanks of an algorithm.[1] The idea is that you define an algorithm as a series of steps, but you force the caller to override some of those steps, as shown in Figure 19-1.

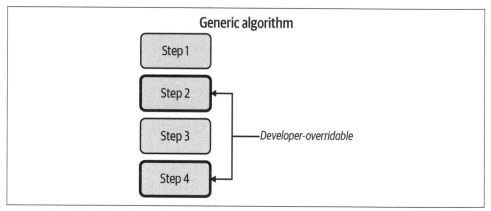

Figure 19-1. The Template Method Pattern

---

1 Erich Gamma, Richard Helm, Ralph E. Johnson, and John Vlissides. *Design Patterns: Elements of Reusable Object-Oriented Software.* Boston, MA: Addison-Wesley Professional, 1994.

First up for the Ultimate Kitchen Assistant is a pizza-making module. While traditional sauce-and-cheese pizzas are great, I want the Ultimate Kitchen Assistant to be more flexible. I want it to handle all sorts of pizza-like entities, from a Lebanese manoush to a Korean bulgogi pizza. To make any of these pizza-like dishes, I want the machinery to perform a similar set of steps, but let developers tweak certain operations to make their style of pizza. Figure 19-2 describes such a pizza-making algorithm.

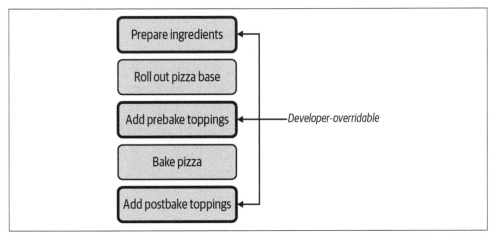

Figure 19-2. Pizza-making algorithm

Each pizza will use the same basic steps, but I want to be able to tweak certain steps (preparing ingredients, adding prebake toppings, and adding postbake toppings). My goal in applying the Template Method Pattern is to make these steps pluggable.

In its simplest incarnation, I can pass functions into the template method:

```
@dataclass
class PizzaCreationFunctions:
    prepare_ingredients: Callable
    add_pre_bake_toppings: Callable
    add_post_bake_toppings: Callable

def create_pizza(pizza_creation_functions: PizzaCreationFunctions):
    pizza_creation_functions.prepare_ingredients()
    roll_out_pizza_base()
    pizza_creation_functions.add_pre_bake_toppings()
    bake_pizza()
    pizza_creation_functions.add_post_bake_toppings()
```

Now, if you want to create a pizza, you just pass in your own functions:

```
pizza_creation_functions = PizzaCreationFunctions(
    prepare_ingredients=mix_zaatar,
    add_pre_bake_toppings=add_meat_and_halloumi,
    add_post_bake_toppings=drizzle_olive_oil
)

create_pizza(pizza_creation_functions)
```

This is incredibly convenient for any pizza, now or in the future. As new pizza-making capabilities come online, developers need to pass their new functions into the template method. These developers can plug in specific parts of the pizza-making algorithm to suit their needs. They don't need to know anything about their use case at all; they are free to grow the system without being bogged down with changing legacy code. Suppose they want to create the bulgogi pizza. Instead of changing create_pizza, I simply need to pass in a new PizzaCreationFunctions:

```
pizza_creation_functions = PizzaCreationFunctions(
    prepare_ingredients=cook_bulgogi,
    add_pre_bake_toppings=add_bulgogi_toppings,
    add_post_bake_toppings=garnish_with_scallions_and_sesame
)

create_pizza(pizza_creation_functions)
```

The Canonical Template Method Pattern

The Template Method Pattern described in the Gang of Four book is a bit different than what I've shown in this section. This is another case where the Gang of Four book leans heavily on class- and inheritance-based design. In the original Template Method Pattern, you are required to write a base class:

```
class PizzaCreator:
    def roll_out_dough():
        # snip
    def bake():
        # snip
    def serve():
        # snip

    def prepare_ingredients():
        raise NotImplementedError()

    def add_pre_bake_toppings():
        raise NotImplementedError()

    def add_post_bake_toppings():
        raise NotImplementedError()
```

To use this base class, you have to subclass and override the three required methods. You then have to find a way to substitute your derived class into any code that needs a pizza maker. You typically have to set up Abstract Factories (another design pattern found in the Gang of Four book) to inject derived classes.

Since Python does not require everything to be in a class and offers first-class support for functions, I prefer using a data class of functions to fill in a template. It involves less boilerplate, but still provides similar flexibility and extensibility. Just be aware that design-pattern purists may prefer the OO pattern described above.

The Strategy Pattern

The Template Method Pattern is great for swapping out select parts of an algorithm, but what if you want to swap out the *entire* algorithm? A very similar design pattern exists for this use case: the Strategy Pattern.

The Strategy Pattern is for plugging entire algorithms into a context.[2] For the Ultimate Kitchen Assistant, consider a module that specializes in Tex-Mex (a regional American cuisine that blends southwestern US and northern Mexican cuisines). A large variety of dishes can be made from a common set of items; you mix and match the different ingredients in new ways.

For instance, you will find the following ingredients on most Tex-Mex menus: tortillas (corn or flour), beans, ground beef, chicken, lettuce, tomato, guacamole, salsa, and cheese. From these ingredients, you can create tacos, flautas, chimichangas, enchiladas, taco salads, nachos, gorditas…the list goes on. I don't want the system to restrict all the different Tex-Mex dishes; I want different groups of developers to supply *how* to make the dish.

To do this with the Strategy Pattern, I need to define what the Ultimate Kitchen Assistant does and what the strategy does. In this case, the Ultimate Kitchen Assistant should provide the mechanisms for interacting with ingredients, but future developers are free to keep adding new Tex-Mex concoctions with a TexMexStrategy.

As with any code designed to be extensible, I need to make sure that the interaction between my Ultimate Kitchen Assistant and the Tex-Mex module agrees on the pre- and postconditions, namely what gets passed into the Tex-Mex module and what comes out.

---

2 Erich Gamma, Richard Helm, Ralph E. Johnson, and John Vlissides. *Design Patterns: Elements of Reusable Object-Oriented Software*. Boston, MA: Addison-Wesley Professional, 1994.

Suppose the Ultimate Kitchen Assistant has numbered bins to put ingredients in. The Tex-Mex module needs to know what bins the common Tex-Mex ingredients are in, so it can use the Ultimate Kitchen Assistant to actually do the prepping and cooking.

```
@dataclass
class TexMexIngredients:
    corn_tortilla_bin: int
    flour_tortilla_bin: int
    salsa_bin: int
    ground_beef_bin: int
    # ... snip ..
    shredded_cheese_bin: int

def prepare_tex_mex_dish(tex_mex_recipe_maker: Callable[TexMexIngredients]);
    tex_mex_ingredients = get_available_ingredients("Tex-Mex")
    dish = tex_mex_recipe_maker(tex_mex_ingredients)
    serve(dish)
```

The function `prepare_tex_mex_dish` collects ingredients, then delegates to the actual `tex_mex_recipe_maker` to create the dish to serve. The `tex_mex_recipe_maker` is the strategy. It's very similar to the Template Method Pattern, but you typically are just passing a single function rather than a collection of functions.

A future developer just has to write a function that does the actual preparation, given the ingredients. They could write:

```
import tex_mex_module as tmm
def make_soft_taco(ingredients: TexMexIngredients) -> tmm.Dish:
    tortilla = tmm.get_ingredient_from_bin(ingredients.flour_tortilla_bin)
    beef = tmm.get_ingredient_from_bin(ingredients.ground_beef_bin)
    dish = tmm.get_plate()
    dish.lay_on_dish(tortilla)
    tmm.season(beef, tmm.CHILE_POWDER_BLEND)
    # ... snip

prepare_tex_mex_dish(make_soft_taco)
```

If they decide they want to provide support for a different dish at some point in the future, they just have to write a new function:

```
def make_chimichanga(ingredients: TexMexIngredients):
    # ... snip
```

Developers can continue to define functions however they want, whenever they want. Just like the Template Method Pattern, they can plug in new functionality with minimal impact to the original code.

As with the Template Method, the implementation I've shown is a bit different than what was originally described in the Gang of Four book. The original implementation involved classes and subclasses that wrap a single method. In Python, it's far easier to just pass the single function.

Plug-in Architectures

The Strategy and Template Method Patterns are great for plugging in small bits of functionality: a class here or a function there. However, the same patterns apply to your architecture as well. Being able to inject classes, modules, or subsystems is just as important. A Python library called stevedore (*https://oreil.ly/AybtZ*) is an incredibly useful tool for managing *plug-ins*.

A plug-in is a piece of code that can be dynamically loaded at runtime. Code can scan for installed plug-ins, select an appropriate one, and delegate responsibilities to that plug-in. This is another example of extensibility; developers can focus on specific plug-ins without touching the core codebase.

There are a number of benefits beyond extensibility to a plug-in architecture:

- You can deploy plug-ins independently from the core, giving you more granularity for rolling out updates.
- Third parties can write plug-ins without modifying your codebase.
- Plug-ins are able to be developed in isolation from the core codebase, reducing the chances of creating tightly coupled code.

To demonstrate how plug-ins work, say I want to support an ecosystem for the Ultimate Kitchen Assistant where users can buy and install modules (such as the Tex-Mex module in the last section) separately from the main kitchen assistant. Each module provides a set of recipes, special equipment, and storage of ingredients for the Ultimate Kitchen Assistant to do work. The real benefit is that each module can be developed separately from the Ultimate Kitchen Assistant core; each module is a plug-in.

The first thing to do when designing plug-ins is determine the contract between the core and the various plug-ins. Ask yourself what services the core platform provides and what you expect the plug-ins to provide. In the case of the Ultimate Kitchen Assistant, Figure 19-3 demonstrates the contract I will be using in the following examples.

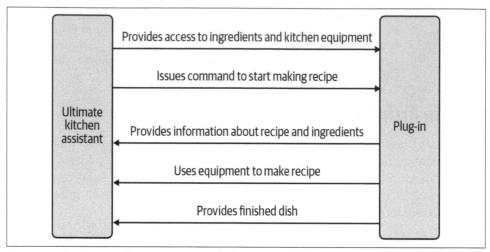

Figure 19-3. Contract between core and plug-in

I want to put this contract into code, so that it is unambiguous what I expect out of a plug-in:

```python
from abc import abstractmethod
from typing import runtime_checkable, Protocol

from ultimate_kitchen_assistant import Amount, Dish, Ingredient, Recipe

@runtime_checkable
class UltimateKitchenAssistantModule(Protocol):

    ingredients: list[Ingredient]

    @abstractmethod
    def get_recipes() -> list[Recipe]:
        raise NotImplementedError

    @abstractmethod
    def prepare_dish(inventory: dict[Ingredient, Amount],
                     recipe: Recipe) -> Dish:
        raise NotImplementedError
```

This serves as the definition of what the plug-in looks like. To create a plug-in that satisfies my expectations, I just need to create a class that inherits from my base class.

```python
class PastaModule(UltimateKitchenAssistantModule):
    def __init__(self):
        self.ingredients = ["Linguine",
                            # ... snip ...
                            "Spaghetti" ]

    def get_recipes(self) -> list[Recipe]:
```

```
        # ... snip returning all possible recipes ...

    def prepare_dish(self, inventory: dict[Ingredient, Amount],
                     recipe: Recipe) -> Dish:
        # interact with Ultimate Kitchen Assistant to make recipe
        # ... snip ...
```

Once you have created the plug-in, you need to register it with stevedore. stevedore matches plug-ins to a *namespace*, or an identifier that groups plug-ins together. It does so by using Python's *entry points*, which allow Python to discover components at runtime.[3]

You register plug-ins with the help of `setuptools` and `setup.py`. Many Python packages use `setup.py` to define packaging rules, one of which being entry points. In the `setup.py` for `ultimate_kitchen_assistant`, I would register my plug-in as follows:

```
from setuptools import setup

setup(
    name='ultimate_kitchen_assistant',
    version='1.0',
    #.... snip ....

    entry_points={
        'ultimate_kitchen_assistant.recipe_maker': [
            'pasta_maker = ultimate_kitchen_assistant.pasta_maker:PastaModule',
            'tex_mex = ultimate_kitchen_assistant.tex_mex:TexMexModule'
        ],
    },
)
```

 If you are having trouble linking your plug-ins, check out the `entry-point-inspector` package (*https://oreil.ly/kbMro*) for debugging help.

I am binding my `PastaMaker` class (in the `ultimate_kitchen_assistant.pasta_maker` package) to a plug-in with the namespace `ultimate_kitchen_assistant.recipe_maker`. I've created another hypothetical plug-in called `TexMexModule`, as well.

Once the plug-ins are registered as entry points, you can use stevedore to load them dynamically at runtime. For instance, if I wanted to collect all recipes from all plug-ins, I could write the following:

---

3 Entry points can be complex in how they interact with Python packaging, but that's beyond the scope of this book. You can learn more at *https://oreil.ly/bMyJS*.

```
import itertools
from stevedore import extension
from ultimate_kitchen_assisstant import Recipe

def get_all_recipes() -> list[Recipe]:
    mgr = extension.ExtensionManager(
            namespace='ultimate_kitchen_assistant.recipe_maker',
            invoke_on_load=True,
        )

    def get_recipes(extension):
        return extension.obj.get_recipes()

    return list(itertools.chain(mgr.map(get_recipes)))
```

I use `stevedore.extension.ExtensionManager` to find and load all plug-ins in the namespace `ultimate_kitchen_assistant.recipe_maker`. I can then map (or apply) a function to every plug-in that gets found to get their recipes. Lastly, I use `itertools` to chain them all together. It doesn't matter how many plug-ins I have set up; I can load them all with this code.

Let's say a user wants to make something from the pasta maker, such as "Pasta with Sausage." All the calling code needs to do is ask for a plug-in named `pasta_maker`. I can load the specific plug-in with a `stevedore.driver.DriverManager`.

```
from stevedore import driver


def make_dish(recipe: Recipe, module_name: str) -> Dish:
    mgr = driver.DriverManager(
        namespace='ultimate_kitchen_assistant.recipe_maker',
        name=module_name,
        invoke_on_load=True,
    )

    return mgr.driver.prepare_dish(get_inventory(), recipe)
```

 Discussion Topic

What parts of your system could use a plug-in architecture? How would this benefit your codebase?

stevedore provides a great way to decouple code; separating the code into plug-ins keeps it flexible and extensible. Remember, the goal of extensible programs is to limit the number of modifications needed in the core system. Developers can create plug-ins in isolation, test them, and integrate them into your core seamlessly.

My favorite part about stevedore is that it actually can work *across* packages. You can write plug-ins in a completely separate Python package than the core. As long as the same namespace is used for the plug-in, stevedore can stitch everything together. stevedore has a load of other features that are worth checking out, such as event notifications, enabling plug-ins through a variety of methods, and automatic plug-in documentation generation. If a plug-in architecture meets your needs, I highly recommend checking out more of stevedore.

 You can technically register any class as a plug-in, regardless of whether it is substitutable for the base class or not. Because the code is separated by an abstract layer with stevedore, your type-checker will not be able to detect this. Consider checking the interface at runtime to catch any mismatches before using the plug-in.

Closing Thoughts

When you create pluggable Python, you give your collaborators the ability to isolate new functionality but still easily integrate it into an existing codebase. Developers can plug into an existing algorithm with the Template Method Pattern, an entire class or algorithm with the Strategy Pattern, or even entire subsystems with stevedore. stevedore is especially useful when you want to split your plug-ins across discrete Python packages.

This concludes Part III, which was all about extensibility. Writing extensible code is adhering to the Open-Closed Principle, where you make it easy to add onto your code without requiring modifications to existing code. Event-driven architectures and plug-in architectures are fantastic examples of designing with extensibility in mind. All of these architectural patterns require you to be aware of dependencies: physical, logical, and temporal. As you find ways to minimize physical dependencies, you'll find that your code becomes composable, and can be rearranged in new compositions at will.

The first three parts of this book focused on changes that can make your code more maintainable and readable and reduce the chance of errors. However, errors still have a chance of showing up; they are an unavoidable part of developing software. To combat this, you need to make it easy to detect errors before they hit production. You'll learn how to do just that with tools like linters and tests in Part IV, "Building a Safety Net".

## PART IV

Building a Safety Net

Welcome to Part IV of the book, which is about the importance of building a safety net around your codebase. Think about a tightrope walker perilously balanced, high in the air. No matter how many times the performer has practiced their routine, there is always a set of safety precautions should the worst happen. The tightrope walker can perform their act with confidence, trusting in the fact that something will break their fall if they slip. You want to provide your fellow collaborators with the same sort of confidence and trust as they work in your codebase.

Even if your code is completely error free, how long will it stay that way? Every change introduces risk. Every new developer coming into a codebase will take time before fully understanding all of its intricacies. Customers will change their minds and ask for the complete opposite of what they asked for six months ago. This is all a natural part of any software development life cycle.

Your development safety net is a combination of static analysis and tests. Much has been written on the topic of testing and how to write good tests. In the chapters that follow, I will focus on *why* you write tests, how to decide which tests you write, and how you can make those tests more valuable. I'll go beyond simple unit and integration testing to talk about advanced testing techniques like acceptance testing, property-based testing, and mutation testing.

## CHAPTER 20

Static Analysis

Before I get to testing, I first want to talk about static analysis. *Static analysis* is a set of tools that inspect your codebase, looking for potential errors or inconsistencies. It's a great asset for finding common mistakes. In fact, you've already been working with a static analysis tool: mypy. Mypy (and other typecheckers) inspect your codebase and find typing errors. Other static analysis tools check for other types of errors. In this chapter, I'll walk you through common static analyzers for linting, complexity checking, and security scanning.

Linting

The first class of static analysis tools that I'll walk you through is called a *linter*. Linters search for common programming mistakes and style violations within your codebase. They get their name from the original linter: a program named *lint* that used to check C programs for common errors. It would search for "fuzzy" logic and try to remove that fuzz (hence, linting). In Python, the most common linter you will come across is Pylint. Pylint is used to check for a myriad of common mistakes:

- Certain style violations of the PEP 8 (*https://oreil.ly/MnCoY*) Python style guide
- Dead code that is unreachable (such as code after a return statement)
- Violations of access constraints (such as private or protected members of a class)
- Unused variables and functions
- Lack of cohesion in a class (no use of self in a method, too many public methods)
- Missing documentation in the form of docstrings
- Common programming errors

Many of these error classes are things that we've discussed previously, such as accessing private members or a function needing to be a free function instead of a member function (as discussed in Chapter 10.) A linter like Pylint will complement all of the techniques you've learned throughout this book; if you violate some of the principles I've been espousing, linters will catch those violations for you.

Pylint is also incredibly handy at finding some common errors in your code. Consider a developer adding code that adds all of an author's cookbooks to an existing list:

```
def add_authors_cookbooks(author_name: str, cookbooks: list[str] = []) -> bool:

    author = find_author(author_name)
    if author is None:
        assert False, "Author does not exist"
    else:
        for cookbook in author.get_cookbooks():
            cookbooks.append(cookbook)
        return True
```

This seems innocuous, but there are two issues in this code. Take a few minutes and see if you can find them.

Now let's see what Pylint can do. First, I need to install it:

```
pip install pylint
```

Then, I'll run Pylint against the example above:

```
pylint code_examples/chapter20/lint_example.py
************ Module lint_example

code_examples/chapter20/lint_example.py:11:0: W0102:
    Dangerous default value [] as argument (dangerous-default-value)
code_examples/chapter20/lint_example.py:11:0: R1710:
    Either all return statements in a function should return an expression,
    or none of them should. (inconsistent-return-statements)
```

Pylint has identified the two issues in my code (it actually found more, such as missing documentation strings, but I've elided them for the purposes of this discussion). First, there is a dangerous mutable default value of an argument in the form of []. Much has been written on this behavior before (*https://oreil.ly/sCQQu*), but it's a common gotcha for errors, especially for people new to the language.

The other error is a bit more subtle: not all branches return the same type. "But wait!" you exclaim. "It's OK, because I assert, which raises an error instead of falling through the if statement (which returns None)." However, while assert statements are fantastic, they can be turned off. When you pass the -O flag to Python, it disables all assert statements. So, when the -O flag is turned on, this function returns None. For the record, mypy does not catch this error, but Pylint does. Even better, Pylint ran in under a second to find those bugs.

It doesn't matter if you don't make those errors, or you if always find them in code review. There are countless developers working in any codebase, and errors can happen anywhere. By enforcing a linter like Pylint, you can eliminate very common, detectable errors. For a full list of built-in checkers, see the Pylint documentation (*https://oreil.ly/9HRzC*).

Shift Errors Left

One of the common tenets of the DevOps mindset is to "shift your errors left." I mentioned this when discussing types, but it applies to static analysis and tests as well. The idea is to think of your errors in terms of their cost. How expensive is it to fix an error? It depends on where you find that error. An error found in production by a customer is costly. Developers have to spend time away from their normal feature development, tech support and testers get involved, and there are risks when you have to do an emergency deployment.

The earlier in the development cycle you are, the less expensive it is to address errors. If you can find errors during testing, you can avoid a slew of production costs. However, you want to find these issues even earlier, before they ever enter into the codebase. I talked at length in Part I about how typecheckers can shift those errors even further left, so that you find the errors right as you develop. It's not just typecheckers that allow you to do this, but static analysis tools such as linters and complexity checkers as well.

These static analysis tools are your first line of defense against errors, even more so than tests. They aren't a silver bullet (nothing is), but they are invaluable in finding problems early. Add them to your continuous integration pipeline and set them up as pre-commit hooks or server-side hooks in your version control system. Save yourself time and money and don't let easy-to-detect errors ever enter your codebase.

Writing Your Own Pylint Plug-in

The real Pylint magic starts to happen when you write your own plug-ins (see Chapter 19 for more information on plug-in architectures). A Pylint plug-in lets you write your own custom *checkers*, or rules. While built-in checkers look for common Python errors, your custom checkers can look for errors in your problem domain.

Take a look at a snippet of code way back from Chapter 4:

```
ReadyToServeHotDog = NewType("ReadyToServeHotDog", HotDog)

def prepare_for_serving() -> ReadyToServeHotDog:
```

```
    # snip preparation
    return ReadyToServeHotDog(hotdog)
```

During Chapter 4, I mentioned that in order for NewType to be effective, you need to make sure that you are only constructing it from *blessed* methods, or methods that enforce the constraints tied to that type. At the time, my advice was to use a comment to give hints to readers of the code. However, with Pylint, you can write a custom checker to find out when you violate this expectation.

Here's the plug-in in its entirety. I'll break it down for you afterward:

```python
from typing import Optional

import astroid

from pylint.checkers import BaseChecker
from pylint.interfaces import IAstroidChecker
from pylint.lint.pylinter import PyLinter

class ServableHotDogChecker(BaseChecker):
    __implements__ = IAstroidChecker

    name = 'unverified-ready-to-serve-hotdog'
    priority = -1
    msgs = {
      'W0001': (
        'ReadyToServeHotDog created outside of hotdog.prepare_for_serving.',
        'unverified-ready-to-serve-hotdog',
        'Only create a ReadyToServeHotDog through hotdog.prepare_for_serving.'
      ),
    }

    def __init__(self, linter: Optional[PyLinter] = None):
        super(ServableHotDogChecker, self).__init__(linter)
        self._is_in_prepare_for_serving = False

    def visit_functiondef(self, node: astroid.scoped_nodes.FunctionDef):
        if (node.name == "prepare_for_serving" and
            node.parent.name =="hotdog" and
            isinstance(node.parent, astroid.scoped_nodes.Module)):

            self._is_in_prepare_for_serving = True

    def leave_functiondef(self, node: astroid.scoped_nodes.FunctionDef):
        if (node.name == "prepare_for_serving" and
            node.parent.name =="hotdog" and
            isinstance(node.parent, astroid.scoped_nodes.Module)):

            self._is_in_prepare_for_serving = False

    def visit_call(self, node: astroid.node_classes.Call):
        if node.func.name != 'ReadyToServeHotDog':
```

```
        return

    if self._is_in_prepare_for_serving:
        return

    self.add_message(
        'unverified-ready-to-serve-hotdog', node=node,
    )

def register(linter: PyLinter):
    linter.register_checker(ServableHotDogChecker(linter))
```

This linter verifies that when someone creates a ReadyToServeHotDog, it is only done in a function that is named prepare_for_serving, and that function must live in a module called hotdog. Now let's say I were to create any other function that created a ready-to-serve hot dog, like this:

```
def create_hot_dog() -> ReadyToServeHotDog:
    hot_dog = HotDog()
    return ReadyToServeHotDog(hot_dog)
```

I can run my custom Pylint checker:

```
PYTHONPATH=code_examples/chapter20 pylint --load-plugins \
    hotdog_checker code_examples/chapter20/hotdog.py
```

Pylint confirms that serving an "unservable" hot dog is now an error:

```
************* Module hotdog
code_examples/chapter20/hotdog.py:13:12: W0001:
    ReadyToServeHotDog created outside of prepare_for_serving.
        (unverified-ready-to-serve-hotdog)
```

This is fantastic. Now I can write automated tooling that checks for errors that a type-checker like mypy can't even begin to look for. Don't let your imagination constrain you. Use Pylint to catch anything you can dream of: business logic constraint violations, temporal dependencies, or a custom style guide. Now, let's go see how this linter works so that you can build your own.

Breaking Down the Plug-in

The first thing I did to write the plug-in was to define a class that inherits from a pylint.checkers.BaseChecker:

```
import astroid

from pylint.checkers import BaseChecker
from pylint.interfaces import IAstroidChecker

class ReadyToServeHotDogChecker(BaseChecker):
    __implements__ = IAstroidChecker
```

You'll also notice some references to `astroid`. The `astroid` library is useful for parsing Python files into an abstract syntax tree (AST). This provides a conveniently structured way of interacting with Python source code. You'll see how that's useful in a little bit.

Next, I define metadata about the plug-in. This provides information such as the plug-in name, messages that get displayed to the user, and an identifier (`unverified-ready-to-serve-hotdog`) that I can refer to later.

```
name = 'unverified-ready-to-serve-hotdog'
priority = -1
msgs = {
 'W0001': ( # this is an arbitrary number I've assigned as an identifier
    'ReadyToServeHotDog created outside of hotdog.prepare_for_serving.',
    'unverified-ready-to-serve-hotdog',
    'Only create a ReadyToServeHotDog through hotdog.prepare_for_serving.'
 ),
}
```

Next, I want to track what function I'm in, so that I can tell if I'm using `prepare_for_serving` or not. This is where the `astroid` library will come to play. As mentioned before, the `astroid` library helps the Pylint checker think in terms of an AST; you don't need to worry about string parsing. If you'd like to learn more about AST and Python parsing, you can check out `astroid`'s documentation (*https://oreil.ly/JvQgU*), but for now, all you have to know is that if you define specific functions in your checker, they will get called when `astroid` parses the code. Each function called gets passed a `node` which represents a specific part of code, such as an expression or a class definition.

```
def __init__(self, linter: Optional[PyLinter] = None):
    super(ReadyToServeHotDogChecker, self).__init__(linter)
    self._is_in_prepare_for_serving = False

def visit_functiondef(self, node: astroid.scoped_nodes.FunctionDef):
    if (node.name == "prepare_for_serving" and
        node.parent.name =="hotdog" and
        isinstance(node.parent, astroid.scoped_nodes.Module)):
            self._is_in_prepare_for_serving = True

def leave_functiondef(self, node: astroid.scoped_nodes.FunctionDef):
    if (node.name == "prepare_for_serving" and
        node.parent.name =="hotdog" and
        isinstance(node.parent, astroid.scoped_nodes.Module)):

        self._is_in_prepare_for_serving = False
```

In this case, I've defined an `__init__` method to save a member variable to track if I'm in the right function. I've also defined two functions, `visit_functiondef` and `leave_functiondef`. `visit_functiondef` will get called whenever `astroid` parses a function definition, and `leave_functiondef` is called whenever the parser stops parsing a function definition. So when the parser encounters a function, I check to see if that function is named `prepare_for_serving`, which is inside a module called hotdog.

Now that I have a member variable to track if I'm in the right function or not, I can write another `astroid` hook to get called whenever a function is called (such as Ready ToServeHotDog(hot_dog)).

```python
def visit_call(self, node: astroid.node_classes.Call):
    if node.func.name != 'ReadyToServeHotDog':
        return

    if self._is_in_prepare_for_serving:
        return

    self.add_message(
        'unverified-ready-to-serve-hotdog', node=node,
    )
```

If the function call is not `ReadyToServeHotDog` or if the execution is in `prepare_serv ing`, this checker sees no issue and returns early. If the function call is `ReadyToServe HotDog` and the execution is not in `prepare_serving`, the checker fails and adds a message to indicate an `unverified-ready-to-serve-hotdog` check failure. By adding a message, Pylint will pass this on to the user and flag it as a failed check.

Lastly, I need to register the linter:

```python
def register(linter: PyLinter):
    linter.register_checker(ReadyToServeHotDogChecker(linter))
```

And that's it! With about 45 lines of Python, I have defined a Pylint plug-in. This was a simple checker, but your imagination is the limit for what you can do. Pylint checks, either built-in or user created, are invaluable for finding errors.

Discussion Topic

What checkers can you create in your codebase? What error cases can you catch with the use of these checkers?

Other Static Analyzers

Typecheckers and linters are often the first things people think of when they hear "static analysis," but there are so many additional tools that can help you write robust code. Each tool acts as a separate line of defense, all stacked together, to protect your codebase. Think about each tool as a piece of Swiss cheese.[1] Each individual piece of Swiss cheese has holes of various widths or sizes, but when multiple pieces are stacked together, it is unlikely that there is an area where all holes align and you can see through the stack.

Likewise, each tool you use to build a safety net will miss certain errors. Typecheckers won't catch common programming mistakes, linters won't check security violations, security checkers won't catch complex code, and so on. But when these tools are stacked together, it's much less likely for a legitimate error to squeak by (and for those that do, that's why you have tests). As Bruce MacLennan says, "Have a series of defenses so that if an error is not caught by one, it will probably be caught by another."[2]

Complexity Checkers

Most of this book has been centered on readable and maintainable code. I've talked about how complex code impacts the speed of feature development. It'd be nice for a tool to indicate which parts of your codebase have high complexity. Unfortunately, complexity is subjective and reducing complexity will not always reduce errors. I can, however, treat complexity measures as a *heuristic*. A heuristic is something that provides an answer, but offers no guarantee that it is an optimal answer. In this case, the question is, "Where can I find the most bugs in my code?" Most of the time, it will be in code with high complexity, but remember that this is not a guarantee.

Cyclomatic complexity with mccabe

One of the most popular complexity heuristics is known as *cyclomatic complexity*, first described by Thomas McCabe.[3] To measure code's cyclomatic complexity, you must view your code as a *control flow graph*, or a graph that maps out the different paths of execution your code can take. Figure 20-1 shows you a few different examples.

---

1 J. Reason. "Human Error: Models and Management." *BMJ* 320, no. 7237 (2000): 768–70. *https://doi.org/10.1136/bmj.320.7237.768.*

2 Bruce MacLennan. "Principles of Programming Language Design." web.eecs.utk.edu, September 10, 1998. *https://oreil.ly/hrjdR.*

3 T.J. McCabe. "A Complexity Measure." *IEEE Transactions on Software Engineering* SE-2, no. 4 (December 1976): 308–20. *https://doi.org/10.1109/tse.1976.233837.*

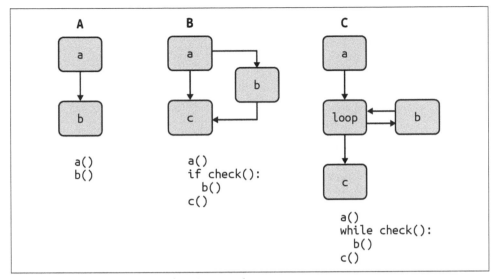

Figure 20-1. Cyclomatic complexity examples

Section A of Figure 20-1 demonstrates a linear flow of statements, which has a complexity of one. An `if` with no `elif` statement, as shown in Section B of Figure 20-1, has two paths (`if` or `else`/fall-through), so the complexity is two. Similarly a `while` loop, like in Section C of Figure 20-1, has two separate paths: either the loop continues or exits. As the code gets more complex, the cyclomatic complexity number gets higher.

You can use a static analysis tool in Python to measure cyclomatic complexity, aptly named `mccabe`.

I'll install it with `pip`:

```
pip install mccabe
```

To test it out, I'll run it on the `mccabe` codebase itself and flag any function that has a cyclomatic complexity greater than or equal to five:

```
python -m mccabe --min 5 mccabe.py
192:4: 'PathGraphingAstVisitor._subgraph_parse' 5
273:0: 'get_code_complexity' 5
298:0: '_read' 5
315:0: 'main' 7
```

Let' take a look at `PathGraphingAstVisitor._subgraph_parse`:

```
def _subgraph_parse(self, node, pathnode, extra_blocks):
    """parse the body and any `else` block of `if` and `for` statements"""
    loose_ends = []
    self.tail = pathnode
    self.dispatch_list(node.body)
```

```
        loose_ends.append(self.tail)
        for extra in extra_blocks:
            self.tail = pathnode
            self.dispatch_list(extra.body)
            loose_ends.append(self.tail)
        if node.orelse:
            self.tail = pathnode
            self.dispatch_list(node.orelse)
            loose_ends.append(self.tail)
        else:
            loose_ends.append(pathnode)
        if pathnode:
            bottom = PathNode("", look='point')
            for le in loose_ends:
                self.graph.connect(le, bottom)
            self.tail = bottom
```

There are a few things going on in this function: various conditional branches, loops, and even a loop nested in an if statement. Each of these paths is independent and needs to be tested for. As cyclomatic complexity grows, code gets harder to read and harder to reason about. There is no magic number for cyclomatic complexity; you will need to inspect your codebase and look for a suitable limit.

Whitespace heuristic

There's another complexity heuristic that I am quite fond of that is a bit simpler to reason about than cyclomatic complexity: whitespace checking (*https://oreil.ly/ i3Dpd*). The idea is as follows: count how many levels of indentation there are in a single Python file. High levels of indentation indicate nested loops and branches, which may signal complex code.

Unfortunately, there are no popular tools at the time of writing that handle whitespace heuristics. However, it is easy to write this checker yourself:

```python
def get_amount_of_preceding_whitespace(line: str) -> int:
    # replace tabs with 4 spaces (and start tab/spaces flame-war)
    tab_normalized_text = line.replace("\t", "    ")
    return len(tab_normalized_text) - len(tab_normalized_text.lstrip())

def get_average_whitespace(filename: str):
    with open(filename) as file_to_check:
        whitespace_count = [get_amount_of_preceding_whitespace(line)
                            for line in file_to_check
                            if line != ""]
        average = sum(whitespace_count) / len(whitespace_count) / 4
        print(f"Avg indentation level for {filename}: {average}")
```

Another possible measure of whitespace is the "area" of indentation per function, where you sum up all the indentation instead of averaging it. I am leaving this as an exercise for the reader to implement.

As with cyclomatic complexity, there is no magic number to check for with whitespace complexity. I encourage you to play around in your codebase and determine what an appropriate amount of indentation is.

Security Analysis

Security is difficult to do right, and hardly anyone ever gets lauded for breach prevention. Instead, it's the breaches themselves that seem to dominate the news. Every month I hear of another breach or data leak. These breakdowns are incredibly costly to a company, be it from regulatory fines or loss of customer base.

Every developer needs to be hyperaware of the security of their codebase. You don't want to hear about how *your* codebase is the root cause of the latest massive data breach in the news. Thankfully, there are static analysis tools that can prevent common security flaws.

Leaking secrets

If you ever want to be terrified, search for the text AWS_SECRET_KEY in your favorite code-hosting tool, like GitHub (*https://oreil.ly/FEm7D*). You will be amazed at how many people commit secret values such as the key that provides access to AWS.[4]

Once a secret is in a version control system, especially a publicly hosted one, it is very hard to remove traces of it. The organization is forced to revoke any leaked credentials, but they have to do it faster than the troves of hackers trawling repositories for keys. To prevent this, use a static analysis tool that specifically looks for leaked secrets, such as dodgy (*https://github.com/landscapeio/dodgy*). If you don't choose to use a prebuilt tool, at least perform a text search on your codebase to make sure that nobody is leaking common credentials.

Security flaw checking

Checking for leaked credentials is one thing, but what about more serious security flaws? How do you find things like SQL injection, arbitrary code execution, or incorrectly configured network settings? When exploited, these sorts of flaws can be

---

4 There are real-world implications to this. A quick search on the internet turns up tons of articles detailing this problem, such as *https://oreil.ly/gimse*.

detrimental to your security profile. But, just like every other problem in this chapter, there is a static analysis tool for handling this: Bandit.

Bandit checks for common security problems. You can find a full list in the Bandit documentation (*https://bandit.readthedocs.io/en/latest*), but here is a preview of the sorts of flaws Bandit looks for:

- Flask in debug mode, which can lead to remote code execution
- Making an HTTPS request without certificate validation turned on
- Raw SQL statements that have the potential for SQL injection
- Weak cryptographic key creation
- Flagging untrusted data influencing code paths, such as unsafe YAML loading

Bandit checks for so many different potential security flaws. I highly recommend running it against your codebase:

```
pip install bandit
bandit -r path/to/your/code
```

Bandit also has a robust plug-in system, so that you can augment the flaw detection with your own security checks.

 While security-oriented static analyzers are very useful, do not make them your only line of defense. Supplement these tools by continuing additional security practices (such as conducting audits, running penetration tests, and securing your networks).

Closing Thoughts

Catching errors early saves you time and money. Your goal is to find errors as you develop code. Static analysis tools are your friends in this endeavor. They are a cheap, quick way to find any problems in your codebase. There are a variety of static analyzers to meet your needs: linters, security checkers, and complexity checkers. Each has its own purpose and provides a layer of defense. And for the errors that these tools don't catch, you extend the static analyzers through the use of a plug-in system.

While static analyzers are your first line of defense, they are not your only line. For the rest of the book, I will focus on tests. The next chapter will focus on your testing strategy. I'll walk through how you need to organize your tests, as well as the best practices surrounding writing tests. You'll learn how to write a testing triangle, how to ask the right questions around testing, and how to write effective developer tests.

## CHAPTER 21

Testing Strategy

Tests are one of most important safety nets you can build around your codebase. It is incredibly comforting to make a change and see that all tests pass afterwards. However, it is challenging to gauge the best use of your time regarding testing. Too many tests and they become a burden; you spend more time maintaining tests than delivering features. Too few tests and you are letting potential catastrophes make it into production.

In this chapter, I will ask you to focus on your testing strategy. I'll break down the different types of tests and how to choose which tests to write. I'll focus on Python best practices around test construction, and then I'll end with some common testing strategies specific to Python.

Defining Your Test Strategy

Before you write tests, you should decide what your *test strategy* will be. A test strategy is a plan for spending time and effort to test your software in order to mitigate risk. This strategy will influence what types of tests you write, how you write them, and how much time you spend writing (and maintaining) them. Everybody's test strategy will be different, but they will all be in a similar form: a list of questions about your system and how you plan on answering them. For example, if I were writing a calorie-counting app, here would be a part of my test strategy:

```
Does my system function as expected?
Tests to write (automated - run daily):
    Acceptance tests: Adding calories to the daily count
    Acceptance tests: Resetting calories on daily boundaries
    Acceptance tests: Aggregating calories over a time period
    Unit tests: Corner Cases
    Unit tests: Happy Path
```

```
Will this application be usable by a large user base?
Tests to write (automated - run weekly):
    Interoperability tests: Phones (Apple, Android, etc.)
    Interoperability tests: Tablets
    Interoperability tests: Smart Fridge

Is it hard to use maliciously?
Tests to write: (ongoing audit by security engineer)
    Security tests: Device Interactions
    Security tests: Network Interactions
    Security tests: Backend Vulnerability Scanning (automated)

... etc. ...
```

 Do not treat your test strategy as a static document that is created once and never modified. As you develop your software, continue to ask questions as they come to mind, and discuss whether your strategy needs to evolve as you learn more.

This test strategy will govern where you put your focus for writing tests. As you start to fill it out, the first thing you need to do is understand what a test is and why you write them.

What Is a Test?

You should understand the *what* and the *why* you are writing the software. Answering these questions will frame your goals for writing tests. Tests serve as a way of verifying *what* the code is doing, and you write tests so that you don't negatively impact the *why*. Software produces value. That's it. Every piece of software has some value attached to it. Web apps provide important services for the general population. Data science pipelines may create prediction models that help us better understand the patterns in our world. Even malicious software has value; the people who are performing the exploit are using the software to achieve a goal (even if there is negative value to anyone affected).

That's *what* software provides, but *why* does anyone write software? Most people answer "money," and I don't want to knock that, but there are other reasons too. Sometimes software is written for money, sometimes it's written for self-fulfilment, and sometimes it's written for advertising (such as contributing to an open source project to bolster a resume). Tests serve as validation for these systems. They go so much deeper than just catching errors or giving you confidence in shipping a product.

If I'm writing some code for learning purposes, my *why* is purely for self-fulfilment, and the value is derived from how much I learn. If I do things wrong, that is still a learning opportunity; I can get by if all my tests are just manual spot checks at the end of the project. However, a company that markets tools to other developers might have a completely different strategy. Developers at that company may choose to write tests to make sure they are not regressing any functionality so that the company does not lose customers (which would translate to a loss of profit). Each of these projects needs a different level of testing.

So, what is a test? Is it something that catches errors? Is it something that gives you confidence to ship your product? Yes, but the true answer goes a little deeper. Tests answer questions about your system. I want you to think about the software you write. What is its purpose? What do you want to always know about the things you build? The things that are important to you form your test strategy.

When you ask yourself questions, you really are asking yourself what tests you find valuable:

- Will my application handle a predicted load?
- Does my code meet the customer's needs?
- Is my application secure?
- What happens when a customer inputs bad data into my system?

Each one of these questions points to a different type of test that you might need to write. Check out Table 21-1 for a list of common questions and the appropriate tests that answer those questions.

Table 21-1. Types of tests and the questions they answer

Test type	Question the test answers
Unit	Do units (functions and classes) act as developers expect?
Integration	Are separate parts of the system stitched together properly?
Acceptance	Does the system do what the end user expects?
Load	Does the system stay operational under heavy duress?
Security	Does the system resist specific attacks and exploits?
Usability	Is the system intuitive to use?

> ## A Note About Manual Testing
>
> Since this is a book about robust Python, I am focusing mostly on your codebase and the tools that support it. This means there is a heavy bias toward automated testing in Python. However, do not take this to mean that manual testing should be tossed to the wayside.
>
> *Manual testing*, which is having a person execute testing steps instead of the computer, has its place. It is fantastic for things such as exploring your codebase in ways that are not easy for a computer, such as validating how a user will interact with your system, checking for security vulnerabilities, or running any other type of test that relies on subjective analysis.
>
> In cases where it is cheaper to run manual tests than automated tests (say for expensive test equipment or other constraints), it may also be appropriate to keep a human in the loop. Before you jump to this conclusion, though, factor in the cost of repetition: think through how often you will run the test. In some cases, the cost of manual testing will overtake the cost of automated testing after just a few test runs.

Notice that Table 21-1 did not say anything about making sure your software is bug free. As Edsger Djikstra wrote, "Program testing can be used to show the presence of bugs, but never to show their absence!"[1] Tests answer questions regarding the *quality* of your software.

Quality is this nebulous, ill-defined term that gets tossed around quite a bit. It's a tough thing to pin down, but I prefer this quote from Gerald Weinberg: "Quality is value to some person."[2] I love how open-ended this quote is; you need to think of anyone who may receive some value from your system. It's not just your direct customers, but your customers' customers, your operations team, your sales, your coworkers, and so on.

Once you've identified who receives the value of your system, you need to measure the impact when something goes wrong. For every test that is not run, you lose a chance to learn whether you are delivering value. What is the impact if that value is not delivered? For core business needs, the impact is pretty high. For features that lie outside of an end user's critical path, the impact may be low. Know your impact, and weigh that against the cost of testing. If the impact's cost is higher than the test, write

---

1 Edsger W. Dijkstra. "Notes on Structured Programming." Technological University Eindhoven, The Netherlands, Department of Mathematics, 1970. *https://oreil.ly/NAhWf*.

2 Gerald M. Weinberg. *Quality Software Management*. Vol. 1: *Systems Thinking*. New York, NY: Dorset House Publishing, 1992.

the test. If it's lower, skip writing the test and spend your time doing something more impactful.

The testing pyramid

In just about any testing book, you are bound to come across a figure similar to Figure 21-1: a "testing pyramid."[3]

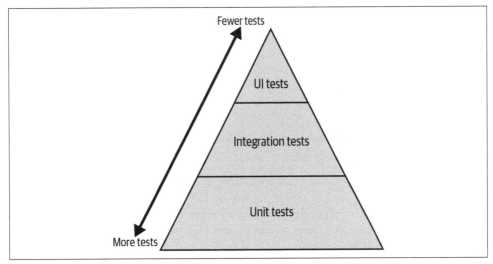

Figure 21-1. The testing pyramid

The idea is that you want to write a lot of small, isolated unit tests. These are theoretically cheaper and should make up the bulk of your testing, hence they're at the bottom. You have fewer integration tests, which are costly, and even fewer UI tests, which are very costly. Now, ever since its inception, developers have argued about the testing pyramid in a multitude of ways, including where the lines get drawn, the usefulness of unit tests, and even the shape of the triangle (I've even seen the triangle inverted).

The truth is, it doesn't matter what the labels are or how you separate your tests. What you want is your triangle to look like Figure 21-2, which focuses on the ratio of value to cost.

---

3 This is known as the testing pyramid, introduced in *Succeeding with Agile* by Mike Cohn (Addison-Wesley Professional). Cohn originally has "Service" level tests in place of integration tests, but I've seen more iterations with "integration" tests as the middle layer.

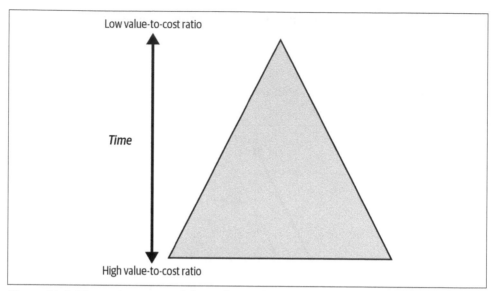

Figure 21-2. The testing pyramid focused on value-to-cost

Write lots of tests that have a high value-to-cost ratio. It doesn't matter if they are unit tests or acceptance tests. Find ways to run them often. Make tests fast so that developers run them multiple times between commits to verify that things are still working. Keep your less valuable, slower, or more costly tests for testing on each commit (or at least periodically).

The more tests you have, the fewer unknowns you have. The fewer unknowns you have, the more robust your codebase will be. With every change you make, you have a bigger safety net to check for any regression. But what if the tests are becoming too costly, far outweighing the cost of any impact? If you feel these tests are still worthwhile, you need to find a way to reduce their cost.

The cost of a test is threefold: the initial cost of writing, the cost of running, and the cost for maintenance. Tests, at a minimum, will have to run for some amount of time, and that does cost money. However, reducing that cost often becomes an optimization exercise, where you look for ways of parallelizing your tests or running them more frequently on developer machines. You still need to reduce the initial cost of writing and ongoing cost of maintaining your tests. Fortunately, everything you've read in this book so far directly applies to reducing those costs. Your test code is just as much a part of your codebase as the rest of your code, and you need to make sure it is robust as well. Choose the right tools, organize your test cases properly, and make your tests clear to read and maintain.

Discussion Topic

Measure the costs of tests in your system. Does time to write, time to run, or time spent maintaining dominate your costs? What can you do to reduce those costs?

Reducing Test Cost

When you examine the value against the cost of a test, you are gathering information that will help you prioritize your testing strategy. Some tests may not be worth running, and some will stand out as the first tests you want to write to maximize value. However, sometimes you run into the case where there is a really important test that you want to write, but it is incredibly costly to write and/or maintain. In these cases, find a way to reduce the costs of that test. The way you write and organize your tests is paramount to making a test cheaper to write and understand.

Using pytest

For the examples in this chapter, I will use the popular testing library pytest (*https://docs.pytest.org/en/stable*). There are fantastic resources for learning pytest, such as *Python Testing with pytest: Simple, Rapid, Effective, and Scalable* by Brian Okken (Pragmatic Bookshelf). Here, I'll cover the basics to give you context for this chapter.

A test in pytest is any function that is prefixed with test_ in a file that is also prefixed by *test_*. Here's a file named *test_calorie_count.py* with a single test:

```
from nutrition import get_calorie_count

def test_get_calorie_count():
    assert get_calorie_count("Bacon Cheeseburger w/ Fries") == 1200
```

Tests contain assertions, or things that should be true. pytest uses the built-in assert statement for assertions. If a test's assertion is false, an AssertionError is raised and the test fails. If the assertion is true, the test continues executing.

If you are hesitant to introduce a dependency on a library, there is a built-in unit testing framework with the unittest module in Python. I prefer pytest because of some advanced features (fixtures, plug-ins, etc.), but all of the principles in this chapter apply to other testing frameworks as well.

AAA Testing

As with production code, focus on readability and maintainability in your test code. Communicate your intent as clearly as possible. Future test readers will thank you if they can see exactly what you are trying to test. When writing a test, it helps for each test to follow the same basic pattern.

One of the most common patterns you'll find in tests is the 3A, or AAA, test pattern.[4] AAA stands for *Arrange-Act-Assert*. You break up each test into three separate blocks of code, one for setting up your preconditions (arrange), one for performing the operations that are being tested (act), and then one for checking for any post-conditions (assert). You may also hear about a fourth A, for *annihilate*, or your clean-up code. I'll cover each of these steps in detail to discuss how to make your tests easier to read and maintain.

Arrange

The *arrange* step is all about setting up the system in a state that is ready to test. These are called the *preconditions* of the test. You set up any dependencies or test data that are needed for the test to operate correctly.

Consider the following test:

```
def test_calorie_calculation():

    # arrange (set up everything the test needs to run)
    add_ingredient_to_database("Ground Beef", calories_per_pound=1500)
    add_ingredient_to_database("Bacon", calories_per_pound=2400)
    add_ingredient_to_database("Cheese", calories_per_pound=1800)
    # ... snip 13 more ingredients

    set_ingredients("Bacon Cheeseburger w/ Fries",
                    ingredients=["Ground Beef", "Bacon" ... ])

    # act (the thing getting tested)
    calories = get_calories("Bacon Cheeseburger w/ Fries")

    # assert (verify some property about the program)
    assert calories == 1200

    #annihilate (cleanup any resources that were allocated)
    cleanup_database()
```

First, I add ingredients to a database and associate a list of ingredients with a dish called "Bacon Cheeseburger w/ Fries." Then I find out how many calories are in the burger, check this against a known value, and clean up the database.

Look how much code there is before I actually get to the test itself (the `get_calories` invocation). Large *arrange* blocks are a red flag. You will have many tests that look very similar, and you want readers to be able to know how they differ at a glance.

---

4 The AAA pattern was first named by Bill Wake in 2001. Check out this blog post (*https://oreil.ly/gdU4T*) for more information.

Large *arrange* blocks may indicate a complicated setup of dependencies. Any user of this code will presumably have to set up the dependencies in a similar way. Take a step back and ask if there are simpler ways to handle dependencies, such as using the strategies described in Part III.

In the preceding example, if I have to add 15 ingredients in two separate tests but set an ingredient slightly differently to simulate substitutions, it will be difficult to eyeball how the tests differ. Giving the tests verbose names indicating their differences is a good step to make, but that only goes so far. Find a balance between keeping the test informative and making it easy to read at a glance.

Consistent preconditions versus changing preconditions.   Look through your tests and ask yourself what preconditions are the same across sets of tests. Extract these through a function and reuse that function across each test. Look how much easier it is to compare the following two tests:

```
def test_calorie_calculation_bacon_cheeseburger():
    add_base_ingredients_to_database()
    add_ingredient_to_database("Bacon", calories_per_pound=2400)

    setup_bacon_cheeseburger(bacon="Bacon")
    calories = get_calories("Bacon Cheeseburger w/ Fries")

    assert calories == 1200

    cleanup_database()

def test_calorie_calculation_bacon_cheeseburger_with_substitution():
    add_base_ingredients_to_database()
    add_ingredient_to_database("Turkey Bacon", calories_per_pound=1700)

    setup_bacon_cheeseburger(bacon="Turkey Bacon")
    calories = get_calories("Bacon Cheeseburger w/ Fries")

    assert calories == 1100

    cleanup_database()
```

By creating helper functions (in this case, `add_base_ingredients_to_database` and `setup_bacon_cheeseburger`), you take all the unimportant boilerplate of the tests and reduce it, allowing developers to hone in on differences between tests.

Use test framework features for boilerplate code.   Most test frameworks provide a way to run code automatically before tests. In the built-in `unittest` module, you can write a `setUp` function to run before every test. In `pytest`, you accomplish something similar with fixtures.

A *fixture* in `pytest` is a way of specifying initialization and teardown code for tests. Fixtures offer a ton of useful features, like defining dependencies on other fixtures (letting `pytest` control initialization order) and controlling initialization so that a fixture is only initialized once per module. In the previous example, we could have used a fixture for the `test_database`:

```python
import pytest

@pytest.fixture
def db_creation():
    # ... snip  set up local sqlite database
    return database

@pytest.fixture
def test_database(db_creation):
    # ... snip adding all ingredients and meals
    return database

def test_calorie_calculation_bacon_cheeseburger(test_database):
    test_database.add_ingredient("Bacon", calories_per_pound=2400)
    setup_bacon_cheeseburger(bacon="Bacon")

    calories = get_calories("Bacon Cheeseburger w/ Fries")

    assert calories == 1200

    test_database.cleanup()()
```

Notice how the test has an argument for `test_database` now. This is the fixture at work; the function `test_database` (as well as `db_creation`) will get called before the test. Fixtures only become more useful as the number of tests grows. They are composable, allowing you to mix them together and reduce code duplication. I won't generally use them to abstract code in a single file, but as soon as that initialization needs to be used in multiple files, fixtures are the way to go.

Mocking. Python offers duck typing (first mentioned in Chapter 2) as part of its type system, which means that you can easily substitute types for one another as long as they uphold the same contract (as discussed in Chapter 12). This means that you can tackle complex dependencies in a completely different way: use a simple mocked object instead. A *mocked* object is something that looks identical to a production object as far as methods and fields go, but offers simplified data.

 Mocks are used a lot in unit tests, but you will see their usage decline the less granular the tests become. This is because you try to test more of the system at a higher level; the services you are mocking are often part of the tests.

For instance, if the database in the previous example was quite complex to set up with multiple tables and schemas, it might not be worth setting up for every test, especially if tests share a database; you want to keep tests isolated from one another. (I'll cover this more in a moment.) The class handling the database might look like this:

```
class DatabaseHandler:

    def __init__(self):
        # ... snip complex setup

    def add_ingredient(self, ingredient):
        # ... snip complex queries

    def get_calories_for_ingredient(self, ingredient):
        # ... snip complex queries
```

Instead of using this class verbatim, create a mock class that just looks like a database handler:

```
class MockDatabaseHandler
    def __init__(self):
        self.data = {
            "Ground Beef": 1500,
            "Bacon": 2400,
            # ... snip ...
        }

    def add_ingredient(self, ingredient):
        name, calories = ingredient
        self.data[name] = calories

    def get_calories_for_ingredient(self, ingredient):
        return self.data[ingredient]
```

With the mock, I'm just using a simple dictionary to store my data. How you mock your data will be different for each scenario, but if you can find a way to substitute the real object with a mock object, you can dramatically reduce the complexity of your setup.

 Some people use *monkeypatching* (*https://oreil.ly/xBFHl*), or swapping out methods at runtime to inject mocks. This is OK in moderation, but if you find your tests littered with monkeypatching, this is an antipattern. It means that you have far too rigid a physical dependency between different modules and should look at finding ways to make your system more modular. (Consult Part III for more ideas on making code extensible.)

Annihilate

Technically, the *annihilate* stage is the last thing you do in a test, but I'm covering it second. Why? Because it's inherently tied to your *arrange* step. Whatever you set up in *arrange* needs to be torn down if it could influence other tests.

You want your tests to be isolated from one another; it will make them easier to maintain. One of the biggest nightmares for a test automation writer is having tests fail depending on what order they run in (especially if you have thousands). This is a sure sign of tests having subtle dependencies on one another. Clean up your tests before you leave them and reduce the chances of tests interacting with one another. Here are some strategies for dealing with test cleanup.

Don't use shared resources. If you can get away with it, share nothing between tests. This isn't always feasible, but it should be your goal. If no tests share any resources, then you don't need to clean anything up. A shared resource can be in Python (global variable, class variables) or in the environment (database, file access, socket pools).

Use context managers. Use a context manager (discussed in Chapter 11) to ensure that resources are always cleaned up. In my previous example, eagle-eyed readers may have noticed a bug:

```python
def test_calorie_calculation_bacon_cheeseburger():
    add_base_ingredients_to_database()
    add_ingredient_to_database("Bacon", calories_per_pound=2400)
    setup_bacon_cheeseburger(bacon="Bacon")

    calories = get_calories("Bacon Cheeseburger w/ Fries")

    assert calories == 1200

    cleanup_database()
```

If the assertion fails, an exception is raised and `cleanup_database` never executes. It would be much better to force usage through a context manager:

```python
def test_calorie_calculation_bacon_cheeseburger():
    with construct_test_database() as db:
        db.add_ingredient("Bacon", calories_per_pound=2400)
        setup_bacon_cheeseburger(bacon="Bacon")

        calories = get_calories("Bacon Cheeseburger w/ Fries")

        assert calories == 1200
```

Put your cleanup code in the context manager so that your test writers never have to actively think about it; it's just done for them.

Use fixtures. If you are using `pytest` fixtures, you can use them much like you could a context manager. You can *yield* values from a fixture, allowing you to return to the fixture's execution after the test finishes. Observe:

```python
import pytest

@pytest.fixture
def db_creation():
    # ... snip  set up local sqlite database
    return database

@pytest.fixture
def test_database(db_creation):
    # ... snip adding all ingredients and meals
    try:
        yield database
    finally:
        database.cleanup()

def test_calorie_calculation_bacon_cheeseburger(test_database):
    test_database.add_ingredient("Bacon", calories_per_pound=2400)
    setup_bacon_cheeseburger(bacon="Bacon")

    calories = get_calories("Bacon Cheeseburger w/ Fries")

    assert calories == 1200
```

Notice how the `test_database` fixture now yields the database. When any test using this function finishes (whether it passes or fails), the database cleanup function will always execute.

Act

The *act* stage is the most important part of the test. It embodies the actual operation that you are testing. In the preceding examples, the *act* stage was getting the calories for a specific dish. You do not want an *act* stage to be much longer than one or two lines of code. Less is more; by keeping this stage small, you reduce the time it takes readers to understand the meat of the test.

Sometimes, you want to reuse the same *act* stage across multiple tests. If you find yourself wanting to write the same test on the same action, but with slightly different input data and assertions, consider *parameterizing* your tests. Test *parameterization* is a way of running the same test on different parameters. This allows you to write *table-driven* tests, or a way of organizing your test data in a tabular form.

Here is the `get_calories` test with parameterization:

```python
@pytest.mark.parametrize(
    "extra_ingredients,dish_name,expected_calories",
    [
        (["Bacon", 2400], "Bacon Cheeseburger", 900),
        ([],   "Cobb Salad", 1000),
        ([],   "Buffalo Wings", 800),
        ([],   "Garlicky Brussels Sprouts", 200),
        ([],   "Mashed Potatoes", 400)
    ]
)
def test_calorie_calculation_bacon_cheeseburger(extra_ingredients,
                                                dish_name,
                                                expected_calories,
                                                test_database):
    for ingredient in extra_ingredients:
        test_database.add_ingredient(ingredient)

    # assume this function can set up any dish
    # alternatively, dish ingredients could be passed in as a test parameter
    setup_dish_ingredients(dish_name)

    calories = get_calories(dish_name)

    assert calories == expected_calories
```

You define your parameters as a list of tuples, one per test case. Each parameter is passed to the test case as an argument. `pytest` automatically will run this test, once per parameter set.

Parameterized tests have the benefit of condensing a lot of test cases into one function. Readers of the test can just go down through the table listed in the parameterization to understand what expected input and output is (Cobb salad should have 1,000 calories, mashed potatoes should have 400 calories, and so on).

 Parameterization is a great way to separate the test data from the actual test (similar to separating policy and mechanisms, as discussed in Chapter 17). However, be careful. If you make your tests too generic, it will be harder to ascertain what they are testing. Avoid using more than three or four parameters if you can.

Assert

The last step to do before cleaning up is *asserting* some property is true about the system. Preferably, there should be one logical assertion near the end of your test. If you find yourself jamming too many assertions into a test, you either have too many actions in your test or too many tests matched into one. When a test has too many responsibilities, it makes it harder for maintainers to debug software. If they make a change that produces a failed test, you want them to be able to quickly find out what the problem is. Ideally, they can figure out what's wrong based on the test name, but at the very least, they should be able to open up the test, look for about 20 or 30 seconds, and realize what went wrong. If you have multiple assertions, you have multiple reasons a test can go wrong, and it will take maintainers time to sort through them.

This doesn't mean that you should only have one *assert* statement; it is OK to have a few *assert* statements as long as they are all involved in testing the same property. Make your assertions verbose as well, so that developers get an informative message when things go wrong. In Python, you can supply a text message that gets passed along with the `AssertionError` to help with debugging.

```
def test_calorie_calculation_bacon_cheeseburger(test_database):
    test_database.add_ingredient("Bacon", calories_per_pound=2400)
    setup_bacon_cheeseburger(bacon="Bacon")

    calories = get_calories("Bacon Cheeseburger w/ Fries")

    assert calories == 1200, "Incorrect calories for Bacon Cheeseburger w/ Fries"
```

`pytest` rewrites assertion statements, which also provides an extra level of debug messages. If the above test were to fail, the message returned to the test writer would be:

```
E       AssertionError: Incorrect calories for Bacon Cheeseburger w/ Fries
E       assert 1100 == 1200
```

For more complex assertions, build up an assertion library that makes it incredibly easy to define new tests. This is like building a vocabulary in your codebase; you want a diverse set of concepts to share in your test code as well. For this, I recommend using Hamcrest matchers (*http://hamcrest.org*).[5]

Hamcrest matchers are a way of writing assertions to read similarly to natural language. The `PyHamcrest` (*https://github.com/hamcrest/PyHamcrest*) library supplies common matchers to help you write your asserts. Take a look at how it uses custom assertion matchers to make tests more clear:

```
from hamcrest import assert_that, matches_regexp, is_, empty, equal_to
def test_all_menu_items_are_alphanumeric():
    menu = create_menu()
    for item in menu:
        assert_that(item, matches_regexp(r'[a-zA-Z0-9 ]'))

def test_getting_calories():
    dish = "Bacon Cheeseburger w/ Fries"
```

---

5 Hamcrest is an anagram of "matchers."

```
    calories = get_calories(dish)
    assert_that(calories, is_(equal_to(1200)))

def test_no_restaurant_found_in_non_matching_areas():
    city = "Huntsville, AL"
    restaurants = find_owned_restaurants_in(city)
    assert_that(restaurants, is_(empty()))
```

The real strength of PyHamcrest is that you can define your own matchers.[6] Here's an example of a matcher for checking if a dish is vegan:

```
from hamcrest.core.base_matcher import BaseMatcher
from hamcrest.core.helpers.hasmethod import hasmethod

def is_vegan(ingredient: str) -> bool:
    return ingredient not in ["Beef Burger"]

class IsVegan(BaseMatcher):

    def _matches(self, dish):
        if not hasmethod(dish, "ingredients"):
            return False
        return all(is_vegan(ingredient) for ingredient in dish.ingredients())

    def describe_to(self, description):
        description.append_text("Expected dish to be vegan")

    def describe_mismatch(self, dish, description):
        message = f"the following ingredients are not vegan: "
        message += ", ".join(ing for ing in dish.ingredients()
                             if not is_vegan(ing))
        description.append_text(message)


def vegan():
    return IsVegan()


from hamcrest import assert_that, is_
def test_vegan_substitution():
    dish = create_dish("Hamburger and Fries")
    dish.make_vegan()
    assert_that(dish, is_(vegan()))
```

---

6 Check out the PyHamcrest documentation (*https://oreil.ly/XWjOd*) for more information, such as additional matchers or integrating with test frameworks.

If the test fails, you get the following error:

```
def test_vegan_substitution():
    dish = create_dish("Hamburger and Fries")
    dish.make_vegan()
>   assert_that(dish, is_(vegan()))
E   AssertionError:
E   Expected: Expected dish to be vegan
E        but: the following ingredients are not vegan: Beef Burger
```

Discussion Topic

Where in your tests can you use custom matchers? Discuss what a shared testing vocabulary would be in your tests and how custom matchers would improve readability.

Closing Thoughts

Just like a tightrope walker's safety net, tests give you comfort and confidence as you work. It's not just about finding bugs. Tests verify that what you build is performing as you expect. They give future collaborators leeway to make more risky changes; they know that if they fall, the tests will catch them. You will find that regressions become more rare, and your codebase becomes easier to work in.

However, tests are not free. There is a cost to writing, running, and maintaining them. You need to be careful how you spend your time and effort. Use well-known patterns in constructing tests to minimize the cost: follow the AAA pattern, keep each stage small, and make your tests clear and readable. Your tests are just as important as your codebase. Treat them with just as much respect and make them robust.

In the next chapter, I will focus on acceptance tests. Acceptance tests have a different purpose than unit or integration tests, and some of the patterns you use will differ.

You will learn about how acceptance tests create conversations, as well as how they make sure your codebase is doing the right thing for your customers. They are an invaluable tool for your codebase in delivering value.

## CHAPTER 22

Acceptance Testing

As a developer, it is easy to focus on the tests that directly surround your codebase: unit tests, integration tests, UI tests, and the like. These tests verify that the code is doing what you intend. They are an invaluable tool to keep your codebase regression free. They are also completely the *wrong* tool for building what a customer expects.

Developers write these tests with full knowledge of the code, which means the tests are biased toward that developer's expectations. There is no guarantee that this tested behavior is actually what the *customer* wants, though.

Consider the following unit test:

```
def test_chili_has_correct_ingredients():
    assert make_chili().ingredients() == [
        "Ground Beef",
        "Chile Blend",
        "Onion",
        ...
        "Tomatoes",
        "Pinto Beans"
    ]
```

This test might be airtight; it passes and catches any regression made in the code. However, when presented to a customer, you might be confronted with: "No, I wanted Texas-style chili! You know, no tomatoes or beans?" All the unit tests in the world won't save you from building the wrong thing.

This is where acceptance testing comes in. *Acceptance tests* check that you are building the correct product. While unit tests and integration tests are a form of *verification*, acceptance tests are *validation*. They validate that you are building what the user expects.

In this chapter, you will learn about acceptance testing in Python. I'll show you the behave framework, which uses the Gherkin language to define requirements in a whole new fashion.[1] You'll walk through behavior-driven development (BDD) as a tool to clarify conversations. Acceptance testing is a crucial part of building a safety net; it will protect you from building the wrong thing.

Behavior-Driven Development

The mismatch between customer expectations and software behavior is as old as software development. The problem stems from translating natural language to programming language. Natural language is rife with ambiguities, inconsistencies, and nuance. Programming languages are rigid. The computer does exactly what you tell it to do (even if it's not what you meant). Even worse, it's like a game of Telephone[2] as the requirements get passed through a few people (customers, sales, managers, testers) before the test is ever written.

As with everything in the software life cycle, this error case only gets more costly the longer it takes to fix. Ideally, you want to find out these issues as you're coming up with user requirements. This is where behavior-driven development comes into play.

The Gherkin Language

Behavior-driven development, first pioneered by Daniel Terhorst-North (*https://oreil.ly/MnziJ*), is a practice that focuses on defining the behaviors in your system. BDD focuses on clarifying communications; you iterate over the requirements with the end user, defining the behaviors they want.

Before you write a single lick of code, you make sure that you have agreement on what the right thing to build is. The set of defined behaviors will *drive* what code you write. You work with the end user (or their proxy, such as a business analyst or product manager) to define your requirements as a specification. These specifications follow a formal language, to introduce a bit more rigidity in their definition. One of the most common languages for specifying requirements is Gherkin.

Gherkin is a specification that follows the *Given-When-Then* (GWT) format. Every requirement is organized as follows:

---

1 The Gherkin language was created by Aslak Hellesøy. His wife suggested that his BDD testing tool be named Cucumber (apparently for no specific reason), and he wanted to distinguish the specfication language from the testing tool itself. Since a gherkin is a small, pickled cucumber, he continued the theme, and the Gherkin specfication language was born.

2 Telephone is a game where everyone sits in a circle, and one person whispers a message to another. The message continues to get whispered around the circle until it reaches the origin. Everyone has a laugh at how the message has gotten distorted.

```
Feature: Name of test suite

    Scenario: A test case
        Given some precondition
        When I take some action
        Then I expect this result
```

For instance, if I wanted to capture a requirement that checks for vegan substitution of a dish, I would write it as follows:

```
Feature: Vegan-friendly menu

    Scenario: Can substitute for vegan alternative
        Given an order containing a Cheeseburger with Fries
        When I ask for vegan substitutions
        Then I receive the meal with no animal products
```

Another requirement might be that certain dishes can't be made vegan:

```
    Scenario: Cannot substitute vegan alternatives for certain meals
        Given an order containing Meatloaf
        When I ask for vegan substitutions
        Then an error shows up stating the meal is not vegan substitutable
```

 If the GWT format feels familiar, that's because it's identical to the AAA test organization you learned about in Chapter 21.

By working with your end users to write your requirements in this fashion, you benefit from a few key principles:

Write using plain language
There's no need to delve into any programming languages or formal logic. Everything is written in a form that is intelligible to both business people and developers. This makes it incredibly easy to home in on what the end user actually wants.

Build a shared vocabulary
As the number of requirements increases, you find that you start having the same clauses in multiple requirements (see above with When I ask for vegan substitutions). This builds up your domain language and will make it easier for all involved parties to understand the requirements.

Requirements are testable
This is probably the biggest benefit of this requirement format. Because you are writing the requirement as GWT, you are inherently specifying an acceptance test to write. With the chili example used in this chapter, imagine if the Gherkin test was specified as such:

```
Scenario: Texas-Style Chili
   Given a Chili-Making Machine
   When a Chili is dispensed
   Then that dish does not contain beans
   And that dish does not contain tomatoes
```

It becomes much clearer what tests need to be written to act as acceptance tests. If the Gherkin test has any ambiguities, you can work with the end user to figure out what a concrete test should be. This can also help with traditionally vague requirements such as, "The Chili-Making Machine should be fast." Instead, by focusing on a concrete test, you end up with a test like this:

```
Scenario: Chili order takes less than two minutes
   Given a Chili-Making Machine
   When a Chili is ordered
   Then the Chili is dispensed to the customer within two minutes
```

These requirements specifications are not a silver bullet to eliminate bugs in requirements. They are instead a mitigation strategy. If you have technical and business people review them before code is written, you will have a better chance of discovering ambiguities or mismatched intentions.

Once you start defining your tests in Gherkin, you can do something awesome: you can make your specifications *executable*.

Executable Specifications

Executable specifications translate a set of requirements directly to code. This means that not only are your requirements *testable*, but they are *tests* as well. When the requirements change, your tests will change at the same time. This is the ultimate form of *traceability*, or the ability to connect your requirements to specific tests or code.

Discussion Topic

How does your organization track requirements? How do you trace those requirements to test cases? How do you handle requirements changing? Discuss how your processes would change if your requirements and tests were the same thing.

The Python module behave (*https://oreil.ly/VywJX*) allows you to back your Gherkin requirements with concrete tests. It does so by associating functions with specific clauses in the requirement.

By default, behave expects your Gherkin files to be in a folder called *features* and your Python functions (called steps) to be in a folder called *features/steps*.

Let's look at the first Gherkin requirement I showed earlier in this chapter:

```
Feature: Vegan-friendly menu

    Scenario: Can substitute for vegan alternative
      Given an order containing a Cheeseburger with Fries
      When I ask for vegan substitutions
      Then I receive the meal with no animal products
```

With **behave**, I can write Python code that maps to each of these GWT statements:

```
from behave import given, when, then

@given("an order containing a Cheeseburger with Fries")
def setup_order(ctx):
    ctx.dish = CheeseburgerWithFries()

@when("I ask for vegan substitutions")
def substitute_vegan(ctx):
    ctx.dish.substitute_vegan_ingredients()

@then("I receive the meal with no animal products")
def check_all_vegan(ctx):
    assert all(is_vegan(ing) for ing in ctx.dish.ingredients())
```

Each step is represented as a decorator that matches the clause of the Gherkin requirement. The decorated function is what gets executed as part of the specification. In the above example, the Gherkin requirement would be represented by the following code (you do not have to write this; Gherkin does it for you):

```
from behave.runner import Context
context = Context()
setup_order(context)
substitute_vegan(context)
check_all_vegan(context)
```

To run this, first install **behave**:

```
pip install behave
```

Then, run **behave** on the folder containing your requirements and steps:

```
behave code_examples/chapter22/features
```

You will see the following as output:

```
Feature: Vegan-friendly menu

  Scenario: Can substitute for vegan alternatives
    Given an order containing a Cheeseburger with Fries
    When I ask for vegan substitutions
    Then I receive the meal with no animal products

1 feature passed, 0 failed, 0 skipped
1 scenario passed, 0 failed, 0 skipped
3 steps passed, 0 failed, 0 skipped, 0 undefined
Took 0m0.000s
```

When this code is run in a terminal or an IDE, all the steps show up as green. If any step fails, the step turns red and you get a stack trace of what went wrong.

Now you can tie your requirements directly to your acceptance tests. If an end user changes their mind, they can write a new test. If the GWT clause already exists for the new tests, that's a win; new tests can be written without the help of a developer. If the clauses do not already exist, that's also a win, because it kick-starts a conversation when the test immediately fails. Your end users and your business people need no Python knowledge to understand what you are testing.

Use the Gherkin specifications to drive conversations about the software that you need to build. behave allows you to tie your acceptance tests directly to these requirements, and they serve as a way of focusing conversations. Using BDD prevents you from jumping right into coding the wrong thing. As the popular saying goes: "Weeks of coding will save you hours of planning."[3]

Additional behave Features

The previous example was a bit bare-bones, but thankfully, behave provides some extra features to make test writing even easier.

Parameterized Steps

You may have noticed that I have two Given steps that are very similar:

```
Given an order containing a Cheeseburger with Fries
```

and

```
Given an order containing Meatloaf
```

---

3 While this quote's author is anonymous, I first came across it on the Programming Wisdom Twitter account (*https://oreil.ly/rKsVj*).

It'd be silly to write two similar functions to link this in Python. behave lets you parameterize the steps to reduce the need for writing multiple steps:

```
@given("an order containing {dish_name}")
def setup_order(ctx, dish_name):
    if dish_name == "a Cheeseburger with Fries":
        ctx.dish = CheeseburgerWithFries()
    elif dish_name == "Meatloaf":
        ctx.dish = Meatloaf()
```

Alternatively, you can stack clauses on a function if needed:

```
@given("an order containing a Cheeseburger with Fries")
@given("a typical drive-thru order")
def setup_order(context):
    ctx.dish = CheeseBurgerWithFries()
```

Parameterizing and reusing steps will help you build up vocabulary that is intuitive to use, which will reduce the cost of writing Gherkin tests.

Table-Driven Requirements

In Chapter 21, I mentioned how you can parameterize tests so that all your preconditions and assertions are defined in a table. behave offers something very similar:

```
Feature: Vegan-friendly menu

Scenario Outline: Vegan Substitutions
  Given an order containing <dish_name>,
  When I ask for vegan substitutions
  Then <result>

Examples: Vegan Substitutable
    | dish_name                | result |
    | a Cheeseburger with Fries | I receive the meal with no animal products |
    | Cobb Salad               | I receive the meal with no animal products |
    | French Fries             | I receive the meal with no animal products |
    | Lemonade                 | I receive the meal with no animal products |

Examples: Not Vegan Substitutable
    | dish_name   | result |
    | Meatloaf    | a non-vegan-substitutable error shows up |
    | Meatballs   | a non-vegan-substitutable error shows up |
    | Fried Shrimp | a non-vegan-substitutable error shows up |
```

behave will automatically run a test for each table entry. This is a great way to run the same test on very similar data.

Step Matching

Sometimes, the basic decorators don't have enough flexibility to capture what you are trying to express. You can tell behave to use regular expression parsing in your decorators. This is useful to make the Gherkin specifications feel more natural to write (especially getting around complex data formats or wonky grammar issues). Here's an example that allows you to specify dishes with an optional "a" or "an" beforehand (so that dish names can be simplified).

```
from behave import use_context_matcher

use_step_matcher("re")

@given("an order containing [a |an ]?(?P<dish_name>.*)")
def setup_order(ctx, dish_name):
    ctx.dish = create_dish(dish_name)
```

Customizing the Test Life Cycle

Sometimes you need to run code before or after your tests run. Say you need to set up a database before all the specifications are set, or tell a service to clear its cache between test runs. Just like `setUp` and `tearDown` in the built-in `unittest` module, behave offers functions that let you hook in functions before or after steps, features, or the entire test run. Use this to consolidate common setup code. To take full advantage of this functionality, you can define specifically named functions in a file named *environment.py*.

```
def before_all(ctx):
    ctx.database = setup_database()

def before_feature(ctx, feature):
    ctx.database.empty_tables()

def after_all(ctx):
    ctx.database.cleanup()
```

Check out the behave documentation (*https://oreil.ly/NjEtf*) for more information on controlling your environment. If you are more comfortable with `pytest` fixtures, check out behave fixtures (*https://oreil.ly/6ZZA4*) for very similar ideas.

 Functions like `before_feature` and `before_scenario` get the feature or scenario, respectively, passed to them. You can key off the names of these features and scenarios to do specific actions for specific parts of your tests.

Using Tags to Selectively Run Tests

behave also offers the ability to tag certain tests with arbitrary text. These tags can be anything you want: @wip for work in progress, @slow for slow running tests, @smoke for a select few tests for running on each check-in, and so on.

To tag a test in behave, just decorate your Gherkin scenario:

```
Feature: Vegan-friendly Menu


    @smoke
    @wip
    Scenario: Can substitute for vegan alternatives
      Given an order containing a Cheeseburger with Fries
      When I ask for vegan substitutions
      Then I receive the meal with no animal products
```

To run just tests with a specific tag, you can pass a --tags flag to your behave invocation:

```
behave code_examples/chapter22 --tags=smoke
```

 If you'd like to exclude tests from being run, prefix the tags with a hyphen, as seen in this example where I exclude tests tagged with wip from being run:

```
behave code_examples/chapter22 --tags=-wip
```

Report Generation

Using behave and BDD to drive your acceptance testing will not pay off if you are not involving your end users or their proxies. Find ways to make it easy for them to understand and use the Gherkin requirements.

You can get a list of all step definitions by invoking behave --steps-catalog.

Of course, you also need a way of showing test results to give your end users an idea of what is working and what is not. behave lets you format outputs in a variety of different ways (and you can define your own). Out of the box, there is also the ability to create reports from JUnit (*https://junit.org/junit5*), a unit-testing framework designed for the Java language. JUnit writes its test results as a XML file, and a lot of tools were built to ingest and visualize the test results.

To generate a JUnit test report, you can pass --junit to your behave invocation. Then, you can use a tool junit2html (*https://github.com/inorton/junit2html*) to get a report for all of your test cases:

```
pip install junit2html
behave code_examples/chapter22/features/ --junit
```

```
# xml files are in the reports folder
junit2html <filename>
```

An example output is shown in Figure 22-1.

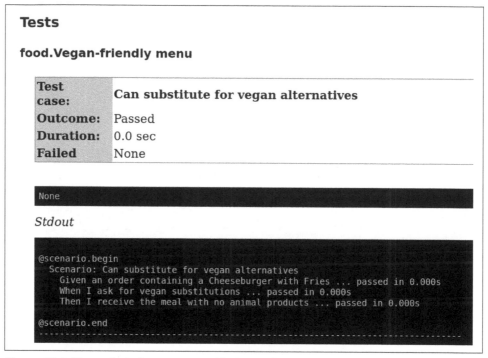

Tests

food.Vegan-friendly menu

Test case:	Can substitute for vegan alternatives
Outcome:	Passed
Duration:	0.0 sec
Failed	None

None

Stdout

```
@scenario.begin
    Scenario: Can substitute for vegan alternatives
        Given an order containing a Cheeseburger with Fries ... passed in 0.000s
        When I ask for vegan substitutions ... passed in 0.000s
        Then I receive the meal with no animal products ... passed in 0.000s

@scenario.end
--------------------------------------------------------------------------------
```

Figure 22-1. Example behave report with `junit2html`

There are plenty of JUnit report generators, so look around for one you like and use it to produce HTML reports of your test results.

Closing Thoughts

If all your tests pass but don't deliver what the end user wants, you have wasted time and effort. It is costly to build the right thing; you want to try and get it right the first time. Use BDD to drive crucial conversations about the requirements for your system. Once you have requirements, use behave and the Gherkin language to write acceptance tests. These acceptance tests become your safety net for ensuring that you deliver what the end user wants.

In the next chapter, you'll continue to learn how to repair holes in your safety net. You'll learn about property-based testing with a Python tool called Hypothesis. It can generate test cases for you, including tests you might never have thought of. You can rest easier knowing that your tests have broader coverage than ever before.

## CHAPTER 23

Property-Based Testing

It is impossible to test absolutely everything in your codebase. The best you can do is be smart in how you target specific use cases. You look for boundary cases, paths through the code, and any other interesting attributes of the code. Your main hope is that you haven't left any big holes in your safety net. However, you can do better than hope. You can fill in those gaps with property-based testing.

In this chapter, you will learn how to do property-based testing with a Python library called Hypothesis (*https://oreil.ly/OejR4*). You'll use Hypothesis to generate test cases for you, often in ways you could never expect. You'll learn how to track failing test cases, craft input data in new ways, and even have Hypothesis create combinations of algorithms to test your software. Hypothesis will guard your codebase against a whole new combination of errors.

Property-Based Testing with Hypothesis

Property-based testing is a form of *generative testing*, where tools generate test cases for you. Instead of writing test cases based on specific input/output combinations, you define *properties* for your system. *Properties* in this context is another name for the invariants (discussed in Chapter 10) that hold true for your system.

Consider a menu recommendation system that selects dishes based on customer-provided constraints, such as total calories, price, and cuisine. For this specific example, I want customers to be able to order a full meal that falls below a specific calorie target. Here are the invariants I define for this function:

- The customer will receive three dishes: an appetizer, a salad, and a main dish.
- When all the dishes' calories are added together, the sum is less than their intended target.

If I were to write this as a `pytest` test that focuses on testing these properties, it would look like the following:

```python
def test_meal_recommendation_under_specific_calories():
    calories = 900
    meals = get_recommended_meal(Recommendation.BY_CALORIES, calories)
    assert len(meals) == 3
    assert is_appetizer(meals[0])
    assert is_salad(meals[1])
    assert is_main_dish(meals[2])
    assert sum(meal.calories for meal in meals) < calories
```

Contrast this with testing for a very specific result:

```python
def test_meal_recommendation_under_specific_calories():
    calories = 900
    meals = get_recommended_meal(Recommendation.BY_CALORIES, calories)
    assert meals == [Meal("Spring Roll", 120),
                     Meal("Green Papaya Salad", 230),
                     Meal("Larb Chicken", 500)]
```

The second method is testing for a very specific set of meals; this test is more specific, but also more *fragile*. It is more likely to break when the production code changes, such as when introducing new menu items or changing the recommendation algorithm. The ideal test is one that only breaks when there is a legitimate bug. Remember that tests are not free. You want to reduce maintenance cost, and reducing the time it takes to tweak tests is a great way of doing so.

In both cases, I am testing with a specific input: 900 calories. In order to build a more comprehensive safety net, it's a good idea to expand your input domain to test for more cases. In traditional test cases, you pick which tests to write by performing *boundary value analysis*. Boundary value analysis is when you analyze the code under test, looking for how different inputs influence control flow, or the different execution paths in your code.

For example, say `get_recommended_meal` raised an error if the calorie limit were below 650. The boundary value in this case is 650; this splits the input domain into two *equivalence classes*, or sets of values that have the same property. One equivalence class is all the numbers underneath 650, and another equivalence class is the values

650 and above. With boundary value analysis, there should be three tests: one with calories under 650 calories, one test exactly at the boundary of 650 calories, and one test with a value higher than 650 calories. In practice, this verifies that no developer has messed up relational operators (such as writing <= instead of <) or has made off-by-one errors.

However, boundary value analysis is only useful if you can easily segment your input domain. If it is difficult to ascertain where you should split the domain, picking boundary values will not be easy. This is where the generative nature of Hypothesis comes in; Hypothesis generates input for test cases. It will find boundary values for you.

You can install Hypothesis through pip:

```
pip install hypothesis
```

I'll modify my original property test to let Hypothesis do the heavy lifting of generating input data.

```
from hypothesis import given
from hypothesis.strategies import integers

@given(integers())
def test_meal_recommendation_under_specific_calories(calories):
    meals = get_recommended_meal(Recommendation.BY_CALORIES, calories)
    assert len(meals) == 3
    assert is_appetizer(meals[0])
    assert is_salad(meals[1])
    assert is_main_dish(meals[2])
    assert sum(meal.calories for meal in meals) < calories
```

With just a simple decorator, I can tell Hypothesis to pick the inputs for me. In this case, I am asking Hypothesis to generate different values of integers. Hypothesis will run this test multiple times, trying to find a value that violates the expected properties. If I run this test with pytest, I see the following output:

```
Falsifying example: test_meal_recommendation_under_specific_calories(
    calories=0,
)
============== short test summary info ======================
FAILED code_examples/chapter23/test_basic_hypothesis.py::
    test_meal_recommendation_under_specific_calories - assert 850 < 0
```

Hypothesis found an error early on with my production code: the code doesn't handle a calorie limit of zero. Now, for this case, I want to specify that I should only be testing with a certain number of calories or above:

```
@given(integers(min_value=900))
def test_meal_recommendation_under_specific_calories(calories)
    # ... snip ...
```

Now, when I run the command with `pytest`, I want to show some more information about Hypothesis. I will run:

```
py.test code_examples/chapter23 --hypothesis-show-statistics
```

This produces the following output:

```
code_examples/chapter23/test_basic_hypothesis.py::
    test_meal_recommendation_under_specific_calories:

  - during generate phase (0.19 seconds):
    - Typical runtimes: 0-1 ms, ~ 48% in data generation
    - 100 passing examples, 0 failing examples, 0 invalid examples

  - Stopped because settings.max_examples=100
```

Hypothesis checked 100 different values for me, without me needing to provide any specific input. Even better, Hypothesis will check new values every time you run this test. Rather than restricting yourself to the same test cases time and time again, you get a much broader blast radius in what you test. Consider all the different developers and continuous integration pipeline systems performing tests, and you'll realize how quickly you can catch corner cases.

 You can also specify constraints on your domain by using `hypothesis.assume`. You can write assumptions into your tests, such as `assume(calories > 850)`, to tell Hypothesis to skip any test cases that violate these assumptions.

If I introduce an error (say something goes wrong between 5,000 and 5,200 calories for some reason), Hypothesis catches the error within four test runs (the number of test runs may vary for you):

```
_____ test_meal_recommendation_under_specific_calories _____

    @given(integers(min_value=900))
>   def test_meal_recommendation_under_specific_calories(calories):

code_examples/chapter23/test_basic_hypothesis.py:33:
- - - - - - - - - - - - - - - - - - - - - - - - - - - - - - - -

calories = 5001

    @given(integers(min_value=900))
    def test_meal_recommendation_under_specific_calories(calories):
        meals = get_recommended_meal(Recommendation.BY_CALORIES, calories)
>       assert len(meals) == 3
E       TypeError: object of type 'NoneType' has no len()

code_examples/chapter23/test_basic_hypothesis.py:35: TypeError
```

```
---------------------- Hypothesis ----------------------------
Falsifying example: test_meal_recommendation_under_specific_calories(
    calories=5001,
)
=========== Hypothesis Statistics ========================
code_examples/chapter23/test_basic_hypothesis.py::
    test_meal_recommendation_under_specific_calories:

  - during reuse phase (0.00 seconds):
    - Typical runtimes: ~ 1ms, ~ 43% in data generation
    - 1 passing examples, 0 failing examples, 0 invalid examples

  - during generate phase (0.08 seconds):
    - Typical runtimes: 0-2 ms, ~ 51% in data generation
    - 26 passing examples, 1 failing examples, 0 invalid examples
    - Found 1 failing example in this phase

  - during shrink phase (0.07 seconds):
    - Typical runtimes: 0-2 ms, ~ 37% in data generation
    - 22 passing examples, 12 failing examples, 1 invalid examples
    - Tried 35 shrinks of which 11 were successful

  - Stopped because nothing left to do
```

When you find an error, `Hypothesis` records the failing error so that it can specifically check that value in the future. You also can make sure that `Hypothesis` always tests specific cases using the `hypothesis.example` decorator:

```
@given(integers(min_value=900))
@example(5001)
def test_meal_recommendation_under_specific_calories(calories)
    # ... snip ...
```

The Hypothesis Database

`Hypothesis` will store examples of failed test cases in a local database (by default, in a folder called *.hypothesis/examples* under the same directory where you ran the tests). It is known as the *example database*. This is used for future test invocations to guide `Hypothesis` in testing common error cases.

There are many alternatives to the local database. An in-memory database will speed up your tests. For example, you can use a Redis (*https://redis.io*) database to back the `Hypothesis` example database. You can even specify multiple databases to use with a `hypothesis.database.MultiplexedDatabase`.

When running `Hypothesis` on a team, I recommend sharing a database, either through a shared drive on a network or through something like `Redis`. That way, CI systems can benefit from a shared history of test failures by using a database, and developers can use failed CI results to check troublesome error cases when they run tests locally. Consider using a `hypothesis.database.MultiplexedDatabase` so that the developers can pull in CI test failures but save their own local failures during development to their local database. You can learn more in the Hypothesis database documentation (*https://oreil.ly/D3cii*).

The Magic of Hypothesis

Hypothesis is very good at generating test cases that will find errors. It seems like magic, but it's actually quite clever. In the previous example, you may have noticed that Hypothesis errored out on the value 5001. If you were to run the same code and introduce an error for values greater than 5000, you'll find that the test errors out at 5001 as well. If Hypothesis is testing different values, shouldn't we all see slightly different results?

Hypothesis does something really nice for you when it finds a failure: it *shrinks* the test case. Shrinking is when Hypothesis tries to find the minimal input that still fails the test. For integers(), Hypothesis will try successively smaller numbers (or bigger numbers when dealing with negatives) until the input value reaches zero. Hypothesis tries to zero in (no pun intended) on the smallest value that still fails the test.

To learn more about how Hypothesis generates and shrinks values, it's worth reading the original QuickCheck paper (*https://oreil.ly/htavw*). QuickCheck was one of the first property-based tools, and even though it deals with the Haskell programming language, it is quite informative. Most property-based testing tools like Hypothesis are descendents from the ideas put forth by QuickCheck.

Contrast with Traditional Tests

Property-based testing can greatly simplify the test-writing process. There are entire classes of problems that you do not need to worry about:

Easier testing of nondeterminism
> Nondeterminism is the bane of most traditional tests. Random behavior, creating temporary directories, or retrieving different records from a database can make it incredibly hard to write tests. You have to create a specific set of output values in your test, and to do that, you need to be deterministic; otherwise, your test will keep failing. You often try to control the nondeterminism by forcing specific behaviors, such as forcing the same folder to always be created or seeding a random number generator.

> With property-based testing, nondeterminism is part of the package. Hypothesis will give you different inputs for each test run. You don't have to worry about testing for specific values anymore; define properties and embrace the nondeterminism. Your codebase will be better because of it.

Less fragility

When testing for specific input/output combinations, you are at the mercy of a slew of hard-coded assumptions. You assume that lists will always be in the same order, that dictionaries won't get any key-value pairs added to them, and that your dependencies will never change their behavior. Any one of these seemingly unrelated changes can break one of your tests.

When tests break for reasons unrelated to the functionality under test, it's frustrating. The tests get a bad reputation for being flaky, and either they get ignored (masking true failures), or developers live with the constant nagging of needing to fix tests. Use property-based testing to add resilience to your testing.

Better chance at finding bugs

Property-based testing isn't just about reducing the cost of test creation and maintenance. It will increase your chances of finding bugs. Even if you write your tests covering every path through your code today, there's still a chance that you haven't caught everything. If your functions change in a backward-incompatible way (say, by now erroring out on a value that you previously thought was fine), your luck depends on if you have a test case for that specific value. Property-based testing, by the nature of generating new test cases, will have a better chance of finding that bug over multiple runs.

Discussion Topic

Examine your current test cases and pick tests that are complicated to read. Search for tests that require a large amount of inputs and outputs to adequately test functionality. Discuss how property-based testing can replace these tests and simplify your test suite.

Getting the Most Out of Hypothesis

I've just scratched the surface of Hypothesis so far. Once you really dive into property-based testing, you start opening up tons of doors for yourself. Hypothesis ships with some pretty cool features out of the box that can improve your testing experience.

Hypothesis Strategies

In the previous section, I introduced you to the integers() strategy. A Hypothesis strategy defines how test cases are generated, as well as how the data gets shrunk when a test case fails. Hypothesis ships with a ton of strategies right out of the box. Similar to passing integers() into your test case, you can pass things like floats(), text(), or times() to generate values for floating-point numbers, strings, or date time.time objects, respectively.

Hypothesis also provides strategies that can compose other strategies together, such as building lists, tuples, or dictionaries of strategies (this is a fantastic example of composability, as described in Chapter 17). For instance, let's say I want to create a strategy that maps dish names (text) to calories (a number between 100 and 2,000):

```
from hypothesis import given
from hypothesis.strategies import dictionary, integers, text

@given(dictionaries(text(), integers(min_value=100, max_value=2000)))
def test_calorie_count(ingredient_to_calorie_mapping : dict[str, int]):
    # ... snip ...
```

For even more complicated data, you can use Hypothesis to define your own strategies. You are allowed to map and filter strategies, which are similar in concept to the built-in map and filter functions.

You can also use the hypothesis.composite strategy decorator to define your own strategies. I want to create a strategy that creates three-course meals for me, consisting of an appetizer, main dish, and dessert. Each dish contains a name and a calorie count:

```
from hypothesis import given
from hypothesis.strategies import composite, integers

ThreeCourseMeal = tuple[Dish, Dish, Dish]

@composite
def three_course_meals(draw) -> ThreeCourseMeal:
    appetizer_calories = integers(min_value=100, max_value=900)
    main_dish_calories = integers(min_value=550, max_value=1800)
    dessert_calories = integers(min_value=500, max_value=1000)

    return (Dish("Appetizer", draw(appetizer_calories)),
            Dish("Main Dish", draw(main_dish_calories)),
            Dish("Dessert", draw(dessert_calories)))

@given(three_course_meals)
def test_three_course_meal_substitutions(three_course_meal: ThreeCourseMeal):
    # ... do something with three_course_meal
```

This example works by defining a new composite strategy called three_course_meals. I create three integer strategies; each type of dish gets its own strategy with its own min/max values. From there, I create a new dish that has a name and a *drawn* value from the strategy. draw is a function that gets passed into your composite strategy and that you use to select values from the strategy.

Once you've defined your own strategies, you can reuse them across multiple tests, making it easy to generate new data for your system. To learn more about Hypothesis strategies, I encourage you to read the Hypothesis documentation (*https://oreil.ly/QhhnM*).

Generating Algorithms

In previous examples, I focused on generating input data to create your tests. However, Hypothesis can go a step further and generate combinations of operations as well. Hypothesis calls this *stateful testing*.

Consider our meal recommendation system. I showed you how to filter by calories, but now I also want to filter by price, number of courses, proximity to user, and so on. Here are some properties I want to assert about the system:

- The meal recommendation system always returns three meal options; it may be possible that not all recommended options fit all of the user's criteria.
- All three meal options are unique.
- The meal options are ordered based on the most recent filter applied. In the case of ties, the next most recent filter is used.
- New filters replace old filters of the same type. For example, if you set the price filter to <$20, and then change it to <$15, only the <$15 filter is applied. Setting something like a calorie filter, such as <1800 calories, does not affect the price filter.

Rather than writing a slew of test cases, I will represent my tests using a hypothesis.stateful.RuleBasedStateMachine. This will let me test entire algorithms using Hypothesis, while checking for invariants along the way. It's a bit complicated, so I'll show the entire code first, and then break it down afterward piece by piece.

```
from functools import reduce
from hypothesis.strategies import integers
from hypothesis.stateful import Bundle, RuleBasedStateMachine, invariant, rule

class RecommendationChecker(RuleBasedStateMachine):
    def __init__(self):
        super().__init__()
        self.recommender = MealRecommendationEngine()
        self.filters = []

    @rule(price_limit=integers(min_value=6, max_value=200))
    def filter_by_price(self, price_limit):
        self.recommender.apply_price_filter(price_limit)
        self.filters = [f for f in self.filters if f[0] != "price"]
        self.filters.append(("price", lambda m: m.price))

    @rule(calorie_limit=integers(min_value=500, max_value=2000))
    def filter_by_calories(self, calorie_limit):
        self.recommender.apply_calorie_filter(calorie_limit)
        self.filters = [f for f in self.filters if f[0] != "calorie"]
        self.filters.append(("calorie", lambda m: m.calories))
```

```
    @rule(distance_limit=integers(max_value=100))
    def filter_by_distance(self, distance_limit):
        self.recommender.apply_distance_filter(distance_limit)
        self.filters = [f for f in self.filters if f[0] != "distance"]
        self.filters.append(("distance", lambda m: m.distance))

    @invariant()
    def recommender_provides_three_unique_meals(self):
        assert len(self.recommender.get_meals()) == 3
        assert len(set(self.recommender.get_meals())) == 3

    @invariant()
    def meals_are_appropriately_ordered(self):
        meals = self.recommender.get_meals()
        ordered_meals = reduce(lambda meals, f: sorted(meals, key=f[1]),
                               self.filters,
                               meals)
        assert ordered_meals == meals
```

```
TestRecommender = RecommendationChecker.TestCase
```

That's quite a lot of code, but it's really cool how it all works. So let's break it down.

First, I will create a subclass of a hypothesis.stateful.RuleBasedStateMachine:

```
from functools import reduce
from hypothesis.strategies import integers
from hypothesis.stateful import Bundle, RuleBasedStateMachine, invariant, rule

class RecommendationChecker(RuleBasedStateMachine):
    def __init__(self):
        super().__init__()
        self.recommender = MealRecommendationEngine()
        self.filters = []
```

This class will be responsible for defining the discrete steps that I want to test in combination. In the __init__ method, I set up self.recommender as a MealRecommendationEngine, which is what I'm testing in this scenario. I also will keep track of a list of filters that are applied as part of this class. Next, I will set up hypothesis.stateful.rule functions:

```
    @rule(price_limit=integers(min_value=6, max_value=200))
    def filter_by_price(self, price_limit):
        self.recommender.apply_price_filter(price_limit)
        self.filters = [f for f in self.filters if f[0] != "price"]
        self.filters.append(("price", lambda m: m.price))

    @rule(calorie_limit=integers(min_value=500, max_value=2000))
    def filter_by_calories(self, calorie_limit):
        self.recommender.apply_calorie_filter(calorie_limit)
        self.filters = [f for f in self.filters if f[0] != "calorie"]
```

```
        self.filters.append(("calorie", lambda m: m.calories))

    @rule(distance_limit=integers(max_value=100))
    def filter_by_distance(self, distance_limit):
        self.recommender.apply_distance_filter(distance_limit)
        self.filters = [f for f in self.filters if f[0] != "distance"]
        self.filters.append(("distance", lambda m: m.distance))
```

Each rule acts as a step of the algorithm that you want to test. Hypothesis will generate tests using these rules as opposed to generating test data. In this case, each of these rules applies a filter to the recommendation engine. I also save the filters locally so that I can check results later.

I then use hypothesis.stateful.invariant decorators to define assertions that should be checked after every rule change.

```
    @invariant()
    def recommender_provides_three_unique_meals(self):
        assert len(self.recommender.get_meals()) == 3
        # make sure all of the meals are unique - sets de-dupe elements
        # so we should have three unique elements
        assert len(set(self.recommender.get_meals())) == 3

    @invariant()
    def meals_are_appropriately_ordered(self):
        meals = self.recommender.get_meals()
        ordered_meals = reduce(lambda meals, f: sorted(meals, key=f[1]),
                               self.filters,
                               meals)
        assert ordered_meals == meals
```

I've written two invariants: one stating that the recommender always returns three unique meals and one that the meals are in the correct order based on the filters chosen.

Finally, I save off the TestCase from the RecommendationChecker into a variable that is prefixed with Test. This is so pytest can discover the stateful Hypothesis test.

```
    TestRecommender = RecommendationChecker.TestCase
```

Once it's all put together, Hypothesis will start generating test cases with different combinations of rules. For instance, with one Hypothesis test run (with an intentionally introduced error), Hypothesis generated the following test.

```
state = RecommendationChecker()
state.filter_by_distance(distance_limit=0)
state.filter_by_distance(distance_limit=0)
state.filter_by_distance(distance_limit=0)
state.filter_by_calories(calorie_limit=500)
state.filter_by_distance(distance_limit=0)
state.teardown()
```

When I introduced a different error, Hypothesis shows me a different test case that catches the fault.

```
state = RecommendationChecker()
state.filter_by_price(price_limit=6)
state.filter_by_price(price_limit=6)
state.filter_by_price(price_limit=6)
state.filter_by_price(price_limit=6)
state.filter_by_distance(distance_limit=0)
state.filter_by_price(price_limit=16)
state.teardown()
```

This is handy for testing complex algorithms or objects with very specific invariants. Hypothesis will mix and match different steps, constantly searching for some ordering of steps that will produce an error.

Discussion Topic

What areas of your codebase contain hard-to-test, highly interrelated functions? Write a few stateful Hypothesis tests as a proof of concept and discuss how these sorts of tests can build confidence in your testing suite.

Closing Thoughts

Property-based testing does not exist to replace traditional testing; it exists to supplement it. When your code has well-defined inputs and outputs, testing with hard-coded preconditions and expected assertions is sufficient. However, as your code gets more complex, your tests become more complex, and you find yourself spending more time than you want parsing and understanding tests.

Property-based testing is simple to use with Hypothesis in Python. It repairs holes in your safety net by generating new tests throughout the lifetime of your codebase. You use hypothesis.strategies to control exactly how your test data gets generated. You can even test algorithms by combining different steps with hypothesis.stateful testing. Hypothesis will let you focus on the properties and invariants of your code and express your tests more naturally.

In the next chapter, I will wrap up the book with mutation testing. Mutation testing is another method of filling gaps in your safety net. Instead of finding new ways of testing your code, mutation code focuses on measuring the efficacy of your tests. It is another tool in your arsenal for more robust testing.

## CHAPTER 24

Mutation Testing

When weaving your safety net of static analysis and tests, how do you know that you are testing as much as you can? Testing absolutely everything is impossible; you need to be smart in what tests you write. Envision each test as a separate strand in your safety net: the more tests you have, the wider your net. However, this doesn't inherently mean that your net is well-constructed. A safety net with fraying, brittle strands is worse than no safety net at all; it gives the illusion of safety and provides false confidence.

The goal is to strengthen your safety net so that it is not brittle. You need a way to make sure your tests will actually fail when there are bugs in your code. In this chapter, you will learn how to do just that with mutation testing. You'll learn how to perform mutation testing with a Python tool called mutmut. You'll use mutation testing to inspect the relation between your tests and code. Finally, you'll learn about code coverage tools, how best to use those tools, and how to integrate mutmut with your coverage reports. Learning how to do mutation testing will give you a way to measure how effective your tests are.

What Is Mutation Testing?

Mutation testing is the act of making changes in your source code with the intent of introducing bugs.[1] Each change you make in this fashion is known as a *mutant*. You then run your test suite. If the tests fail, it's good news; your tests were successful in

---

[1] Mutation testing was first proposed in 1971 by Richard A. DeMillo, Richard J. Lipton, and Fred G. Sayward in "Hints on Test Data Selection: Help for the Practicing Programmer," *IEEE Computer*, 11(4): 34–41, April 1978. The first implementation was developed in 1980 by Tim A. Budd, "Mutation Analysis of Program Test Data," PhD thesis, Yale University, 1980.

eliminating the mutant. However, if your tests pass, that means your tests are not robust enough to catch legitimate failures; the mutant survives. Mutation testing is a form of *meta-testing*, in that you are testing how good your tests are. After all, your test code should be a first-class citizen in your codebase; it requires some level of testing as well.

Consider a simple calorie-tracking app. A user can input a set of meals and get notified if they exceed their calorie budget for the day. The core functionality is implemented in the following function:

```python
def check_meals_for_calorie_overage(meals: list[Meal], target: int):
    for meal in meals:
        target -= meal.calories
        if target < 0:
            display_warning(meal, WarningType.OVER_CALORIE_LIMIT)
            continue
        display_checkmark(meal)
```

Here is a set of tests for this functionality, all of which pass:

```python
def test_no_warnings_if_under_calories():
    meals = [Meal("Fish 'n' Chips", 1000)]
    check_meals_for_calorie_overage(meals, 1200)
    assert_no_warnings_displayed_on_meal("Fish 'n' Chips")
    assert_checkmark_on_meal("Fish 'n' Chips")

def test_no_exception_thrown_if_no_meals():
    check_meals_for_calorie_overage([], 1200)
    # no explicit assert, just checking for no exceptions

def test_meal_is_marked_as_over_calories():
    meals = [Meal("Fish 'n' Chips", 1000)]
    check_meals_for_calorie_overage(meals, 900)
    assert_meal_is_over_calories("Fish 'n' Chips")

def test_meal_going_over_calories_does_not_conflict_with_previous_meals():
    meals = [Meal("Fish 'n' Chips", 1000), Meal("Banana Split", 400)]
    check_meals_for_calorie_overage(meals, 1200)
    assert_no_warnings_displayed_on_meal("Fish 'n' Chips")
    assert_checkmark_on_meal("Fish 'n' Chips")
    assert_meal_is_over_calories("Banana Split")
```

As a thought exercise, I'd like you to look over these tests (ignoring the fact that this is a chapter about mutation testing) and ask yourself what your opinion would be if you found these tests in production. How confident are you that they are right? How confident are you that I didn't miss anything? How confident are you that these tests will catch bugs if the code changes?

The central theme of this book is that software will always change. You need to make it easy for your future collaborators to maintain your codebase in spite of this change.

You need to write tests that catch not only errors in what you wrote, but errors other developers make as they change your code.

It doesn't matter if a future developer is refactoring the method to use a common library, changing a single line, or adding more functionality to the code; you want your tests to catch any errors that they introduced. To get into the mindset of mutation testing, you need to think about all the possible changes that can be made to the code and check if your tests would catch any erroneous change. Table 24-1 breaks down the above code line by line and shows the outcome of the tests if that line is missing.

Table 24-1. Impact of each line removed

Code line	Impact if removed
`for meal in meals:`	Tests fail: Syntax errors and code does no looping
`target -= meal.calories`	Tests fail: no warnings are ever displayed
`if target < 0`	Tests fail: all meals show a warning
`display_warning(meal, Warning Type.OVER_CALORIE_LIMIT)`	Tests fail: no warnings are shown
`continue`	Tests pass
`display_checkmark(meal)`	Tests fail: checkmarks are not displayed on meals

Look at the row in Table 24-1 for the `continue` statement. If I delete that line, all tests pass. This means one of three scenarios occurred: the line isn't needed; the line is needed, but not important enough to test; or there is missing coverage in our test suite.

The first two scenarios are easy to handle. If the line isn't needed, delete it. If the line isn't important enough to test (this is common for things such as debug logging statements or version strings), you can ignore mutation testing on this line. But, if the third scenario is true, you are missing test coverage. You have found a hole in your safety net.

If `continue` is removed from the algorithm, both a checkmark and a warning will show up on any meal that is over the calorie limit. This is not ideal behavior; this is a signal that I should have a test to cover for this case. If I were to just add an assertion that meals with warnings also have no checkmarks, then our test suite would have caught this mutant.

Deleting lines is just one example of a mutation. There are numerous other mutants I could apply to the code above. As a matter of fact, if I change the `continue` to a `break`, the tests still pass. Going through every mutation I can think of is tedious, so I want an automated tool to do this process for me. Enter `mutmut`.

Mutation Testing with mutmut

mutmut (*https://pypi.org/project/mutmut*) is a Python tool that does mutation testing for you. It comes with a pre-programmed set of mutations to apply to your codebase, such as:

- Finding integer literals and adding 1 to them to catch off-by-one errors
- Changing string literals by inserting text inside them
- Exchanging `break` and `continue`
- Exchanging `True` and `False`
- Negating expressions, such as converting `x is None` to `x is not None`
- Changing operators (especially changing from `/` to `//`)

This is by no means a comprehensive list; `mutmut` has quite a few clever ways of mutating your code. It works by making discrete mutations, running your test suite for you, and then displaying which mutants survived the testing process.

To get started, you need to install `mutmut`:

```
pip install mutmut
```

Then, you run `mutmut` against all your tests (warning, this can take some time). You can run `mutmut` on my code snippet above with the following:

```
mutmut run --paths-to-mutate code_examples/chapter24
```

 For long-running tests and large codebases, you may want to break up your `mutmut` runs, as they do take some time. However, `mutmut` is intelligent enough to save its progress in a folder called *.mutmut-cache*, so if you exit in the middle, it will pick up execution at the same point on future runs.

`mutmut` will display some statistics as it runs, including the number of surviving mutants, the number of eliminated mutants, and which tests were taking a suspiciously long time (such as accidentally introducing an infinite loop).

Once execution completes, you can view the results with `mutmut results`. In my code snippet, `mutmut` identifies three surviving mutants. It will list mutants as numeric IDs, and you can show the specific mutant with the `mutmut show <id>` command.

Here are the three mutants that survived in my code snippet:

```
mutmut show 32
--- code_examples/chapter24/calorie_tracker.py
+++ code_examples/chapter24/calorie_tracker.py
@@ -26,7 +26,7 @@
 def check_meals_for_calorie_overage(meals: list[Meal], target: int):
     for meal in meals:
         target -= meal.calories
-        if target < 0:
+        if target <= 0:
             display_warning(meal, WarningType.OVER_CALORIE_LIMIT)
             continue
         display_checkmark(meal)

mutmut show 33
--- code_examples/chapter24/calorie_tracker.py
+++ code_examples/chapter24/calorie_tracker.py
@@ -26,7 +26,7 @@
 def check_meals_for_calorie_overage(meals: list[Meal], target: int):
     for meal in meals:
         target -= meal.calories
-        if target < 0:
+        if target < 1:
             display_warning(meal, WarningType.OVER_CALORIE_LIMIT)
             continue
         display_checkmark(meal)

mutmut show 34
--- code_examples/chapter24/calorie_tracker.py
+++ code_examples/chapter24/calorie_tracker.py
@@ -28,6 +28,6 @@
         target -= meal.calories
         if target < 0:
             display_warning(meal, WarningType.OVER_CALORIE_LIMIT)
-            continue
+            break
         display_checkmark(meal)
```

In each example, mutmut shows the result in *diff notation*, which is a way of representing the changes of a file from one changeset to another. In this case, any line prefixed with a minus sign "-" indicates a line that got changed by mutmut. Lines starting with a plus sign "+" are the change that mutmut made; these are your mutants.

Each of these cases is a potential hole in my testing. By changing <= to <, I find out I don't have coverage for when the calories of a meal exactly match the target. By changing 0 to 1, I find out that I don't have coverage at the boundaries of my input domain (refer back to Chapter 23 for discussion of boundary value analysis). By changing a continue to a break, I stop the loop early and potentially miss marking later meals as OK.

Fixing Mutants

Once you identify mutants, it's time to fix them. One of the best ways to do so is to apply the mutants to the files you have on disk. In my previous example, my mutants had the numbers 32, 33, and 34. I can apply them to my codebase like so:

```
mutmut apply 32
mutmut apply 33
mutmut apply 34
```

 Only do this on files that are backed up through version control. This makes it easy to revert the mutants when you are done, restoring the original code.

Once the mutants have been applied to disk, your goal is to write a failing test. For instance, I can write the following:

```
def test_failing_mutmut():
    clear_warnings()
    meals = [Meal("Fish 'n' Chips", 1000),
             Meal("Late-Night Cookies", 300),
             Meal("Banana Split", 400)
             Meal("Tub of Cookie Dough", 1000)]

    check_meals_for_calorie_overage(meals, 1300)

    assert_no_warnings_displayed_on_meal("Fish 'n' Chips")
    assert_checkmark_on_meal("Fish 'n' Chips")
    assert_no_warnings_displayed_on_meal("Late-Night Cookies")
    assert_checkmark_on_meal("Late-Night Cookies")
    assert_meal_is_over_calories("Banana Split")
    assert_meal_is_over_calories("Tub of Cookie Dough")
```

You should see this test fail (even if you have only one of the mutations applied). Once you are confident you have caught all mutations, revert the mutants and make sure the tests now pass. Rerunning mutmut should show that you eliminated the mutants as well.

Mutation Testing Reports

mutmut also provides a way to export its results to JUnit report format. You've seen other tools export to JUnit reports already in this book (such as in Chapter 22), and mutmut is no different:

```
mutmut junitxml > /tmp/test.xml
```

And just like in Chapter 22, I can use `junit2html` to produce a nice HTML report for the mutation tests, as seen in Figure 24-1.

Figure 24-1. Example mutmut *report with* junit2html

Adopting Mutation Testing

Mutation testing is not widespread in the software development community today. I believe this to be for three reasons:

- People are unaware of it and the benefits it provides.
- A codebase's tests are not mature enough yet for useful mutation testing.
- The cost-to-value ratio is too high.

This book is actively working to improve the first point, but the second and third points certainly have merit.

If your codebase does not have a mature set of tests, you will see little value in introducing mutation testing. It will end up providing too high of a noise-to-signal ratio. You will see much more value from improving your test suite than trying to find all the mutants. Consider running mutation testing on smaller parts of your codebase that do have mature test suites.

Mutation testing does have a high cost; it's important to maximize the value received in order to make mutation testing worth it. Mutation tests are slow, by virtue of running test suites multiple times. Introducing mutation testing to an existing codebase is painful, as well. It is far easier to start on brand-new code from the beginning.

However, since you are reading a book about improving the robustness of potentially complex codebases, there's a good chance you are working in an existing codebase. Hope is not lost if you'd like to introduce mutation testing, though. As with any method of improving robustness, the trick is to be selective in where you run mutation testing.

Look for areas of code that have lots of bugs. Look through bug reports and find trends that indicate that a certain area of code is troublesome. Also consider finding areas of code with high churn, as these are the areas that are most likely to introduce a change that current tests do not fully cover.[2] Find the areas where mutation testing will pay back the cost multifold. You can use `mutmut` to run mutation testing selectively on just these areas.

Also, `mutmut` comes with an option to mutation test only the parts of your codebase that have *line coverage*. A line of code has *coverage* by test suite if it is executed at least once by any test. Other coverage types exist, such as API coverage and branch

---

2 You can find code with high churn by measuring files with the highest number of commits. I found the following Git one-liner after a quick Google search: `git rev-list --objects --all | awk '$2' | sort -k2 | uniq -cf1 | sort -rn | head`. This was provided by sehe on this Stack Overflow question (*https://oreil.ly/39UTx*).

coverage, but `mutmut` focuses on line coverage. `mutmut` will only generate mutants for code that you actually have tests for in the first place.

To generate coverage, first install `coverage`:

```
pip install coverage
```

Then run your test suite with the `coverage` command. For the example above, I run:

```
coverage run -m pytest code_examples/chapter24
```

Next, all you have to do is pass the `--use-coverage` flag to your `mutmut` run:

```
mutmut run --paths-to-mutate code_examples/chapter24 --use-coverage
```

With this, `mutmut` will ignore any untested code, drastically reducing the amount of noise.

The Fallacy of Coverage (and Other Metrics)

Any time a way of measuring code emerges, there is a rush to use that measurement as a *metric*, or a goal that acts as a proxy predictor of business value. However, there have been numerous ill-advised metrics through software development history, and none more infamous than using lines of code written as an indicator of project progress. The thinking went that if you could directly measure how much code any one person was writing, you would be able to directly measure that person's productivity. Unfortunately, this led developers to game the system and try to write intentionally verbose code. This backfired as a metric, because the systems ended up complex and bloated, and development slowed due to poor maintainability.

As an industry, we have moved past measuring lines of code (I hope). However, where one metric disappears, two more come to take its place. I've seen other maligned metrics emerge such as number of bugs fixed or number of tests written. At face value, these are good things to be doing, but the problem comes when they are scrutinized as a metric tied to business value. There are ways to manipulate data in each of these metrics. Are you being judged by the number of bugs fixed? Then, just write more bugs in the first place!

Unfortunately, code coverage has fallen into the same trap in recent years. You hear goals such as "This code should be 100% line covered" or "We should strive for 90% branch coverage." This is laudable in isolation, but it falls short of predicting business value. It misses the point of *why* you want these goals in the first place.

Code coverage is a predictor of the absence of robustness, not quality as many assume. Code with low coverage may or may not do everything you need; you don't know with any reliability. It is a sign that you will have challenges with modifying the code, as you do not have any sort of safety net built around that part of your system.

You should absolutely look for areas with very low coverage and improve the testing story around them.

Conversely, this causes many people to assume that high coverage is a predictor of robustness, when it really isn't. You can have every line and every branch covered by tests, and still have abysmal maintainability. The tests could be brittle or even flat-out useless.

I once worked in a codebase that was beginning to adopt unit testing. I came across a file with the equivalent of the following:

```python
def test_foo_can_do_something():
    foo = Thingamajiggy()
    foo.doSomething()
    assert foo is not None

def test_foo_parameterized_still_does_the_right_thing():
    foo = Thingamajiggy(y=12)
    foo.doSomethingElse(15)
    assert foo is not None
```

There were about 30 of these tests, all with good names and following the AAA pattern (as seen in Chapter 21). But they were all effectively useless: all they did was make sure that no exception was thrown. The worst part of all of this was the tests actually had 100% line coverage and near >80% branch coverage. It's not bad that the tests were checking that no exception was thrown; it was bad that they didn't actually test the actual functions, despite indicating otherwise.

Mutation testing is your best defense against poor assumptions about code coverage. When you are measuring the efficacy of your tests, it becomes much harder to write useless, meaningless tests while still eliminating mutants. Mutation testing elevates coverage measurements to become a truer predictor of robustness. Coverage metrics still won't be a perfect proxy for business value, but mutation testing certainly makes them more valuable as an indicator of robustness.

 As mutation testing becomes more popular, I fully expect "number of mutants eliminated" to be the new buzzword metric replacing "100% code coverage." While you definitely want fewer mutants to survive, beware any goal tied to one metric out of context; this number can be gamed just like all the others. You still need a full testing strategy to ensure robustness in your codebase.

Closing Thoughts

Mutation testing will probably not be the first tool you reach for. However, it's a perfect complement for your testing strategy; it finds holes in your safety net and brings them to your attention. With automated tools such as `mutmut`, you can leverage your existing test suite to perform mutation testing effortlessly. Mutation testing helps you improve the robustness of your test suite, which in turn will help you write more robust code.

This concludes Part IV of this book. You started by learning about static analysis, which provides early feedback at a low cost. You then learned about testing strategies and how to ask yourself what sorts of questions you want your tests to answer. From there, you learned about three specific types of testing: acceptance testing, property-based testing, and mutation testing. All of these serve as ways of enhancing your existing testing strategy, building a denser and stronger safety net around your code-base. With a strong safety net, you will give future developers the confidence and flexibility to evolve your system as they need.

This also concludes the book as a whole. It's been a long journey, and you've learned a variety of tips, tools, and methods along the way. You've dived deep into Python's type system, learned how writing your own types benefit the codebase, and discovered how to write extensible Python. Each part of this book has given you building blocks that will help your codebase stand the test of time.

While this is the end of the book, this is not the end of the story of robustness in Python. Our relatively young industry continues to evolve and transform, and as software continues to eat the world, the health and maintainability of complex systems become paramount. I expect continuing changes in how we understand software, and new tools and techniques to build better systems.

Never stop learning. Python will continue to evolve, adding features and providing new tools. Each one of these has the potential to transform how you write code. I can't predict the future of Python or its ecosystem. As Python introduces new features, ask yourself about the intentions that feature conveys. What do readers of code assume if they see this new feature? What do they assume if that feature is not used? Understand how developers interact with your codebase, and empathize with them to create systems that are pleasant to develop in.

Furthermore, take every single thing you've read in this book and apply critical thought to it. Ask yourself: what value is provided and what does it cost to implement? The last thing I want readers to do is take the advice in this book as completely prescriptive and use it as a hammer to force codebases to adhere to the standards that "the book said to use" (any developer who worked in the '90s or '00s probably remembers "Design Pattern Fever," where you couldn't walk 10 steps without running into an `AbstractInterfaceFactorySingleton`). Each of the concepts in this book should be seen as a tool in a toolbox; my hope is that you've learned enough of the background context to make the right decisions about how you use them.

Above all, remember that you are a human working on a complex system, and other humans will work on these systems with you and after you. Each person has their own motivations, their own goals, their own dreams. Everybody will have their own challenges and struggles. Mistakes will happen. We will never eliminate them all. Instead, I want you to look at these mistakes and push our field forward by learning from them. I want you to help the future build off of your work. In spite of all the changes, all the ambiguities, all the deadlines and scope creep, and all the tribulations of software development, I want you to be able to stand behind your work and say: "I'm proud I built this. This was a good system."

Thank you for taking the time to read this book. Now go forth and write awesome code that stands the test of time.

Index

communication methods, cost versus proximity, 9
complexity
    necessary and accidental, 17, 217
    type annotating complex code, 99
complexity checkers, 292-295
    cyclomatic complexity with mccabe tool, 292
    whitespace heuristic, 294
composability, 243-257
    composing on a smaller scale, 251-257
        algorithms, 255-257
        decorators, 252-255
        functions, 251
    cost of, 250
    designing code for, 247
    Hypothesis strategies, 332
    operators in RxPy, 268
    policy versus mechanisms, 247-250
composite protocols, 194
composite types, 123
composition, 171
    using instead of inheritance, 183
conditionally checking arguments in derived
    class's overridden functions, 181
config files, specifying in different places
    (mypy), 81
constraining types, 45-60
    Annotated types, 56
    Final types, 59
    Literal types, 55
    NewType, 57-59
    Optional types, 46-51
    Union types, 51-55
consumers of events, 259
    (see also producers–consumers of events)
context managers, 145, 167-170
    using in annihilate stage of AAA testing,
    308
continuous integration
    dependencies and, 228
    pipelines with third-party integrations, poli-
    cies versus mechanisms, 248
control flow graph, 292
cost versus proximity in communication meth-
    ods, 9
cost-benefit analysis for adopting typechecking,
    96
costs

for communication methods, 9
for tests, 302
coupling
    composition as weaker form of, 184
    decoupling of producers and consumers of
    events, 260
    dependencies contributing to, 227
    introduction with extensibility, 223
customer expectations and software behavior,
    mismatch between, 316
cyclomatic complexity, 292-294

D

daemon mode (mypy), 85
data access, protecting for classes, 147
data classes, 123-134
    adding methods to, 127
    benefits and limitations of, 134
    classes versus, 137
    creating, 125
    deciding whether to use, 152
    versus dictionaries, 132
    Fraction class example, 123
    modeling with pydantic, 205
    versus namedtuple, 133
    nesting data classes and other user-defined
        types in, 124
    versus TypedDict, 133
    usage, 128-132
        equality checks, 128
        immutability, 130
        relational comparisons, 129
        string conversions, 128
datetime type, 26
debugging
    of event-driven architectures, 261
    PyPubSub options for, 264
decorators, 252-255, 319
    regular expression parsing in behave, 322
dependencies, 225-242
    architectural design patterns and, 281
    creating by linking policies, 248
    extensible code leading to, 223
    large arrange blocks and, 305
    logical, 232-234
    physical, 228-232
    pinning or not pinning, 227
    reduction with composability, 243
    relationships, 226-228

about, 215-217
bidirectional, of event-driven architectures,
    260
drawbacks of, 223
Open-Closed Principle, 221-223
    detecting OCP violations, 222
    redesign of notification system, 217-221
extension points, 271

F

fan-in and fan-out, 240
Final types, 59, 132
fixtures, 305, 309
flags, using with Enums, 117
    Flag base class, 118
fragile tests, 326
    less fragility with property-based tests, 331
frozen (data classes), 130
function signatures in stub files, 103
functional programming, 251
functions
    in clean code, 3
    composing, 251
    deciding whether to place inside a class, 151
    decorators, 252-255
    return type annotations, 38
    visualizing function calls, 238
functools module, 251

G

generative testing, 325
generators, 13
generics
    collections, 69-70
    disallowing Any type for, 82
    using for types other than collections, 70
__getitem__ method, 166
getters and setters, 150
    writing for every private class member, 149
Gherkin language, 316-318
GitHub repo for this book, 103
Given-When-Then (GWT) format, 316
    parameterized steps in behave, 320
    writing Python code that maps to, 319
graphs, 69
    defining Graph class to use for generic
        types, 69
GraphViz library, 236
    converting .dot file to .png, 239

green-field projects, 95
__gt__ method, 166

H

Hamcrest matchers, 311
hard-to-use code, characteristics of, 156
has-a relationship, 183
hashable, 131
heterogeneous versus homogeneous collec-
    tions, 63-67
    data classes, representing heterogeneous
        data, 133
    making heterogeneous collection user-
        defined type, 64
    single type in homogeneous collections, 63
    TypedDict, using to store heterogeneous
        data in a dictionary, 67
    uses of heterogeneous collections, 65
heuristics, 292
high cost, high proximity communications, 10
high cost, low proximity communications, 10
higher-order functions, 251
Hoare, C.A.R., 46
homogeneous collections, 63
    (see also heterogeneous versus homogene-
        ous collections)
Hypothesis
    getting the most from, 331-336
        generating algorithms, 333-336
        Hypothesis strategies, 331
    property-based testing with, 327-331
        contrast with traditional tests, 330-331
        Hypothesis database, 329
        magic of Hypothesis, 330

I

immutability, 137
    (see also invariants)
    in reactive programming, 268
    specifying for data classes, 130
imports, visualizing, 237
indexing
    dynamic versus static, for collections, 14
    static indexing of tuples, 113
inheritance, 171-176
    deciding between protocols and, 194
    denoting when defining derived class, 173
    different behaviors in derived class, 174
    effects on maintainability, 175

Redis, 264
regular expression parsing in decorators, 322
relational comparisons using data classes, 129
remote cache (mypy), 85
report generation in behave, 323
reporting (mypy), 83
reports on mutation testing, 342
representable state space, 53
requirements
    backing with concrete tests, 318
    specifying using Gherkin language, 316-318
    table-driven, in behave, 321
retry logic, 252
return types, annotations, 37
robustness, 1-5
    about, 2
    dependencies and, 241
    duck typing and, 32
    embracing change, 2
    importance of clean code, 3
    maintainability of code, 4
    static versus dynamic typing, 30
    strong versus weak typing, 29
    type annotations and, 36
    typechecking and, 44
    types and, 27
    why it matters, 4
runtime checkable protocols, 195
RxPy, 266
    observables, 267
    observers subscribing to observables, 267
    pipable operators, 267

S

sanitizer functions, 90
security
    dependencies broadening attack surface, 227
    security tests, questions answered by, 299
    static analysis of, 295-296
        leaking secrets, 295
        security flaw checking, 295
self argument in class instantiations, 137
self.data, using with user collection classes, 73
semantic representation of types, 25
sets, 13, 63
    collections.abc.Set, 74
setup.py, 279
setuptools, 279

shared resources, not using in tests, 308
shifting errors left, 199, 287
"shotgun surgery", 217
shrinking the test case (Hypothesis), 330
side effects of functions, 251
simple events, 262
Single Responsibility Principle, 142
software value, 4
SOLID design principles, 142
"spaghetti code", 225
speeding up mypy, 84
stateful testing (Hypothesis), 333-336
static analysis, 41, 285-296
    linting, 285-291
        Pylint, 285-287
            writing your own Pylint plug-in, 287-291
        other analyzers, 291-296
            complexity checkers, 292-295
            security analysis, 295-296
        shifting errors left, 287
static call graph generators, 238
static versus dynamic typing, 30
step matching (behave), 322
stevedore, 277
    ability to work across packages, 281
    loading plug-ins dynamically at runtime, 279
    registering plug-ins with, 279
strategies (Hypothesis), 331
Strategy Pattern, 275-277
streaming events, 266-269
strictness (typecheckers), 80
string conversions, using data classes, 128
strings, 13
strong versus weak typing, 28
structural subtyping, 189
stub files, 103
subclasses, 172
subclassing
    implications of extending code through, 175
    protocols and, 195
subscribing to a topic, 262
substitutability, 176-182
    Liskov Substitution Principle, 179
    logical dependency introducing, 233
subtyping, 171-185
    design considerations in, 182-185

About the Author

Patrick Viafore has been working in the software industry for over 14 years, building and maintaining mission-critical software systems including lightning detection, telecommunications, and operating systems. Working with statically typed languages has influenced his approach to dynamically typed languages such as Python, and how we can make them safer and more robust. He also is an organizer of the HSV.py meetup, where he can observe common Python obstacles, and loves helping beginners and experts alike. His goal is to make computer science/software engineering topics more approachable to the developer community.

Patrick currently works at Cloud Software Group, working on desktop and application virtualization. He also does software consulting and contracting through his business, Kudzera, LLC.

Colophon

The animal on the cover of *Robust Python* is a Nile crocodile (*Crocodylus niloticus*), which lives near freshwater lakes, rivers, and swamplands throughout sub-Saharan Africa. It is an aggressive apex predator that hunts by submerging itself in the water and waiting to ambush any aquatic or terrestrial animal that comes near. They eat a wide variety of prey, including birds, fish, mammals, and other reptiles. They are also dangerous to humans, with hundreds of attacks and deaths occurring every year.

Crocodiles have incredibly strong bite force, as well as conical teeth designed to fasten tight to their prey rather than tear flesh. These traits enable them to quickly grab even large animals and hold them underwater to drown. This species is the largest crocodile in Africa, averaging around 12–16 feet long and 500–1,600 pounds in weight (though females are about 30% smaller than males). They have dark backs and mottled yellow-green sides that camouflage them in the water.

Nile crocodiles are social animals that share basking spots and kills that are too large to eat alone. Females lay between 25 to 80 eggs, and protect hatchlings for a time (though juvenile crocodiles hunt for themselves). Despite the mother's efforts, it's estimated that only 10% of eggs hatch, and 1% of those grow to adulthood, due to predation by species like the Nile monitor, waterbirds, and other crocodilians.

Many of the animals on O'Reilly covers are endangered; all of them are important to the world.

The cover illustration is by Karen Montgomery, based on a black-and-white engraving from *Meyers Kleines Lexicon*. The cover fonts are Gilroy Semibold and Guardian Sans. The text font is Adobe Minion Pro; the heading font is Adobe Myriad Condensed; and the code font is Dalton Maag's Ubuntu Mono.

Milton Keynes UK
Ingram Content Group UK Ltd.
UKHW051538210924
448609UK00002B/10